Unwin Critical Library

GENERAL EDITOR: CLAUDE RAWSON

ROBINSON CRUSOE

Unwin Critical Library

GENERAL EDITOR: CLAUDE RAWSON

Robinson Crusoe PAT ROGERS

Shakespeare's Sonnets KENNETH MUIR

Physics HUGH KENNER

Paradise Lost G. K. HUNTER

Robinson Crusoe

PAT ROGERS
Professor of English, University of Bristol

London
GEORGE ALLEN & UNWIN
Boston   Sydney

First published in 1979

GEORGE ALLEN & UNWIN LTD
40 Museum Street, London WC1A 1LU

© George Allen & Unwin (Publishers) Ltd, 1979

British Library Cataloguing in Publication Data

Rogers, Pat
    'Robinson Crusoe'. – (Unwin critical library).
    1. Defoe, Daniel. Robinson Crusoe
    I. Title
    823'.5   PR3403.Z5   79–40291

    ISBN 0–04–800002–7

Typeset in 10 on 11 point Plantin by Trade Linotype Limited, Birmingham
and printed in Great Britain
by Hollen Street Press, Slough, Berkshire

PREFACE

The English novel has a long prehistory, but finally *Robinson Crusoe* appeared. Its publication in 1719 marked a decisive moment in literary history. Until then we are dealing essentially with the archaeology of fiction; it takes Ernest A. Baker two and a half volumes to reach Defoe in his *History of the English Novel,* and of course there are significant prose narratives along the way by Nashe, Sidney, Aphra Behn and others. But it is only with *Crusoe* that this sporadic and remote tradition turns into a live and unbroken career at the very centre of literary practice. We must be careful of reasoning *post hoc, ergo propter hoc* – especially as the English and French novelists who followed Defoe seem to have paid him very little attention. Nevertheless, *Crusoe* was a real turning-point, and the book's historical interest is contingent upon its artistic qualities.

'Artistic' might seem a strange word to use of a work written without obvious grace and conspicuously lacking in the kind of skilful *ordonnance* we find in writers such as Jane Austen, Henry James or even (in his different way) James Joyce. The truth is, however, that the first part of *Robinson Crusoe* exhibits, along with sustained mastery of narrative, a capacity to dramatise spiritual and psychological experience which opened up fictional possibilities which have still not been exhausted. In his apparently clumsy fashion Defoe gave the English novel new expressive powers, and Crusoe stands as one of the most deeply observed characters in all prose fiction. He has a strong physical identity – he eats, drinks, sleeps, falls ill, feels fear and pain, and even his sexlessness is made to appear natural in context. At the same time he has a profound inner life: a strong religious sense, but also a wider moral being, which emerges, for example, in his dealings with the Spanish captain. Crusoe possesses, notoriously, distinct social and economic characteristics: he is recognisably a man of his age, recognisably English, recognisably Protestant, recognisably a member of the trading community. Yet these disparate attributes are fused in Defoe's portrayal of the cautious adventurer. For all his typicality, we get to know him in his full individuality, just as with the men and women in Shakespeare. We live in enforced intimacy with the castaway on his island, sharing the most ordinary moments in diurnal existence. However often we read the book, we are startled afresh by the vivid details – the three Dutch cheeses stored in a seaman's chest; the large tortoise which suddenly provides variety in Crusoe's diet; the 'preposterous' effort to make a canoe out of a cedar-tree, a hundred yards away from the nearest water; and so on. These are no casual felicities, but the instinctive touches of a great writer in full imaginative possession of his material.

Above all, Defoe made external narrative carry with it interior meanings. *The Pilgrim's Progress* had also employed a sort of adventure framework to convey spiritual experience, and Bunyan is unquestionably closer kin to Defoe than are Fielding, Sterne or Laclos. Nevertheless, there is something archaic about Bunyan's methods: when Christian meets Apollyon in the Valley of Humiliation, the data presented to us are consistent, believable in their own terms, but quite without ordinary human redundancy:

> He was clothed with scales like a fish (and they are his pride) he had wings like a dragon, feet like a bear, and out of his belly came fire and smoke, and his mouth was as the mouth of a lion.

The biblical cadences here consort easily with a diagrammatic clarity of outline, and a total absence of non-representative detail. On the other hand, Crusoe's symbolic grains of corn include an element of 'noise', that is to say, strictly irrelevant components that afford them independent life in our minds – there are ten or twelve ears, they are perfect green barley, they sprouted from a bag of chicken's meat carelessly shaken out by the hero. Defoe is no less an allegorical writer than Bunyan, but his allegory has, so to speak, come to terms with the phenomenology of modern living. *The Pilgrim's Progress* has the heightened intensity of a dream (which is its literal form). *Robinson Crusoe* traces the deliberately flattened curve of a flattened life-history, even at one point the banal prosiness of a daily journal. Each book in its way encompasses the ordinary and the transcendental – Bunyan sublimely, Defoe doggedly.

Crusoe did not just happen. It was the consummation of a long literary career, and its cultural roots are many and complex. Subsequent chapters of this book will explore particular aspects of the novel, as they were informed by Defoe's concerns and those of the age at large. These topics range from attitudes towards travel, discovery and colonialism to social, philosophical and religious themes such as solitude and self-help. I have also tried to set out the major narrative models available to Defoe. The aim is not to explain away the book's originality but, rather, to show the density of its imaginative world. For *Robinson Crusoe*, with all its ideological strands, is not itself an ideological tract. With all its spiritual messages it is not just an expression of the spiritual life – until its third part, anyway. *Crusoe* is a story of physical adventure and of moral discovery, and it was in uniting these elements that the modern novel found a role, finally separating it off from fable, idyll, epic and romance.

GENERAL EDITOR'S PREFACE

Each volume in this series is devoted to a single major text. It is addressed to serious students and teachers of literature, and to knowledgeable non-academic readers. It aims to provide a scholarly introduction and a stimulus to critical thought and discussion.

Individual volumes will naturally differ from one another in arrangement and emphasis, but each will normally begin with information on a work's literary and intellectual background, and other guidance designed to help the reader to an informed understanding. This is followed by an extended critical discussion of the work itself, and each contributor in the series has been encouraged to present in these sections his own reading of the work, whether or not this is controversial, rather than to attempt a mere consensus. Each volume also contains a historical survey of the work's critical reputation, including an account of the principal lines of approach and areas of controversy, and a selective (but detailed) bibliography.

The hope is that the volumes in this series will be among those which a University teacher would normally recommend for any serious study of a particular text, and that they will also be among the essential secondary texts to be consulted in some scholarly investigations. But the experienced and informed non-academic reader has also been in our minds, and one of our aims has been to provide him with reliable and stimulating works of reference and guidance, embodying the present state of knowledge and opinion in a conveniently accessible form.

University of Warwick

ACKNOWLEDGEMENTS

The principal source for this book has been, of course, the body of Daniel Defoe's own writings. This has been supplemented by the work of many distinguished Defoe scholars, including Arthur W. Secord, John Robert Moore and (happily still active) James Sutherland. Among recent students I am indebted especially to Ian Watt, Maximillian E. Novak, George A. Starr and J. Paul Hunter. My understanding of the wider currents of international history owes much to a number of books by J. H. Parry and C. R. Boxer. I should add that Peter Earle's book *The World of Defoe* appeared when my own research was well advanced. But this is not to suggest that our reading overlapped in every particular, or that I derived no correctives or fresh insights from Mr. Earle's fascinating book – quite the contrary.

On a personal level I have been taught much about Defoe and his age by many friends and colleagues, particularly Christine Rees, Bill Speck, Paul Davies, Michael Treadwell, Clive Probyn and Alan Downie. To the General Editor of this series, C. J. Rawson, I am indebted for wise counsel, and for the opportunity to embark on a stimulating task. The faults which remain are the product of my own unquenchable ignorance. I began the book as a strong admirer of *Robinson Crusoe*, and this feeling has been enhanced by further study. My hope is that readers of this book will equally return to Defoe's masterpiece with enriched interest and enjoyment.

CONTENTS

	page
Preface	vii
General Editor's Preface	ix
Acknowledgements	x
A Note on the Texts	xiii
Abbreviations	xiii
Map Illustrating Crusoe's Travels	xvi
1 Preliminary	1
2 Travel, Trade and Empire	25
3 Religion and Allegory	51
4 Social and Philosophic Themes	73
5 Literary Background	92
6 Structure and Style	110
7 Critical History	127
Appendix A Woodes Rogers's Narrative of Selkirk	155
Appendix B Richard Steele's Narrative of Selkirk	160
Appendix C The Illustrators of *Robinson Crusoe*	163
Appendix D Table of Dates	165
Appendix E Gazetteer	168
Appendix F Biographical Index	170
Bibliography	172
General Index	179

A NOTE ON THE TEXTS

There is no complete collected edition of Defoe's works; as yet no volumes have appeared in the series to be published by the Southern Illinois University Press. I have therefore adopted this set of priorities in textual matters:

(1) Where a good modern edition exists, such as the Oxford English Novels volumes, I have used this. *The Life and Strange Surprizing Adventures of Robinson Crusoe* is quoted from J. Donald Crowley's edition in that series (1972), which is based on the text of the first edition.

(2) Failing this, I have had recourse to an accessible reprint where the text is not hopelessly corrupt. For the second and third parts of *Robinson Crusoe*, I use *The Works of Daniel Defoe*, ed. G. H. Maynadier (Boston, Mass., 1903–4), Vols II and III. This is a modernised but reasonably accurate text.

(3) If there is no other available source, I quote from the original edition, or in certain cases from a collected edition published in Defoe's lifetime.

This procedure has one unfortunate consequence, in that my quotations present a mosaic of modern- and old-spelling texts. The alternative was to confine myself to largely inaccessible editions, many of them available only in the great libraries of the English-speaking world. I have chosen what seems to me the lesser of two evils.

ABBREVIATIONS

The following cue-titles are used for works which are frequently mentioned:

Byrd   Max Byrd (ed.), *Daniel Defoe: A Collection of Critical Essays* (Englewood Cliffs, NJ, 1976).

CH   P. Rogers (ed.), *Defoe: The Critical Heritage* (London and Boston, Mass., 1972).

Checklist   J. R. Moore, *A Checklist of the Writings of Daniel Defoe* (Bloomington, Ind., 1960; rev. edn. 1971).

Citizen   J. R. Moore, *Daniel Defoe: Citizen of the Modern World* (Chicago, Ill., 1958).

Earle   P. Earle, *The World of Defoe* (London, 1976).

Ellis   F. H. Ellis (ed.), *Twentieth Century Interpretations of Robinson Crusoe* (Englewood Cliffs, NJ, 1969).

Gildon   Charles Gildon, *The Life and Strange Surprizing Adventures of Mr D—— DeF—* (London, 1719).

History of Pyrates   *A General History of the Pyrates*, ed. M. Schonhorn (London, 1972).

Hunter   J. P. Hunter, *The Reluctant Pilgrim: Defoe's Emblematic Methôd and Quest for Form in Robinson Crusoe* (Baltimore, Md., 1966).

Hutchins   H. C. Hutchins, *Robinson Crusoe and Its Printing 1719–1731* (New York, 1925).

Lee   W. Lee, *Daniel Defoe: His Life, and Recently Discovered Writings,* 3 vols. (London, 1869; reprinted Hildesheim, 1968).

Letters   *The Letters of Daniel Defoe,* ed. G. H. Healey (Oxford, 1955).

Library   *Librorum ex Bibliothecis Philippi Farewell, D.D. et Danielis Defoe, Gen. Catalogus* (1731).

Little   B. Little, *Crusoe's Captain* (London, 1960).

Novak, *Economics*   M. E. Novak, *Economics and the Fiction of Daniel Defoe* (Berkeley and Los Angeles, Calif., 1962; reprinted New York, 1976).

Novak, *Nature*   M. E. Novak, *Defoe and the Nature of Man* (Oxford, 1963).

RC1   *The Life and Strange Surprizing Adventures of Robinson Crusoe* (1719). Text and page references follow the edition by J. Donald Crowley (Oxford English Novels, London, 1972).

RC2   *The Farther Adventures of Robinson Crusoe* (1719). See p. xiii.

RC3   *Serious Reflections . . . of Robinson Crusoe* (1720). See p. xiii.

Review   Daniel Defoe, *The Review,* ed. A. W. Secord, 22 vols. (New York, 1938).

Secord   A. W. Secord, *Studies in the Narrative Method of Defoe* (Urbana, Ill., 1924; reprinted New York, 1963).

Shinagel   M. Shinagel, *Daniel Defoe and Middle-Class Gentility* (Cambridge, Mass., 1968).

Starr   G. A. Starr, *Defoe and Spiritual Autobiography* (Princeton, NJ, 1965).

Sutherland   J. Sutherland, *Defoe,* 2nd edn. (London, 1950).

Tour   Daniel Defoe, *A Tour through the Whole Island of Great Britain,* ed. G. D. H. Cole (London, 1927; reprinted 1968).

Watt   I. Watt, *The Rise of the Novel* (London, 1957; paperback, Harmondsworth, 1963).

OTHER ABBREVIATIONS

ECS	*Eighteenth Century Studies*
EIC	*Essays in Criticism*
ELH	*ELH: A Journal of English Literary History*
HLQ	*Huntington Library Quarterly*
JEGP	*Journal of English and Germanic Philology*
MLN	*Modern Language Notes*
MLQ	*Modern Language Quarterly*
MP	*Modern Philology*
N & Q	*Notes and Queries*
OED	*Oxford English Dictionary*
OEN	Oxford English Novels
PBSA	*Papers of the Bibliographical Society of America*

PMLA   *PMLA: Publications of the Modern Language Association of America*
PQ   *Philological Quarterly*
RES   *Review of English Studies*
SEL   *Studies in English Literature 1500–1900*
SP   *Studies in Philology*
TLS   *Times Literary Supplement*

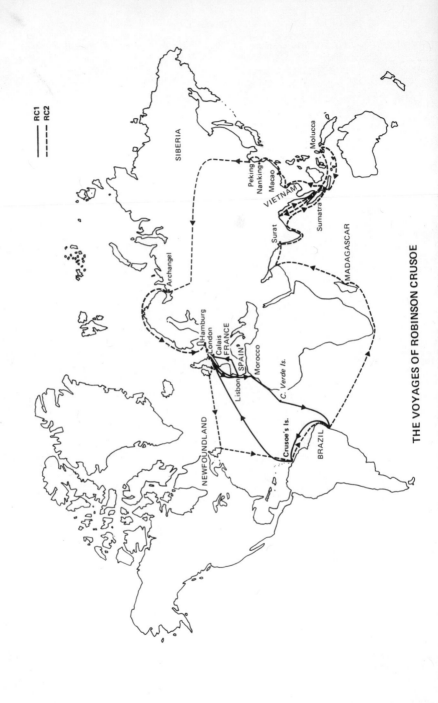

RC1 ———
RC2 - - - -

SIBERIA

Archangel

Peking
Nanking
Macao

Molucca

VIETNAM

Surat

Sumatra

MADAGASCAR

Hamburg
London
Calais
FRANCE
SPAIN
Lisbon
Morocco
C. Verde Is.

NEWFOUNDLAND

Crusoe's Is.

BRAZIL

THE VOYAGES OF ROBINSON CRUSOE

For Ian Jack
scholar, teacher and wise friend

CHAPTER 1

Preliminary

DEFOE'S LIFE

Robinson Crusoe is generally regarded as the first English novel, but its author was by no conceivable stretch of imagination a beginner.[1] Defoe had been writing for thirty of his sixty-nine years when the first part of *Crusoe* appeared in 1719. The three parts form items 412, 417 and 436 in Moore's *Checklist* of Defoe's writings; a few earlier items in the list may not have been written by Defoe, but we can be certain that he *did* write other works not identified to fill the blanks.[2] (Moore's final tally amounts to some 560 books, pamphlets and journals.) No one writing his 412th work can begin with a totally blank literary sheet, and even though *Crusoe* was a deeply innovative production it necessarily drew on a long apprenticeship in the author's craft. We might estimate, very roughly, that of the previous 411 books something like half were, in the broadest sense, political. They included tracts on controversial topics such as the Sacheverell dispute of 1709–10; pamphlets on the politics of religion, and especially the condition of dissenters; and clusters of items concerned with a specialised interest, such as Scottish affairs. In addition Defoe had been widely active as a poet, with *The True-Born Englishman* (1701) his most popular single work. From the time of his verse meditations in 1681, he had aspired to success as a poet, and in 1703 almost a hundred pages of *Poems on State Affairs* (the most widely read verse of the day) were occupied by his compositions.[3] But after 1710 he restricted himself more and more to prose, and by 1720 he allowed himself only a very occasional return to poetry.

Experienced as he was, Defoe had not yet found his entire range as an author. It is often supposed that his background as a writer of criminal biography was a major help to his fictional technique; and yet, as A. W. Secord pointed out, 'the biographies known to have been written by Defoe previously to 1719 . . . are neither very numerous nor very significant'.[4] His lives of Jack Sheppard and Jonathan Wild come *after*, not before, *Moll Flanders* and *Colonel Jack*. What might be called Defoe's 'social' concerns grew much more prominent in the 1720s; it was in his last decade that he produced most of his important works on crime, economics, the family and class. We might almost say that it was his novels which led him to an interest in social affairs, rather than the other way round. In other words, although Defoe was quite an elderly man when he came to *Crusoe*, he was still only on the verge of discovering some of his most characteristic styles as a writer.

The reason for Defoe's late efflorescence may be at bottom no more than this: he finally had time to write undistractedly. His had been an eventful progress through life up to that time. He was born in 1660, most likely in the autumn; the event probably took place in Cripplegate, just outside the historic walls of the City of London, near legendary Grub Street. He was actually Daniel Foe; his father was James Foe, later a City liveryman, a merchant whose Flemish ancestors had originally settled in the English midlands. Arriving in the world contemporaneously with the restoration of Charles II, and facing as a result some hard-line legislation, little Daniel became in his innocence a dissenter (in fact a Presbyterian) at the age of 2, when his entire family was forced to decide whether they could subscribe to the new tests of allegiance to the Church of England. When he was 5 the Great Plague hit London, and he was evacuated to the country; the superb descriptions in *A Journal of the Plague Year* (1722) owe more to research and imagination than to direct recollection. In his teens the young Foe attended a prominent dissenting academy just outside London, seemingly in the expectation of becoming a minister. But he did not do this: instead, he established himself as a merchant just off Cornhill, in the business heart of London. By 1684 he was in a position to marry, and marry well; his bride, Mary Tuffley, brought him a dowry of £3,700, worth perhaps £60,000 or $120,000 at present-day values.

It looked as if he was heading for a life of prosperity and respectability. True, he did incautiously go off to fight for the Duke of Monmouth, the Protestant pretender to the throne of Catholic James II, in 1685. He even got himself captured, but was lucky to escape with a royal pardon, when hundreds went to the gallows. Having weathered this, he should have done doubly well when William III dispatched James in 1688 – he actually rode to meet the 'invader' on his way to London, and joined the entourage at Henley. By this time he was a member of a City livery company, that is, one of the bodies which controlled business life: Daniel Foe was admitted to the Butchers' Company, by reason of his father's membership. He was beginning to write and to be published; he had good contacts on the fringe of the Court; and all seemed set fair. But he over-reached himself. After one doomed effort to raise civet-cats in Stoke Newington (he owned seventy cats for manufacturing perfume), in the course of which he managed to cheat his own mother-in-law, he found himself in severe financial difficulties.[5] He had been engaged in a wide variety of ventures, including a project to construct a diving engine to help salvage some lucrative wrecks which lay round the coast of Britain. But it was a more respectable occupation, marine insurance partly designed against these very wrecks, which brought him down. Along with eighteen other merchants he failed because the French were too successful in seizing English vessels during the war now enveloping Europe. A petition to Parliament looked as if it might succeed, and allow the merchants to compose with his creditors; but in the end the House of Lords rejected the measure.[6] In fact Daniel Foe, as he still was, found himself in the Fleet gaol: there could scarcely be a more symbolic eighteenth-century landscape than the debtor's prison, and yet the novelist made no use of it as he did of Newgate.

Slowly, in the middle 1690s, he began to climb once more. He became Defoe, so much more aristocratic in tone, and he acquired substantial public offices. In 1697 his first important literary work, significantly entitled *An Essay upon Projects*, came before the public. With his capital renewed – perhaps owing to a royal gift – he put money into a brick-making concern at Tilbury. The year 1701 saw the publication of *The True-Born Englishman*, satirising hostility towards those of foreign ancestry (like himself). It sold, according to report, 80,000 copies: there were twelve separate pirated editions. But again things went awry. Defoe's patron William III died, to be succeeded by the High Church Queen Anne. His satire on the extreme Tory position, called *The Shortest Way with the Dissenters* (namely, embark on a pogrom), earned official displeasure. He went into hiding but was found concealed at a house in Spitalfields. He was sent to Newgate and ultimately, in July 1703, stood in the pillory on three successive days. Meanwhile his brick works had failed and he was bankrupt for a second time. The autumn of 1703 marks the nadir of what had been an exceedingly chequered career.

He owed his rescue to Robert Harley, a moderate Tory politician who was to be his most enduring patron. Harley arranged for a royal pardon, as well as giving Defoe employment intermittently for the next ten years. It was somewhere between a public and a private post. Defoe served as a one-man intelligence agency, travelling around the country to test the political temperature, and writing extensively on behalf of Harley. From 1704 to 1713 he had single-handed responsibility for *The Review*, a journal of opinion rather than fact. Defoe also wrote a long series of pamphlets in support of Harley; many of these concern the Union with Scotland, for which Defoe acted as promoter and publicist. When Harley fell in 1708, Defoe was taken on by his successor, Godolphin. Again he went all over England and Scotland to report, spy and ferret out disaffection. In 1710 the situation was reversed. Godolphin was ousted, and a strong new Tory administration headed by Robert Harley took over. During the next four years Defoe wrote many of his most influential political pamphlets, in spite of many Whig attempts to gag him. With the death of Queen Anne and the collapse of the Tory Party in 1714,

Defoe found himself a suspected person. For the next few years he had to tread most carefully; his health was bad, and he never became *persona grata* with the Hanoverian court. But he did not stop writing, and the first two parts of *Robinson Crusoe* were among sixteen items listed under the year 1719. No doubt many people had written him off; no one could have guessed that his great creative period was still to come.

The early 1720s witnessed the appearance of the books by which he lives today. After *Crusoe* in quick succession came *Memoirs of a Cavalier, Captain Singleton, Moll Flanders, A Journal of the Plague Year, Colonel Jack* and *Roxana*, all within five years. His non-fictional output is just as remarkable in its way. It included a life of Sir Walter Ralegh, his favourite historical subject; the invaluable *Tour* through Britain; a *History of the Pyrates*; biographies of major and minor criminals; *The Complete English Tradesman*, a deeply characteristic production; and works on demonology and magic. He was in harness to the end, and when he died – fleeing from creditors yet again – in April 1731 the flow had not quite ceased. A few unpublished works have come to light, most notably *The Compleat English Gentleman*, as though the organism had gone on, posthumously secreting its natural juice – words on the page. It is an astonishing record of diligence, will and courage, and would be remarkable even if the books had not been very good. Most of them were, but *Crusoe* stands above all.

EARLY EDITIONS

The first part of *Robinson Crusoe* (henceforward *RC1*) was entered in the Stationers' Register on 23 April 1719.[7] This was on the way to being an obsolete mode by which a publisher claimed the property in a book; the Stationers' Company retained comprehensive powers in theory, but the need for a new Copyright Act in 1709 had shown its practical impotence in the face of pirates. The 'whole share' in Defoe's work was claimed by William Taylor: we do not know how much he had paid for the copyright, but at a very rough guess one might expect a figure of £50 or so. Newspaper advertisements are not precise to within a day, but *RC1* must have appeared to the public on or around 25 April. The title-page opens with the words 'The Life and Strange Surprizing Adventures of Robinson Crusoe, of York, Mariner' (typography normalised), followed by fifty-three words of sub-title. Then comes, within rules, the statement '*Written by Himself*', and the imprint, describing the book as 'printed for' W. Taylor. The whole is enclosed within double rules. Taylor (d.1724) had been associated with Jacob Tonson and Bernard Lintot in publishing the official votes of the House of Commons since 1715. He was a less prominent figure in the book trade than either of his associates; suitably to the ethos of *Crusoe*, he might be termed a publisher of the middle rank. His name is linked to few other works of any historical importance.[8]

There was only one issue of the first edition of *RC1*. A few trifling changes were made while the book was in the press, including the substitution of a semi-colon for a colon in the imprint; but these represent variant states of the same printing. The work is in octavo and consists of 186 leaves; the text ends on page 364 and it is followed by four pages of advertisements by the publisher. A list of errata on page 365 is found in all states of this edition. The famous frontispiece of Crusoe in his sheepskin outfit, a gun slung over each shoulder, was designed by Clark and Pine. As A. Edward Newton wrote, 'This illustration has outlasted several centuries of criticism. We always look for it and are disappointed when we do not find it. . . . It has come to be the accepted portrait; no legend is required: one knows that he is looking at Robinson Crusoe.'[9] The book was priced at 5 shillings, a reasonably modest price even by the standards of the day; an octavo of this length might easily have cost 6 shillings or more.

Defoe's name did not appear on this or any other of the early editions. There is nothing surprising or sinister in that. He had been brought up in the world of controversial pamphleteering, where anonymity was more or less ubiquitous. Of the more than 500 items in the *Checklist*, only a handful carry an unambiguous statement of authorship. Some of these are among his shortest productions, like *Daniel Defoe's Hymn for the Thanksgiving* (1706) (item 119), or *De Foe's Answer to Dyer's Scandalous News Letter* (1707) (153). Occasionally initials are used, as with the '*D. F. Gent.*' found in *The Complete Art of Painting* (1720) (430). Defoe sometimes signed a preface, as in *The History of the Union* (1709) (161); or a dedication, as in *Caledonia* (1706) (129). Letters included in the body of a work may provide evidence of authorship. More often Defoe appears under a sobriquet such as 'the Author of the True Born Englishman', common between 1702 and 1707; or 'the Author of the Review', which first appears in 1706 (see item 110) and is much used around 1711. After the Hanoverian accession Defoe grew if anything more prone to concealment, and his *Appeal to Honour and Justice* (1715) (307) is among the last signed works. In this period Defoe became addicted to pseudonyms; his favourite is perhaps 'Andrew Moreton, Esq.', but there are also 'Captain Charles Johnson', 'H.D. late Clerk to Justice R——', and many others. He poses as a clergyman, a Quaker, a Member of Parliament, a Scottish officer, a merchant, a stock-jobber, and many other things. Only very seldom did *The Genuine Works of Mr. Daniel D'Foe* appear in their undisguised state (440).

Now it is usual to link this phenomenon with Defoe's service as an undercover agent for Harley, when he communicated under the names 'Alexander Goldsmith' or 'Claude Gilot'; or to attribute it to a psychological need for mystification and secrecy. In fact there were good practical reasons for keeping his identity to himself, among which the well-grounded fear of prosecution was paramount. In any case, we should recall that *Gulliver's Travels* appeared anonymously, not to mention Swift's pamphlets on controversial subjects of the day; so did *The Dunciad* and *Joseph Andrews*. Samuel Richardson is on the title-page of *Clarissa*, but only as printer. Above all, we have to remember the formal pretence that Crusoe is indeed the author ('*Written by Himself*'). The mention of any real human being – as opposed to the unidentified 'Editor' who writes the preface – would spoil the effect; Defoe *could* not put his name to his masterpiece.

The first thorough investigation of the printing of *Crusoe* was carried out in the 1920s by Henry C. Hutchins. Most of his conclusions have been ratified by later inquiries, but he made one significant mistake. On the basis of some tenuous evidence, Hutchins decided that Taylor was his own printer, and indeed that the formula 'printed for' habitually means 'printed by'. Neither this general assumption nor the particular deduction is justified. Using more sophisticated techniques developed by modern bibliography, K. I. D. Maslen has shown that three printers – who did not include Taylor – were employed in the early editions. However, the first edition of *RC1* was printed throughout by the same printer, identified by Maslen from ornaments as Henry Parker of Goswell Street. Parker is not celebrated in the annals of typography; he did a fair amount of work for the Tory publisher John Morphew (who regularly issued Swift's works a few years earlier). The standard size of printing for the early editions was 1,000 copies, and it is likely that this was the size of Parker's original batch. This compares with 2,500 copies of *Three Hours after Marriage*, by John Gay and others (1716), 2,500 of Pope's duodecimo *Iliad*, volumes 5 and 6 (1719), and 4,000 of some of the Bangorian pamphlets around 1717. Quoting these figures, Maslen justifiably argues that they do not warrant the belief that Defoe had succeeded in 'breaking open a charmed circle' of Augustan élitist readers.[10] Even when we take the subsequent editions into account, *Crusoe* was never a bestseller on quite the scale of *Gulliver's Travels*, though it was an undoubted commercial success from the start.

The second edition was called for by 9 May, that is, a fortnight after the first. Again, this exists in the form of a single issue. Most of the text was again printed by Parker, but this time later portions were farmed out to Hugh Meere and William Bowyer, doubtless owing to the need for haste in forestalling pirates. The same advertisements as in the first edition appear, although they have been reset. Once more the edition size was 1,000 copies, a fact which can be established from Bowyer's paper-ledgers. This was in effect a page-for-page reprint; there are a large number of minor variants but no grounds whatever for believing these to have any authorial origin.

Around 6 June came the third authorised edition, though by this time the pirates were probably in the market. Again, the same three printers can be identified as contributing to the edition. There are two issues of this version, for which the printers took a different share of the responsibility in either case. A number of substantive variants appear in the text of the separate issues, but even here neither can be regarded as more authoritative in any literary sense. The fourth edition appeared about 7 August, by which time the second part of *Crusoe* (*RC2*) was almost ready. A map was included for the first time. Parker seems to have printed both issues of this edition – perhaps a sign that the rush for copies was dying down. Throughout this period 1,000 apparently remained as the standard scale of printing, although 1,500 was often reckoned the most economical number. Thereafter the pace slackened. The fifth edition was published in 1720, perhaps in November, by which time the third part of *Crusoe* (*RC3*) had appeared. Again a map was inserted, folded in opposite the title-page; there was some tinkering with the frontispiece. The text was rather better printed, with more careful attention to spacing. The sixth edition came out in 1722, with six new plates dispersed about the text and red type used alongside black on the title-page. In June 1722 another 'sixth' edition appeared, the first of the duodecimo versions of *RC1*. This ran to 296 pages and contained eight plates. Textually it is different from the sixth octavo edition, though it is not clear who is responsible for the changes – probably not Defoe. From this time the authorised editions regularly appear in duodecimo, the octavo sheets having been exhausted. This applies to the seventh edition (1726), published by William Mears and Thomas Woodward (Taylor having died); the eighth (1736), issued by Woodward alone; the ninth (1747), with the imprint of Woodward and J. Osborn; and the tenth (1753), published by T. and T. Longman and J. and J. Rivington. In general these successive editions of *RC1* were sold along with new versions of *RC2*.

Piracies of the first part were quick to appear. One of the earliest was a Dublin edition – a common situation when there was no effective copyright agreement between England and its off-shore province. This was set up from a copy of the first London edition and may have appeared as soon as the beginning of June 1719. More annoying to Taylor were the home-grown illegal versions. A comparatively rare duodecimo has become known as the 'O' edition; it was set up from the later issue of the fourth edition, and thus dates probably from August or September 1719. It is not absolutely certain that Taylor knew of this particular volume, issued by the 'booksellers' – a euphemism for pirates.

One of which he certainly was aware was a duodecimo published by Thomas Cox in London, stated to give the text of *Crusoe* 'abridg'd' and

made 'more portable'. Some have thought that Defoe himself may have
been involved in this work; Hutchins suspected Charles Gildon. There
were several repercussions. Taylor put a notice in the *St James's Post*
for 7 August 1719, complaining about Cox's alleged improvement, as it
consisted 'only of some scattered Passages, incoherently tacked together'.
This advertisement was included as a note in the preface to *RC2*, which
appeared around 20 August. Taylor, as threatened in his notice, began a
suit against Cox in Chancery. Cox made a long and vigorous reply in
the *Flying Post* for 29 October 1719, referring in passing to Defoe as
'one of the most prostituted pens in the whole world'. The Chancery
suit, like many of its kind, apparently faded quietly into nothingness,
and by the time the third part of *Crusoe* appeared Taylor was looking
back on his struggles with some equanimity.

Meanwhile two other pirate versions had made their appearance.
The novel was serialised in the *Original London Post, or Heathcot's
Intelligence,* in seventy-eight instalments between 7 October 1719 and
30 March 1720. Inevitably the need to fit the text within the confines
of a single-sheet newspaper meant that savage condensation was carried
out. This was one of the very earliest, if not *the* first, among reprints
of English fiction in the popular press, and it is an important sign of the
currency which *Crusoe* had gained. It might be noted here that *RC2*
received the same treatment at Heathcot's hands, in issues between 1
April 1720 (directly following the conclusion of *RC1*) and 19 October
of the same year. This completes the list of known piracies of the first
part. Abridgements can be left aside for a moment, since they typically
involve two if not three parts of the entire work.

The Farther Adventures of Robinson Crusoe (*RC2*) was published by
Taylor, as just noted, on 20 August 1719. The title-page described this
as 'the Second and Last Part of his Life', which is true in so far as the
third part is not properly biographic in scope. The map of the world
which first appeared in the fourth edition of *RC1*, published a fortnight
earlier, is included here, too. It is based on the kind of map found in
Dampier's *New Voyage* and Woodes Rogers's *Cruising Voyage.* The
prominence of various localities, especially in Asia, which figure in *RC2*
suggests that this map was included largely to satisfy readers of the
second part; by comparison *RC1*, even at the beginning and end of the
book, is a static affair. There were two issues of this first edition of *RC2*,
distinguished mainly by a resetting of the text by two or three different
printers, together with the presence or absence of a warning (already
mentioned) against Cox's piracy of *RC1*. It is likely, though not con-
clusively proved, that a somewhat larger print was ordered for the
second part. In the last sentence of *RC1* Defoe (or rather Crusoe) had
given a hint that there might be a sequel forthcoming, no doubt on the
assumption that sales would justify writing such a book. By the end of

July 1719 gossip confirmed that a continuation would be appearing: 'Robinson Crusoe I have not read yet', wrote one cleric to another, 'but they say it was wrote by Daniel de Foe and that a second part is coming out.'[11]

Before the end of the year a second edition of *RC2* had been published by Taylor. It was again an octavo, but economies of spacing made it possible to reduce the number of pages from 384 to 352. This edition was commonly sold together with the fifth edition of *RC1*. It was followed by a third edition (1722), where the text was squeezed even further to make a volume of 320 pages. The press work was, however, superior to that found in most of the early versions; the text was based on the second issue of the first edition, rather than the slightly corrupted second edition. Six plates were inserted, illustrating some of the more dramatic moments of a not always dramatic narrative. Taylor's last edition of *RC2*, the fourth, appeared as a duodecimo in 1722; it was advertised together with the 'sixth' edition of *RC1* on 7 June of that year. The subsequent fortunes of *RC2* are not of great consequence. It appeared as follows: fifth edition (Mears and Woodward), with *RC1* seventh edition, 1726; sixth (Woodward), with *RC1* eighth edition, 1736; seventh (Woodward and Osborn), with *RC1* ninth edition, 1747. All these were in duodecimo. As time went on, the intervals between each printing became longer; normally a fresh edition of the first part brought with it a new version of the *Farther Adventures*. Piracy of *RC2* was less extensive, a clear indication that the sequel enjoyed a lower degree of popular appeal. The Dublin booksellers who had brought out their own *RC1* in 1719 soon coupled the second part to it, following the first issue of the first edition. Otherwise *RC2* fell mainly into the hands of abridgers, of whom more presently.

The original and presumably definitive *Crusoe* was completed on 6 August 1720, with the appearance of *Serious Reflections during the Life and Surprising Adventures of Robinson Crusoe: with his Vision of the Angelick World* (*RC3*). Despite Taylor's understandable attempt to retain the notion of adventures in the title, this third part is closer to a manual of piety than to a novel. From the start it enjoyed much less popularity and, as Hutchins says, 'quite evidently failed to catch the fancy of the public'. There were translations into French (1721), German (1721) and Dutch (1722), but one legitimate edition of the English text seems to have satisfied demand more than amply. The 'Vision' is separately paginated, making 84 pages to follow the 270 occupied by the reflections proper. A map of Crusoe's island is inserted opposite the title-page. Minor variants in the text represent different states of the same issue.

The after-life of *RC3* was confined to its presence in a number of abridgements of the entire work. The most important among these first appeared in 1722, as a duodecimo of 376 pages. All three parts have been squeezed into a single volume, and as one might expect it is the *Reflections* which is least in evidence. The title-page lists Edward Midwinter as printer, with four booksellers (headed by Edmund Curll's frequent associate Arthur Bettesworth) also named. In subsequent editions (1724, 1726, 1733) the booksellers undergo some mutation, and actually include men with an interest in the legitimate version. It looks as if the copyright-owners were unwilling or unable to discourage the abridgement – if, indeed, they did not support it. According to Hutchins, 'by the mid-century, the book was more or less public property'; the abridgers seem to have anticipated this situation. There was in addition a more drastic curtailment of the text, which claimed to 'epitomize' all three volumes within 154 pages (1734) – again, Bettesworth was involved. One or other abridgement, almost certainly the first of those mentioned, must have been prepared by Thomas Gent, a printer who had been apprenticed to Midwinter. In his *Life*, written *c*.1746 although not published until 1832, Gent described his share in such an enterprise; other references in the text – to the imprisonment of Bishop Atterbury particularly – indicate that the abridgement was made around late 1722 or early 1723. It is likely enough that the '1722' abridgement was dated according to the Old Style, which would mean it could have been issued as late as the end of March 1723.

For some reason Taylor divided the rights of *Crusoe* into two shares, although he apparently owned both. After his death on 5 May 1724 the rights were put up for auction at a sale held on 3 February 1726. Lots 34 and 35 consisted of the first two parts, and the catalogue states that £10 is to be paid (to Defoe?) for every 1,000 of the first part, plus 10 guineas more 'when every 1,000 of the 2d Part is put to printing, and £5 more when 500 of the 2d vol. are sold'. Lot 36 was the third part, with 15 guineas to be paid 'on every Impression of 1,000'. In the margin of the catalogue this lot is marked 'not sold'. As for the first two parts, one half-share fetched £15, the other mysteriously commanded 15 guineas. The immediate gainers would have been Taylor's widow, who had subsequently married another bookseller, William Innys. Meanwhile, in August 1724, Thomas Longman, founder of the famous publishing house, had bought Taylor's stock of printed books from the executors (Innys and John Osborn). Both Osborn and Longman purchased a number of rights at the Taylor sale and, as we have seen, they figure among the publishers of *Crusoe* in later editions.

THE LATER PROGENY

This somewhat muddled story reflects the confused reaction of the book trade to what must have been an unexpected success. The first part was an immediate bestseller, and retained some appeal for the rest of the century – though its great days were to lie ahead in the Victorian era. Initially *RC2*, though less popular, was borne along by the success of its predecessor; not until a generation later does the first part commonly appear by itself. The third part never attained any degree of significant readership. After the immediate rush, piracies became less of a business proposition, but the flow of abridgements has never completely dried up. By 1900 there were at least 200 English editions, including abridged texts; 110 translations; 115 revisions and adaptations; and 277 imitations, headed by works such as *Quall, Peter Wilkins* and *The Swiss Family Robinson*. At that time fifty French versions were traced, twenty-one German and five Dutch. Few works of imaginative literature can have entered the syllabus of a naval college, but in 1815 *Robinson Crusoe* was 'revised and corrected for the advancement of nautical education, illustrated by technical and geographical annotation and embellished with maps and engravings'. The perpetrator of this act was the hydrographer of the *Naval Chronicle*; he deserves to be remembered, for among all the uses to which *Crusoe* had been put by its adaptors this must be the one of which Defoe would have wholeheartedly approved.

In each of these categories there is striking testimony to the enduring vitality of *Crusoe*. After 1750 the pace slackened a little as regards 'authentic' editions, though what was termed the 'twelfth' was reached in 1761 – by this time the work was long out of copyright, which strictly should have lapsed in 1733. The so-called 'fifteenth' edition appeared in 1778, published by a distinguished consortium of booksellers including Strahan, Caslon and Longman. A notable version was the Stockdale edition of 1790, with the second volume containing a life by George Chalmers (see below, pp. 133–4). This contained seventeen plates; those illustrating the text were designed by Thomas Stothard and engraved by Thomas Medland (see below, pp. 163–4). The volumes were published by subscription – the first and, I think, the only subscription *Crusoe*. There are 207 ordinary subscribers and 77 booksellers, with Charles Dilly, a large wholesale merchant as well as a retailer, taking 100 copies. In all more than 660 copies were subscribed for – a larger than average total. The names listed include William Pitt (as well as his brother the second Earl of Chatham), together with prominent men such as James Boswell, Sir Joseph Banks, Charles Macklin, Henry James Pye and James Bindley.

In the nineteenth century *Crusoe* was reprinted much more frequently, and the Victorian average is two 'authentic' editions per year. It was included in collected editions of Defoe such as the Tegg (1839–41); it appeared in the Novelist's Library (1831) and in Tauchnitz (1845); the Globe edition of 1867 carried a not very good introduction by Henry Kingsley. A so-called facsimile of the first edition (1883) contained a

preface by Austin Dobson; but the accuracy of the text was lower than
might have been hoped (Dobson had nothing to do with this side of the
production). As for reworkings, they appeared in several languages and
in every guise: *Robinson Crusoe in Words of One Syllable* (1867) is the
choicest example, but there are many strong competitors – Crusoe in
short words, Crusoe's farmyard for children, Crusoe in verse, Crusoe
and other old friends.

Translations begin with the French version of all three parts, published
in Amsterdam (1720–20–21); German renderings of *RC1* and *RC2*
(Hamburg, 1720); and a Dutch translation of the entire work
(Amsterdam, 1721–2). French versions continued to appear regularly
throughout the century: one, published in Frankfurt, The Hague and
Leipzig (1769), attributed the work to Richard Steele. One of the more
interesting is the version by the poet and salon *habitué* Pétrus Borel, with
a life of Defoe by Philarète Chasles and 'une dissertation religieuse par
l'Abbé La Bouderie' (Paris, 1836). German translations were only
slightly less numerous, though Ullrich records only one version of *RC3*
(Amsterdam, 1721). The earliest Italian *Crusoe* listed dates from Venice
in 1731; Danish, from Copenhagen in 1745; Swedish, from Stockholm
in the same year; Finnish, not until 1847. In Spain the book was placed
on the Index, and the earliest Spanish translation appeared in Paris in
1835. Other languages represented in Ullrich's bibliography include
Arabic, Armenian, Bengali, Coptic, Estonian, ancient Greek, Hebrew,
Hungarian, Maltese, Maori, Persian, Polish, Portuguese, Turkish and
Welsh. There is also an Eskimo version known.

Among the imitations and Robinsonades, priority apparently belongs
to two English items, of which the most successful was [?W. R.
Chetwood] *The Voyages, Dangerous Adventures, and Imminent Escapes
of Captain Richard Falconer* (1720). This was often reprinted and was
translated into German. Other popular imitations include *Der Sächsische
Robinson* (1722) and *Gustav Landcron*, the 'Swedish Robinson' (1724),
both of which were known in several languages. In time this was to be
the model of innumerable variants: there was a Dutch Crusoe, a German
Crusoe, a French Crusoe, an American Crusoe, a Norwegian Crusoe, a
Danish Crusoe, an Icelandic Crusoe, a Bohemian Crusoe, a Berliner
Crusoe, one from the Hartz mountains and one from Leipzig, a Spanish
Crusoe, an Austrian Crusoe, a Magyar Robinson, a Swedish Crusoe and
very many more. The formula reached its consummation in the hugely
popular book by Johann Rudolf Wyss, *Der Schweizerische Robinson*
(1812–27). This has become a world book almost on the scale of its
progenitor; the first English translation appeared in 1814 (*The Family
Robinson*), and by 1849 *The Swiss Family Robinson* incorporated all
four portions of the work. Several new translations were made, and the
undaunted Mary Godolphin followed her work on *Crusoe* with *The*

Swiss Family Robinson in Words of One Syllable (1869). It should not be thought that only nationalities were brought into play: we find a *Chemisch-Technologischer Robinson* (1809), *Le Robinson des glaces* (1835), *Le Petit Robinson de Paris* (1840), *La Petite Fille de Robinson* (1844), *Le Robinson des sables du désert* (1845), *The Arctic Crusoe* (1854), *The Catholic Crusoe* (1862), and even *Les Petits Robinson des caves, ou le siège de Paris* (1872). Other transformations include Crusoe as a boy, as a girl, *The Dog Crusoe* (1860), *Le Robinson noir* (1877), as a doctor, and as an idyllic lover. Titles listed by Ullrich are *Robinson Crusoe's Money, Crusoe in New York, Les Robinsons pour rire, Le Robinson des airs, Un Robinson de six ans, Robinson et Robinsonette, Le Dernier Robinson* (1860: not so), *Six Hundred Robinson Crusoes* (1877), *Les Robinson historiques* and *Robinson in Australien*. Crusoe was transported all over the globe, with the Alps and the prairies of North America favourite locations. Meanwhile Le Sage's *Gil Blas* was translated, nonsensically, as *Der Spanische Robinson* (1726); Fenimore Cooper's *The Crater* became *Le Robinson américain* (1851); Captain Marryat's *Masterman Ready* appeared in German (1843) as *Robinson Ready*.

A number of adventure-stories, loosely tied to the Crusoe theme, attained special prominence. In 1727 a book entitled *The Hermit* was published in London, describing fifty years of solitude on a South Sea island experienced by Philip Quarll. The author has been identified as Peter Longueville. There were a dozen or more editions by 1800 in England and America, quite apart from translations and chapbook versions. Almost as successful, and even further from *Crusoe*, was a book by Robert Paltock (1697–1767): this was *The Life and Adventures of Peter Wilkins, a Cornish Man* (1751). It tells of a shipwrecked mariner who reaches a world within the earth where the inhabitants can fly; the flow of editions has still not quite died out, and in the Romantic era Coleridge, Shelley, Lamb, Leigh Hunt and Scott were all admirers. A widely read German Robinsonade was written by Johann Gottfried Schnabel and published in Bordhausen (1731); it is generally known as *Die Insel Felsenburg,* and had its own imitators. However, the most important of all the books in this class was undoubtedly Joachim Hendrik Campe's *Robinson der Jüngere* (Hamburg, 1779–80), which followed the original into all the major European languages – indeed, it appeared in Spanish, Russian, Latin, Lettic and possibly others earlier than did *Crusoe*. Campe's adaptation stays closer to Defoe than does the ordinary Robinsonade; he has Crusoe wrecked without any tools or utensils, and generally prunes the story so as to provide nourishing moral fare for young people. In the eighteenth century *Crusoe* had not yet become a children's classic: some guardians of the public weal experienced anxiety on the score of its religious orthodoxy. But Campe was inoffensive to almost all schools of moral and educational thought: hence his universal acceptability (some 120 editions by 1900).

Since the turn of the century, the flow has continued unabated. *Crusoe* takes up thirty-five columns in the British Library catalogue; merely to list new versions eats up several centimetres annually. It is odd that there is still no truly definitive edition, although the one by J. Donald Crowley (OEN, 1972; paperback, 1976) is adequate within the limits of that series. *RC1* now stands by itself, almost invariably, but where contemporaries abridged the text modern needs have produced an edition garnished with notes, critical commentaries, background materials and bibliographies (see the Norton Critical Edition, 1975). There has been a recent Soviet translation by D. M. Urnov, with *Colonel Jack* (Pravda Publishing House, 1974), as well as a volume of selections from Defoe. The book has been rewritten within the confines of a 1,200-word vocabulary; it was the victim of a new-spelling study (World Book-Fame Reasons) as long ago as 1888. Luckily Defoe's Robinson is great enough to withstand such treatment as it has in its time endured adaptation as an opera by Offenbach (at the Opéra Comique, 1867), Bunuel's surrealist film, an ice-show by Tom Arnold, and countless British pantomime renditions.

A few of the chapbook versions have a thin charm, but it is the pantomime which has extracted the richest sustenance from *Crusoe*. Even before the modern entertainment was invented, Robinson entered the repertoire of popular theatre. At Drury Lane on 30 January 1781 the curtain went up on an afterpiece called *Robinson Crusoe: or Harlequin Friday*. It was what the eighteenth century termed a pantomime, that is, a comic extravaganza built around *commedia dell'arte* characters with much emphasis on dance, mime and spectacle. This particular show was probably put together either by Richard Brinsley Sheridan or by his wife. The text does not survive, but accounts which are preserved suggest that it made for some enjoyable theatre, with particularly striking effects by the great designer Philip Loutherberg. The first act was still within hailing distance of Defoe's story, despite the entrance of Harlequin and his friends. With the second act for some reason the action moved to Spain, and all sight of the original was soon lost. The show proved popular enough to be performed in Oxford and in a private theatre. It would be a fascinating thing to witness a revival of this piece – did the book survive – and to compare it with, say, the Grand Comic Christmas Pantomime of *Robinson Crusoe*, put on at the Alexandra Theatre in Liverpool in 1878–9. No one will wish to argue that suitability for adaptation into pantomime form is a major test of a great artistic creation; but I cannot resist the feeling that the same mythic quality underlies Crusoe's enduring success in both modes.[12]

A flourishing branch of the Crusoe industry continues to be the

production of abridgements, designed ostensibly for children. One recent
example may serve to exemplify many such efforts. It is described as
'Daniel Defoe's classic tale, retold by Derry Moffatt' (London, 1974).
The cover of this paperback is garnished with still photographs from a
recent television performance and indeed part of the lure is that the story
is 'now dramatized in a spectacular new BBC television production
starring Stanley Baker'. Derry Moffatt's version begins in this way:

> Way back in the year 1632 within the noble City of York, a boy was
> born into a middle-class family. Because of a series of strange
> adventures he was later to become very famous. His name was
> Robinson Crusoe. He was blessed with wise and loving parents. As a
> child he had the advantage of being educated both at home and at a
> country school, an asset in those far-off times. His father had been a
> prosperous merchant. Now retired, he cared deeply for his son, wishing
> him to settle down to a comfortable home life.
>
> Robinson Crusoe cherished other plans. Ever since he could
> remember, his mind had been obsessed with one main ambition . . .
> to go to sea. He longed for adventure and freedom, yearned to explore
> fascinating, far-away countries. Constant thoughts of life on a sailing-
> ship, fellow sailors, boisterous green waves, flying spray and a canopy
> of spray overhead fascinated him by day . . . haunted his dreams by
> night.
>
> Robinson Crusoe's father, a shrewd and grave man, was worried
> by his son's vision. Such reveries he was convinced, would surely end
> in disillusionment and drama. One day he sent for his son, determined
> to have a serious talk. Old Mr Crusoe suffered painfully from gout.
> When Robinson Crusoe entered his father's study, he was seated in a
> deep, high-backed chair, his afflicted foot resting on a gout stool.
>
> 'Robinson, my boy,' he boomed, 'it is high time that you and I
> discussed your future. . . .'

Despite some obvious infelicities (is 'a comfortable home life' what
Crusoe's father envisaged for his son?), there is a certain chastity about
the writing which makes it not wholly unfaithful to the original – at any
rate until we come to the green waves and flying spray. Like many
abridgers, Derry Moffatt divides the story into chapters – sixteen in all.
The proportions of the narrative are quite well preserved, with Friday's
entrance occurring at the end of Chapter 8. There is no recourse to
flashback, as in a recent French television serial.

It should be added that more serious recensions continue to be made,
often remoulding the narrative in the manner of Michel Tournier
(*Vendredi*, 1969) and Adrian Mitchell, who install Friday as the tutor
and Crusoe as the bemused convert. A more oblique adaptation is that
of Muriel Spark in her early novel *Robinson* (1958). Here, as a result

of a plane crash, the heroine, January Marlow, is cast with two companions on to an island in the North Atlantic, named after its lone occupier, Robinson. There are echoes of Defoe's plot and some significant twists. Rather than twenty-eight years, two months and nineteen days, the sojourn is set at two months and twenty-nine days, beginning on 20 May 1954. Robinson has bought his island from the Portuguese, a different mode of proprietorship from Crusoe's but equally indisputable in the context of the story. The name 'January' seems to reflect very dimly the naming of Friday. The subtle metaphysics and ironic narrative manner are far less Defoe-like, and Mrs Spark patently writes with a consciousness of *Lord of the Flies*. All the same, it is a book whose central fable depends on our recognition of the Crusoe story, however transmuted and distanced. If not an imitation of *Robinson Crusoe*, it is an allusive version of the myth.

COMPOSITION

Nobody can say quite how and when Defoe came to conceive of *Robinson Crusoe*. Many of the interests displayed in the book had been a lifelong concern. Centrally, for its author, the theme is divine providence; and that is something already apparent in the 21-year-old Defoe's verse *Meditacions*. Travel, discovery, piracy and like subjects had fascinated him from youth. Recent commentators have stressed – perhaps over-stressed – the role of economic ideas in the design of *Crusoe*, and this, too, was a topic on which Defoe had written extensively for twenty years and more. There is little in the first part of the story, indeed, which its author could not have composed at any time in the previous decade. He was busy about his normal literary activities, during that spring of 1719. After a slight lull in the early Hanoverian years, when illness and official intimidation had caused his annual tally of publications to fall below twenty, he was back to his prolific best in the last years of the decade. Immediately preceding *Crusoe* in the standard bibliography comes a contribution to the so-called 'Bangorian' controversy, that is to say, a theological pamphlet:[13] *Merry Andrew's Epistle to his Old Master Benjamin, A Mountebank at Bangor-Bridge On the River Dee near Wales* (somehow confusion has arisen between Bangor, near Caernarvon, where the episcopal see was, and Bangor-on-Dee; but since Bishop Hoadly had never been to his see the mistake is forgivable). After this we know of no fresh publications for twelve weeks, a suspiciously long interval. As I have suggested, Defoe *could* have kept his novel lying in a drawer for nine years; but the likelihood is that he wrote it immediately prior to publication, around February, March and April 1719. He was almost certainly contributing to Mist's *Weekly Journal* at this time; but for Defoe that scarcely counted as a distraction.

The argument here assumes that the famous narrative of Alexander Selkirk served only as a trigger to Defoe's imagination. This story broke seven years earlier, with the appearance of Woodes Rogers's *Cruising Voyage Round the World* and Edward Cooke's *Voyage to the South Sea*. Selkirk's fame had spread with the article by Richard Steele on his career, which was printed in *The Englishman* in 1713. He lived out the rest of his fairly grubby existence in relative obscurity and died in 1721. Biographers have not scrupled to imagine scenes in which Defoe conducted a personal interview with Selkirk, and these are generally set in 1711 or 1712, shortly after the return of Woodes Rogers's expedition in October 1711. Since, however, Selkirk has always been an essential part of the Crusoe myth, it is necessary to say something here of his strange life.[14]

Alexander Selkirk was born in Fife in 1676. A fractious and uncompanionable man, he had set sail as master of a privateering ship in 1703 along with another galley commanded by the famous William Dampier. Perpetual quarrels dogged the enterprise when the ships reached the South Sea (that is, Pacific), and finally matters came to a head in a bitter dispute between Selkirk and one Thomas Stradling, another commander. In September 1704, Selkirk was by his own volition set down alone on Juan Fernandez, specifically the island of Mas a Tierra, 400 miles from the coast of Chile, in the latitude of Valparaiso. It was a rugged volcanic outcrop, broadly triangular in shape, 15 miles long, less than half of that in width. There was a large bay on the eastern side, and there were extensive woods to the north.

It was not a desperately inhospitable place; the earth was fertile and the climate by no means extreme, despite the proximity of the tropic. Selkirk was provided with a good stock of basic equipment, ranging from a gun, a knife and navigation instruments to his tobacco and a Bible. There he spent more than four years, until his rescue by another privateering expedition in February 1709. This was led by the celebrated Bristol mariner Woodes Rogers,* and included the veteran buccaneer

---

*Perhaps the most important figure in the background of *Robinson Crusoe*, Woodes Rogers (1678/9–1732) came from an old Dorset family, the son of a sea captain. He was himself apprenticed to a mariner in 1697, by which time he had moved to Bristol. In 1705 he married the daughter and joint heiress of Rear-Admiral Sir William Whetstone, a prominent naval officer in the war against France. Around 1707 Rogers turned to privateering after a number of losses in merchant shipping, and in July 1708 he set out on his famous expedition, backed by a consortium of Bristol businessmen. There were two ships, *Duke* and *Dutchess*, each carrying rather more than a hundred men on board. They were away for three years and two months; and when they returned there were three, for one of the convoy was a Spanish galleon they had taken as a prize in December 1709. Their route had been in the normal westerly direction, that is, along the eastern coast of South America, round the Horn,

Dampier, the inventive quack Dr Thomas Dover[15] and other notable men. (Carleton Vanbrugh, brother of the dramatist, was one of the number; he died before the expedition got back to London.) Selkirk was appointed mate of one of the privateering vessels, and went with the expedition along the western coast of Chile and Peru, then to Mexico. Eventually he reached home with the rest of the party, eight years after leaving England.

Undeniably there were elements in Selkirk's experiences which found an echo in *Crusoe*. There are similarities in the topography of Mas a Tierra and Crusoe's island, while Selkirk's basic survival-kit is paralleled in the novel. So, for that matter, is his goatskin dress. As for more inward matters, there are points of contact there, too:

> Alexander Selkirk's loneliness had not been absolutely unbroken from 1704 to 1709. He had sighted various passing Spanish coasters or French traders. Only once men had landed, the intruders being Spaniards from whom he fled, and who nearly caught him. Psychologically speaking, his main trouble, at least in the first eight months while he grew inured to his loneliness, had been sheer melancholy and fear of his solitude. He had helped himself in his conquest of this condition by reading, prayer, and the singing of psalms. He claimed that in his solitude his Christianity had been more real than before or, as he reckoned, in future.[16]

It would be incorrect to say that Crusoe precisely replicates this pattern of living, but there are clear links in his gradual acceptance of isolation, with religion proving the main consolation. We may note that Crusoe (having landed on 30 September) begins to explore his island in earnest

---

then via Chile, Peru and Mexico to the Gulf of California. They had crossed the Pacific to Guam and made they way through the Moluccas to Batavia; then home via the Cape route. The most dramatic events took place in the first half of the voyage: the rescue of Selkirk from Juan Fernandez in January 1709, a number of prizes seized in the South Sea, and especially the capture of the well-laden galleon *Nuestra Señora de la Encarnación Disengaño* off lower California. This ship had been bound on the famous run from Manila to Acapulco; her cargo was chiefly made up of costly oriental silks and drapery. In the course of their voyage the privateers took large quantities of coin and bullion, and the plunder ran into hundreds of thousands of pounds. Ultimately the syndicate of backers had something like £150,000 to distribute, of which the crew got a third; investors reaped a profit of about 100 per cent. Rogers wrote his account and possibly spoke in person to Defoe. In 1718 he was sent out as Governor of the Bahamas in an attempt to root out the pirate stronghold at New Providence. In 1721 he came back to England and a few years later suffered imprisonment for debt. However, he was reinstated as governor and he returned to the Bahamas for the last years of his life. See Little, *passim*.

only as late as the following 15 July, following his recovery from sickness. This represents a similar period of adjustment to that of Selkirk; the vivid dream Crusoe experiences during his illness occurs on 27 June, that is, 270 days after his shipwreck. Whether or not there is some arcane spiritual significance in this term – so close to the period of human conception – I have not been able to discover; but it is generally agreed that the dream marks a watershed in Crusoe's revival.

The rest of Selkirk's career has a predictable quality of anticlimax. On his return to England he had some conversations with Richard Steele, then at the height of his fame as essayist and opinion-former. In his paper *The Englishman*, on 3 December 1713, Steele gave a circumstantial account of Selkirk's sojourn on the island. By that time Selkirk had already been taken to court for an assault upon a Bristol shipwright, and before his death in 1721 he had added bigamy to the list of his dubious doings. Two important narratives of his experiences had made him famous in his lifetime before *Crusoe* appeared. One was by Edward Cooke, a Bristol-based privateer who had served as one of Rogers's principal lieutenants on his expedition. Cooke's *Voyage to the South Sea, and Round the World* (1712) announced on its title-page an account of Selkirk's 'Manner of living' during his four years' isolation. It was soon followed by the more celebrated narrative by Woodes Rogers himself, *A Cruising Voyage Round the World*. Curiously the bookseller Bernard Lintot, who in this very year published the first version of *The Rape of Lock*, had a share in both the rival accounts. The commander-in-chief was certainly a more accomplished and sensitive writer, but Cooke supplies more abundant detail on many points. Rogers's bent of mind seems closer to that of Defoe, particularly in his statement of the need for the British to build up a powerful South Sea trade in opposition to the Spanish Empire. This had long been an issue of obsessive importance to Defoe (see below, pp. 26–7). We do not know whether Defoe actually met Rogers, but it is likelier that he knew the two expedition-leaders than that he conferred with Selkirk himself. Incidentally, Cooke's work was dedicated to the Earl of Oxford, Defoe's principal patron at this date.

Selkirk would have retained a flimsy immortality even without Defoe. He was the occasion of a moving poem by William Cowper (1782), whose stern Calvinistic sentiments end on a true Crusoesque note:

> There is mercy in every place:
>   And mercy, encouraging thought!
> Gives even affliction a grace,
>   And reconciles man to his lot.

The grace of affliction is undeniably one of the major themes of *RC1*, expressed pervasively and sometimes explicitly – as in Crusoe's reflections after four years on the island (pp. 128–32). It is possible, too, that

Cowper's great poem 'The Castaway' (1799) has some involvement with
Selkirk, although it deals ostensibly with a ship's mate washed overboard
into the Atlantic during Anson's voyage of the 1740s.

Poets tend to be opportunistic and even blurred in their treatment of
sources: Cowper had not read Anson's story for many years when he
wrote 'The Castaway'. Novelists are often more direct in their borrowings,
and in principle we could suppose Defoe to have kept Selkirk's experiences very strongly in mind as he composed his book. It is certain that
he must have known the versions by Rogers and Cooke exceedingly well,
and it is by no means impossible that he did have some contact with
Selkirk – though the legend has an unsatisfactory basis.[17] But none of
this can prove the imaginative impact of Selkirk upon Defoe's mind.
The recent Oxford English Novels edition only mentions Selkirk once,
very briefly, almost in passing; none of its explanatory notes makes any
cross-reference to the long-accepted 'source'. In my view that is going
too far: Selkirk is not the whole of Crusoe, but his story is an important
component of the fiction. We can agree with John Robert Moore that
'the roots of *Robinson Crusoe* lay deeper in [Defoe's] life';[18] but the
trunk of the book, so to speak, is Selkirk.

Dampier's *New Voyage* appeared again during 1717, whilst Rogers'
Cruising Voyage reached a second edition in 1718; but none of the other
supposed sources for the book was particularly recent in 1719. It would
therefore seem that Defoe had kept the idea at the back of his mind
until professional necessity drew the work out of him. According to
Moore, the onset of war with Spain in the summer of 1718 was the most
direct spur.[19] What had happened was that Spain under Cardinal
Alberoni came into conflict with the empire of Charles VI. It seemed
that there was a real threat of Spain's taking possession of Sardinia,
which by the Treaty of Utrecht (1713) was to be guaranteed neutrality.
The English ministry under Stanhope felt obliged to honour the treaty
and dispatched Admiral Sir George Byng to engage with the Spanish
fleet. On 11 August 1718 he achieved a clear-cut victory off Cape
Passaro. The Spanish response, amongst other measures, was to support
the half-hearted Jacobite rising then brewing, which culminated in the
so-called 'Attempt' of 1719. England formally declared war on Spain
just before Christmas, and soon France joined in. The rising failed,
Alberoni fell at the end of 1719, and by 1720 the whole affair had
fizzled out.

By that time the English people had their heads filled with a different
worry, the South Sea Bubble. But in 1719 there was a good deal of anti-
Spanish feeling, superimposed on the pervasive hostility to papacy
which underlay so much of national life. One might have expected Defoe
to capitalise on this prejudice with a picture of lone Englishmen warding
off hordes of Spaniards, but this is absent from the first part of *Crusoe*.

He was certainly anxious to see Britain grab more of the South Sea trade, and the war with Spain (though it was a small-scale European contest) focused attention yet again upon this matter. If there *was* a single reason for the fact that *RC1* appeared when it did, then this is the strongest probability, although the references to Spain are amazingly pacific except on one occasion (*RC1*, pp. 171–2).

It has been suggested that the figure in Defoe's mind was not so much Selkirk as another old seaman with a dubious past, Robert Drury.[20] It was Defoe, in all probability, who later wrote up Drury's career in *Madagascar* (1729); and since Drury was living in Stoke Newington, near to Defoe, after his retirement in 1708, he would have been a possible informant and spur to the novelist's imagination. But, although Drury had his own spell of captivity, there is nothing in his life-history as dramatic or immediately exploitable as Selkirk's isolation on Juan Fernandez.

Under the heading of composition one further matter needs to be considered. It belongs to the realm of myth rather than legend; but it carries with it the tenacity of myth. The story is, then, that the novel – or at least *RC1* – was written not by Defoe at all, but by Robert Harley. It was first retailed in public by Thomas Warton the Younger, who made an entry about it in his notebook for 10 July 1774,[21] and subsequently passed it on in a letter.[22] The notebook entry runs:

> In the year 1759 I was told by the Revd Mr Benj. Holloway, rector of Middleton-Stoney in Oxfordshire, then about seventy years old, and in the early part of his life domestic chaplain to Lord Sunderland, that he had often heard Lord Sunderland say, that Lord Oxford, while a prisoner in the Tower of London, wrote the first volume of the History of *Robinson Crusoe*, mainly as an amusement under confinement, and gave it to Daniel De Foe, who frequently visited Lord Oxford in the Tower, and was one of his pamphlet-writers – that De Foe, by Lord Oxford's permission, published it as his own and managed [*word obliterated*] its extraordinary success, and [?wrote] himself the second volume, the inferiority of which is generally acknowledged. (Mr Holloway also told me from Lord Sunderland, that Lord Oxford dictated some parts of the manuscript to Defoe.)

There follows an endorsement of Holloway's reliability as 'a grave conscientious clergyman, not vain of telling anecdotes'.

Since this story was first published in 1788 almost every subsequent biographer has felt compelled to trot out this story, if only to rebut it. There are in fact no grounds whatsoever for giving any credence to the tale. To mention only the most obvious difficulties: Robert Harley (1661–1724), first Earl of Oxford, was indeed a prisoner in the Tower between 1715 and 1717 facing impeachment for his conduct as first minister (1710–14). But there is no evidence that Defoe visited him there; or that Harley had any creative urges, let alone talents; or that he devoted himself to literary labours at this time. Moreover, it is of course quite untrue that *RC1* was published as Defoe's own; our certainty that Defoe was the author derives from other factors. We have no means whatever of knowing how Sunderland, the third Earl (1674–1722), might have acquired the supposed information. Harley and he had been on bad terms at least since 1706, when Sunderland was foisted unwillingly upon the Godolphin–Harley administration. By the time of Harley's impeachment Sunderland stood at the head of the Whig ministry pressing charges of treason against him. The story is absurd; by comparison the Baconian heresy appears well founded and credible.[23] A refinement of the theory has the true author of the novel as none other than Francis Bacon, presumably in the intervals of his labour on the text of Shakespeare. In this version Harley figures as owner of the papers, duly lent from his notable collection of manuscripts to a grateful compiler. It is at least a picturesque thought.

Other conjectures have been made from time to time regarding the inception of *Crusoe*. Only one of these deserves mention here. It is the suggestion that Defoe was covertly praising the refugees from the Rhine Palatinate, Protestant 'martyrs' forced from their homeland in 1709. Defoe was certainly interested in these people, and wrote about their plight in the *Review*; years later he was still advertising the scheme he had drawn up to help them settle. Nevertheless, the main body of Protestants left England, many of them for Pennsylvania. Whether Crusoe is really an embodiment of their hardy pioneering spirit may be doubted; but there may be some remote link between his unwilling colonialism and their quest for a new home.[24]

'Background' can never explain a great book; for the genesis of creative literature is, in the last analysis, internal rather than external. But *Robinson Crusoe* may well have had an *occasion*, which is something logically distinct. It is perfectly proper to remind ourselves that Defoe was a man of nearly 60, with a rich life-history to look back on; and that Selkirk's adventures would have triggered off a host of ideas and impressions in his mind. The trouble is that this applies to other men alive in 1719. Defore differed not by social situation or even quite by literary training: he was marked off by his genius, and there is really no accounting for that.

NOTES
(for abbreviations used, see p. xiii)

1   The best-connected narrative remains Sutherland, although *Citizen* is more detailed and comprehensive in some respects. This chapter draws on both. For earlier biographies, see pp. 132–41.

2 Recent scholarship would query certain inclusions in the *Checklist*, e.g. items 286, 288, 293, 294 and 432. Other items remain in the dubious class.

3 For informative editions by F. H. Ellis of Defoe's major satiric poetry, see *Poems on Affairs of State* (New Haven, Conn., 1963–75), Vols VI and VII.

4 Secord, p. 15.

5 On this episode see Sutherland, pp. 40–1, and T. F. M. Newton, 'The civet-cats of Newington Green', *RES*, Vol. XIII (1937), pp. 10–19.

6 *Citizen*, pp. 89–103, is the best treatment; for Defoe in the Fleet prison, see my article in *RES*, n.s. Vol. XXII (1971), pp. 451–5.

7 The standard authority is Hutchins, on which this section is chiefly based. For certain corrections and additions, see Hutchins' own article, 'Two hitherto unrecorded editions of *Robinson Crusoe*', *The Library*, Vol. VIII (1928), pp. 58–72; K. I. D. Maslen, 'The printers of *Robinson Crusoe*', *The Library*, Vol. VII (1952), pp. 124–31: and Maslen, 'Edition quantities for *Robinson Crusoe*, 1719', *The Library*, Vol. XXIV (1969), pp. 145–50. L. L. Hubbard in *PBSA*, Vol. XX (1926), pp. 1–76, painstakingly charts the textual changes in successive Taylor editions.

8 See Hutchins, pp. 183–6, for Taylor's entries in the Stationers' Register.

9 ibid., p. xvii.

10 Maslen, 'Edition quantities', p. 149.

11 Hutchins, pp. 103–4n.

12 *CH*, pp. 22–4, gives other details. The fullest treatment of the *Robinsonade* (the word used in both French and German) is still that of Hermann Ullrich, *Robinson und Robinsonaden* (Weimar, 1898). Voyages on the model of *Crusoe* are discussed by P. B. Gove, *The Imaginary Voyage in Prose Fiction* (rev. edn. 1961). For the pantomime, see G. H. Nettleton, *TLS*, 25 December 1943, 1 January 1944; and *The Dramatic Works of Richard Brinsley Sheridan*, ed. C. Price (Oxford, 1973), Vol. II, pp. 784–7.

13 *Checklist*, p. 162.

14 R. L. Mégroz, *The Real Robinson Crusoe* (London, 1939), is a respectable popular life. See also Little, *passim*.

15 Dover is the subject of a brisk little biography by L. A. G. Strong, *Dr Quicksilver 1660–1742* (London, 1955): a substantial portion of this book (pp. 74–132) is concerned with the privateering expedition led by Rogers. There is a good modern edition of the *Cruising Voyage*, by G. E. Manwaring (London, 1928). On Rogers and Defoe see also *History of Pyrates*, p. xxixn.

16 Little, pp. 69–70.

17 Essentially the story (embellished by nineteenth-century biographers) comes from Mrs Damaris Daniel, a testimony suspect on more than one count. See Little, pp. 166–7, and for further reservations concerning Defoe's Bristol links my article, 'Daniel Defoe, John Oldmixon and the Bristol Riot of 1714', *Transactions of the Bristol and Gloucestershire Archaeological Society*, Vol. XCII (1973), pp. 145–56.

18 *Citizen*, p. 224. The most judicious review of the point comes in Little's chapter, 'The genesis of Crusoe', pp. 151–67.

19 *Citizen*, pp. 223–4.

20 For Drury, see A. W. Secord, 'Defoe in Stoke Newington', *PMLA*, Vol. LXVI (1951), pp. 211–25; and *Robert Drury's Journal and Other Studies* (Urbana, Ill., 1961), pp. 1–45. Secord's admirably thorough research shows Drury to have been an intriguing figure, with whom Defoe may

well have been glad to discuss Madagascar pirates and slaving; but I see no direct hint for *Crusoe* in his career, now it is more fully recorded.

21 British Library, Add. MS 11395, ff. 41–2: transcribed by James Means, 'Lord Oxford and the authorship of *Robinson Crusoe*', *The Scriblerian*, Vol. IX (1977), pp. 139–40, from which I take the text. See further J. A. Downie, in *The Scriblerian*, Vol. X (1977), p. 62.

22 First printed by Sir Henry Ellis (ed.), *Original Letters of Eminent Literary Men* (London, 1843), p. 320: see Lee, Vol. I, p. 294.

23 As Means remarks, 'The idea of Harley, like a latter-day Raleigh, devoting his dreary days of confinement to the Muse is so charming that one almost wishes the anecdote were true' (p. 140). Sunderland remained one of the most eager to bring Oxford to trial for his 'high crimes and misdemeanours', but in the end Robert Walpole reversed his position and helped to get Oxford released in 1717. The theory was propounded by W. L. Purves, *The Authorship of Robinson Crusoe* (1903), but Harley's recent biographer, Elizabeth Hamilton, very properly ignores the story: see *The Backstairs Dragon* (London, 1969).

24 O. F. W. Fernsemer, 'Daniel Defoe and the Palatinate Emigration of 1709', *JEGP*, Vol. XIX (1920), pp. 94–124.

CHAPTER 2

Travel, Trade and Empire

A WIDER WORLD

One of the best-attested facts concerning Defoe in his absorption in travel.[1] He took immense pride in his knowledge of geography; his library was well stocked with atlases and works on discovery and navigation; he was forever surrounded by maps and charts.[2] He was himself a considerable traveller by the standards of the age. In his early days as a merchant he had visited France, the Low Countries, Spain, probably Italy and Germany, too. He made a series of trips around Great Britain, so that he came to know the ports of the coasting trade as well as provincial towns and industrial centres. He regretted the fact that he did not have the opportunity to go farther abroad than the Continent. But at least it was possible for him (as he advised young men to do in *The Compleat English Gentleman*) to 'go round the Globe with Dampier and Rogers'.[3] It is unwise normally to identify Crusoe too closely with his creator, but the 'distemper of wandering' to which he alludes (*RC2*, p. 230) was an urge common to both. The direct impress of Defoe's travels is necessarily slight in *Crusoe*, since nearly all the action occurs in regions of the world he had not been able to visit. But there are unmistakable echoes of his reading in the novel – and it would be strange if there were not.[4]

Travel provided one of the main literary genres in this era. Both real and imaginary voyages proliferated; the distinction was not always clear, and Defoe was not alone in fooling a gullible public with pseudo-veracious narratives.[5] More striking than the popularity of any individual work was the extraordinary appeal of *collections* of travels – multi-volume sets which often went into numerous editions. The most important of these were William Hacke's *A Collection of Original Voyages* (1969), Awnsham and John Churchill's *A Collection of Voyages and Travels* (1704), John Harris's *Navigantium atque Itinerantium Bibliotheca* (1705), and John Stevens's *A New Collection of Voyages and Travels* (1708–10). Most of these were expanded as time went on: thus, Hacke (which Defoe probably used in writing his own *New Voyage Round the World*) appeared together with Dampier's voyages in a set published in 1729. The Churchill compilation increased from four to eight volumes; Harris – the most influential of all – underwent major revision by John Campbell. It can be safely asserted that Defoe was familiar with virtually all these collections, besides the innumerable single volumes which dealt with travel and exploration.[6]

It is true that the heroic age of reconnaissance had passed by the time Defoe was born. In the words of Peter Earle:

> Defoe's lifetime coincides with a lull in the tempo of exploration. The dates of the latest discoveries [as shown in Defoe's *Atlas Maritimus*, 1728] give the game away. Most of them are Australasian discoveries made by the Dutchmen in the early 1640s, though Dampier's Straits between New Guinea and New Britain (1700) is a sign that the freelance buccaneering explorer still existed. But neither Dampier nor the Dutchmen thought much of what they had seen in Australasia and it was left to Captain Cook a generation after Defoe's death to fill the gaps. Defoe was aware of these gaps and of the much larger ones that existed in man's knowledge of the interior of continents. . . . Since no one else would explore, Defoe had to do it himself. Most of the geographical discoveries made in Defoe's lifetime were made by his own fictional characters. Some of these discoveries were so realistic that they were accepted as true long after Defoe's death.[7]

These putative explorations are headed, of course, by the traverse of central Africa made by Captain Singleton (OEN, pp. 47–137), a distance he estimates at 1,800 miles. An even more sustained treatment occurs in *A New Voyage Round the World* ('1725' for 1724), which contains some imaginative and not wholly inaccurate reorientation of Polynesia, and then a hazardous journey across South America, right through the Andes, along the latitude of Baldivia in Chile. In fact Defoe underestimated the rigours of this undertaking; he put the distance at half its true size, he invented a non-existent river, and generally he was misled by the map of Chile included in Herman Moll's *Complete Geographer* (1709).[8] By comparison Crusoe is a conservative animal; the trans-Siberian trek he makes in *RC2* (pp. 401–26) was a rare but not unique feat for a European to undertake. Even so, if he does not exactly pioneer travel-routes, he certainly spends most of his time in regions where very few Englishmen had penetrated.

In any case, while discovery as such was not in a rapid state of advance, colonisation and commercial expansion certainly were. The whole point of the South American adventures in the *New Voyage* is to support a plan to set up an English trading colony in Chile, with the idea of wresting some of Spain's rich plunder in this corner of the world. Defoe had first put forward this project in the reign of William III, but this was the time of the ill-fated Darien expedition and it made no headway. In 1711, just at the period of the formation of the South Sea

Company, Defoe renewed his proposals in a long memorandum to Robert Harley, suggesting that trading bases should be established on both the east and west coasts of South America, presumably around the latitude of 40° South.[9] Again nothing came of it, despite the fact that a similar scheme was presented to Harley by a seaman with wide first-hand experience of the southern climes – Thomas Bowrey, whom Defoe had got to know a few years earlier.[10] Not at all daunted, Defoe returned to this unquenchable enthusiasm in his *Historical Account of the Voyages and Adventures of Sir Walter Ralegh* (1720). In this book Defoe also described some of the possibilities for continuing Ralegh's gold-prospecting near the mouth of the Orinoco (that is, the mainland most adjacent to Crusoe's island). As Frank H. Ellis observes, 'The gold-mines of Guiana were soon worked out, but the by-product, *The Life and Strange Surprizing Adventures of Robinson Crusoe*, proved to be infinitely more rewarding'.[11] We may find it strange to regard *Crusoe* as the by-product of a commercial plan, involving naked colonial expansion and a direct challenge to Spanish empire; but there is a good deal of evidence to show that this was the case. It is absolutely clear that Defoe was led into fiction by strong quasi-polemical drives; today we may be tempted to dismiss such concerns as (at best) catalysts of the true artistic creation, but we should not suppose that Defoe would have agreed with us.

SOURCES AND MODELS

Among the travel-books which Defoe read, a handful are of the most direct importance to *Crusoe*. These are the works whose influence upon the text can be established with reasonable confidence. At various times perhaps a hundred or more alleged 'sources' have been reported, but most can be dismissed as serious contenders. Some of them were not published in Defoe's lifetime, and even where this is recognised it can lead to tortuous lines of argument by which (for example) Defoe and Author X each independently heard an oral account of a given event. In other cases the work only existed in a language of which, so far as we know, Defoe was quite ignorant – his authenticated knowledge extends to Latin, Greek (probably a bit hazy), French and Italian.[12] In most instances the supposed parallel is too vague or trivial to form solid evidence for any influence. Fifty years ago A. W. Secord convincingly sorted out the wheat from the chaff, and subsequent investigators have not disturbed his main conclusions, though some critics have challenged their relevance. The items he listed as 'certain' among the sources are still widely accepted, and few of his rejections can be reinstated in the light of later knowledge. Indeed, as we come to learn more about the development of the picaresque tradition, it seems less and less plausible to assimilate *Crusoe* within this genre. Secord had firmly resisted the view, once commonly held, that *The English Rogue* by Richard Head and Francis Kirkman (1665–71) had supplied Defoe with the genesis of his hero's wandering adventures. The term 'picaresque' is now more strictly used; but in any case it is hard to see how Crusoe could in the loosest terms fit this description – neither his experiences nor his outlook are remotely those of the *picaro*.[13]

Other sources to which Secord allotted little or no importance may be itemised briefly:

(1) Hendrik Smeek, *Krinke Kesmes* (Amsterdam, 1708; German translation 1721). Secord, pages 96–106, discusses the island episode in this story; it has been translated by L. L. Hubbard as *The Narrative of the El-Ho Sjouke Gabbes* (Ann Arbor, 1921).

(2) Hans Jacob Christoph von Grimmelshausen, *Der abenteurliche Simplicissimus* (1668–9). Secord, pages 95–6, considers the desert-island episode; again, there was no English translation in Defoe's lifetime.

(3) Henry Nevile, *The Isle of Pines* (1668).

(4) Garcilaso de la Vega, *The Royal Commentaries of the Yncas*, translated by Sir Paul Rycaut (1688). It contains the narrative of Peter Serrano; see Secord, page 31.

Secord accepted as minor sources the following: (1) the *Navigations* of Hakluyt and *Purchas's Pilgrimes*, as pervasive rather than particular influences; (2) *A Relation of the Great Sufferings and Strange Adventures of Henry Pitman* (1689) – some details possibly used in connection with Crusoe's manner of getting food and shelter, and also with his final deliverance (Secord, pp. 90–2); (3) Maximilien Misson, *A New Voyage to the East Indies* (1707) – an imaginary voyage long believed to be true, with small hints for Crusoe's life on the island (Secord, pp. 92–3); (4) A. O. Exquemelin, *The Bucaniers of America* (1678; English translation 1684–5) – certainly used by Defoe for *Captain Singleton* and the *New Voyage*, just possibly the source of Crusoe's rebellion against his parents' wishes, although only in an exceedingly general way (Secord, pp. 93–4); (5) John Ogilby's *Africa* (1670) – employed for the Sallee episode (Secord, pp. 87–8). None of these sources can be traced in the text of *Crusoe* for any extended duration.

For other possible analogies, see pages 92, 95, below.

The most important of the accepted sources all relate to Crusoe's period on his island in *RC1*. Secord gives most weight to the story of Robert Knox, whose published account may even have been supplemented (he believes) by private communication with Defoe. Knox (1641–1720) described his experiences in *An Historical Relation of Ceylon*

(1681). He had been captured along with crew-mates in 1659; after more than nineteen years in captivity in Ceylon (the modern Sri Lanka) he managed to escape with a single associate, returning to England in 1680. The famous scientist Robert Hooke interviewed Knox and presented an account to the Royal Society. Knox's *Relation*, possibly compiled with the aid of Hooke, was dedicated to the East India Company directors, who subsequently gave Knox a command in their service. He became engaged in the slave trade, and later still a privateer (feeling himself ill-used by the Company). In 1700 he retired from the sea, and passed the remainder of his days in and around London. He died on 19 June 1720, before the appearance of *RC3*.[14]

It is not seriously in dispute that Defoe borrowed some items from the *Relation* to provide incident for *Captain Singleton*, published in the year of Knox's death. Secord attempted to go further and suggested, first, that Knox supplied the most important model for Crusoe's captivity; secondly, that Defoe may have seen Knox's own manuscript additions to his *Relation*, if indeed he did not confer directly with the old sailor.[15] Secord devotes considerable space to the issue, and in summarising his views I incur some risk of falsifying them. It is best to admit that the particular parallels discovered are not always convincing, for example, the fact that both castaways speak Portuguese, or that they emerge from their ordeal with a long beard. However, the general similarities noted by Secord are sufficiently impressive to bear recital.

Secord remarks on a considerable resemblance between the careers of Robert Knox and of Crusoe:

> Each goes to sea against the wishes of his father. . . . Both Crusoe and Knox begin their career with a successful voyage, and both become captives on the second voyage. . . . After Crusoe escapes from Salee [he] becomes a planter in Brazil; it has already been mentioned that Knox became a slaver subsequently to his deliverance from captivity.

Nor does this exhaust the points of contact:

> Upon deliverance from his island, each returns to London where he finds himself a stranger after twenty-three or thirty-five years absence. . . . Each looks up his relatives. Knox finds his brother and his sister, who married to a second husband had several children. Crusoe going into Yorkshire finds 'all the family extinct' except two sisters and two of the children of one of his brothers.

Both find that surviving relatives are unable to make due provision for them as family wills had laid down; however, each man receives a gift from sponsors (Knox twenty pounds; Crusoe 'almost two hundred

Pounds Sterling', *RC1*, p. 279). Secord admits that 'for the rest of their careers there is little beyond a general similarity', but he makes what he can of this:

> Crusoe first settles down for several years of quiet before revisiting his island and setting out for the East Indies upon a trading voyage covering several years more. Knox, meanwhile, has returned to his trading in the Indies, and during the last decade of the century must, so to speak, many times have been in the vicinity of the imaginary Crusoe. Finally in 1700 and 1705 Knox and Crusoe, respectively, retire from the sea to spend their last days in London. Both comment upon their ages and their expectation of death. Knox was still alive (as Crusoe is supposed to have been) in 1719 when parts one and two of 'Robinson Crusoe' were published.[16]

It will be noted that the latter stages of this argument require Defoe to have gained some knowledge of Knox's career subsequent to the phase chronicled in his *Relation*. If this were granted, Secord would be prepared to see close parallels to all three parts of *Crusoe*, not least in Knox's manuscript autobiography with its 'pious ejaculations and quotations from the Bible' as echoed in the *Serious Reflections*. The most striking individual connection Secord makes, in respect of *RC3*, relates to the two authors' treatment of the thanksgivings for the English victory at Ramillies in 1706. As with other portions of the story (the management of goats on the island, or the practices each castaway resorts to for clothing himself), Secord offers plausible but not totally irrefragable evidence. It is possible that he overstated the contribution of Knox, in reaction to uncritical presentation of rival sources (or mindless repetition of the Selkirk legend). Nevertheless, Defoe certainly did know Knox's *Relation* and he was not above plagiarising from it when it suited his needs. Perhaps the unconscious or subliminal influence was greater still; Secord was surely right to point to a common theme of isolated struggle in the two narratives. *Crusoe* is emphatically very much more than a fictional replay of real-life action, but Knox may have supplied part of the framework for the novel.

We are on firmer ground when we come to a second major source, that is, William Dampier's *Voyages*, issued in four parts between 1697 and 1709 (some portions, as was the case with Knox's *Relation*, were printed in John Harris's *Navigantium Bibliotheca*, 1705).[17] The debts are in general slighter, that is, concerned with individual details, but they are correspondingly less vague in character. Dampier (1652–1715) was the most famous traveller of the age.[18] He had been a captain in the Royal Navy, a plantation-manager, a logwood-cutter (an occupation strongly in evidence in the *History of the Pyrates*), a buccaneer in the

Caribbean, a commodore of privateering vessels, a marooned isolate, a Dorset gentleman, a master-gunner, an official surveyor – all in all, a walking, or sailing, embodiment of the age of piracy. Not only was he a member of Woodes Rogers's party when *Duke* rescued Selkirk; there are strong indications that the two had quarrelled back in 1704, when Selkirk had been left on Juan Fernandez. Selkirk seems even to have had a moment of doubt as to whether he *should* allow himself to be rescued in view of Dampier's presence. Dampier may have circumnavigated the globe twice, but he was not a good leader. Happily his gifts did extend to literature, or at least solid and knowledgeable reportage. His *Voyages* has become an enduring classic and it was already celebrated in Defoe's lifetime. Swift makes Gulliver, in his prefatory letter, refer to 'my cousin *Dampier*', and indeed Sir Walter Scott thought that 'the character of the imaginary traveller is exactly that of Dampier, or any other sturdy nautical wanderer of the period'.[19]

A New Voyage Round the World (1697–9) actually furnished Defoe with the title for his last novel proper. It reached a sixth edition in 1717, and it would be hard for any contemporary to ignore these bestselling narratives. It would be just about impossible for anyone so obsessed with the literature of travel as was Defoe not to feel a strong impress from Dampier. Secord's detailed argument shows that the *Voyages* was particularly useful in plotting the route taken by Crusoe in *RC2*, that is, the progress through eastern waters from Sumatra to Tonquin (*RC2*, pp. 359–69). It is Secord's conclusion that Defoe 'also made use of Dampier's map of the East Indies; for some of the matters gathered by Defoe from Dampier appear more clearly on the map than in the text'.[20]

As regards the more famous sections of *Crusoe*, Secord points to the likely influence of Dampier upon the Brazilian episode in *RC1*: he shows how the description of Bahia and its hinterland in *A Voyage to New Holland* (1703) is put to use in the early part of the novel (pp. 34–40). Moreover, Crusoe's own island is stocked with flora and fauna described by Dampier; it may even be based on a small island off the coast of Venezuela which figures in the *New Voyage*, although the geographic location has been changed. Dampier, too, had described the experiences of an Indian who had spent a period of solitude on Juan Fernandez; his reunion with a fellow-countryman has affinities to Friday's joyful recognition of his father (*RC1*, p. 238). Other detailed parallels in such matters as building a shelter are listed by Secord.[21] A final basis of comparison is judiciously appraised by E. A. Baker:

> It is perhaps supererogatory to look in Dampier for the germ of such an incident as the finding of the footprint; but on the dramatic side, at any rate, his mention of the marks of trampling that might have been the track of hostile Spaniards . . . is a more likely source, were

one needed, than the tamer incident in Smeeks or that where Knox
and his mate walk backwards on sandy ground to mislead pursuers.[22]

So far as can be traced, there is no extensive passage in *Crusoe* which
directly reproduces clear features of Dampier's text in an 'unprocessed'
state. With such a famous book, Defoe could scarcely hope to get away
with that kind of bare transcription, hospitable as the age was to
plagiarism. On the other hand the *Voyages* was every contemporary's
idea of a travel-book, and Crusoe's fictional journeys do draw heavily
on Dampier's mode of observation and his account of foreign parts.

A briefer treatment will suffice for the next two sources, though no one
has challenged the status which Secord granted them. Louis Daniel Le
Comte's *Memoirs and Observations . . . Made in a late Journey through
the Empire of China* (1696; English translation 1697), the work of a
Jesuit missionary, furnished all the relevant material for Crusoe's stay
in China (*RC2*, pp. 377–96). Defoe even has his hero travel in company
with a French priest called Father Simon, a backhanded or ironic tribute
to his source. Secord finds it a little surprising that the dependence lies
in this way, for there were other accounts of China in plenty; one might
add that Le Comte had gone through several English editions and was
not an obscure authority by any means. By the end of *RC2* Defoe was
increasingly careless about covering his tracks; and in *RC3* (p. 131) he
actually alludes to Le Comte as a source of information.[23]

For the next section of his journey, Crusoe once more has a convenient
guide in the shape of Everard Ysbrants Ides's *Three Years Travels from
Moscow Overland to China*, a Dutch work published in 1704 and translated into English two years later. The book recounts a journey by the
ambassador of the Czar of Muscovy to the court of the Emperor of China
at Peking. Defoe's narrative in *RC2* (pp. 396–427) reverses the direction,
of course, and in its later stages is forced to depart from Ides – the
ambassador's party had travelled from Moscow to Tobolsk, whereas
Crusoe rather eccentrically heads to Archangel from the latter town.
Secord was unable to discover a source for this final section, covering
the ultimate stages of Crusoe's lifelong wandering. In fact he observed
that between Tobolsk and Archangel 'Defoe's geography apparently runs
wild; for some of the towns and rivers which he finds in that region are
discoverable upon no maps which I have seen, either ancient or modern'.
Secord was unable to decide whether Defoe wearily resorted to 'a half-
hearted attempt to invent names of non-existent towns and streams'
or whether his spelling 'studiedly careless all through the later portion
of part two' degenerated so far as to make recognition impossible.[24] In
view of Defoe's known habits the latter explanation seems to me the
likelier, but I, too, have been unable to locate the unidentified places
named by Crusoe. It would be hard to blame Defoe, in any case, if he

felt that on the last two pages of his narrative he had got away from any pursuers in the form of source-hunters.

There remain the three main published accounts of Selkirk's life on Juan Fernandez. Two of these, by Rogers and Steele respectively, have a special interest and are reprinted in Appendixes A and B below. It would be rash to suppose that Defoe did not read Cooke's story as well, but there are fewer points of substance in his case. The precise extent of Defoe's indebtedness to the Selkirk narratives has long been in dispute and, to be blunt, the issue cannot be resolved. As Secord remarked, 'Defoe's invention begins where history leaves off. . . . The sources of Defoe are not literature; his best works are.'[25] A desert-island story written in 1719 inevitably carried with it echoes of Selkirk, the most celebrated real-life castaway, then as now; but how long Selkirk stayed in the mind of Defoe (with his wealth of reading in other travellers' tales) is now a matter of pure conjecture.

It is possible that there are other direct sources not yet located. Defoe may well have had at the back of his mind narrative of various kinds which supplied a framework too vague and diffused to show up in any kind of scholarly inquiry. John Robert Moore once listed a number of parallels between *Crusoe* and the plot of *The Tempest*. He showed that Defoe's knowledge of Shakespeare was wider than had been realised, and speculated that the Davenant-Dryden version may have lain somewhere behind this novel. It is also clear that Defoe knew something of the sources for *The Tempest*, that is, the accounts of early seventeenth-century Bermuda voyages. Some of the quarrels of the early settlers are brought strongly to mind in the events reported in *RC2* as having taken place during Crusoe's absence. Direct dependence cannot be established. But Moore's indication of a broad literary kinship between *Crusoe* and *The Tempest* seems to me altogether sound. So long as we do not press equivalences too far (that is, Prospero equals Robinson, Caliban equals Friday), then the inner congruence is suggestive – from shipwreck to deliverance. Walter de la Mare wrote that 'unlike Prospero's island in *The Tempest*, Crusoe's asks little of the imagination'; yet he was constrained to add, 'it asks of that little its all'. Of course, the quality of imaginative response is different: the underlying situation provides a common mythic core.[26]

Some critics – notably J. Paul Hunter (see below, pp. 52–3) – believe that the sources of Crusoe have been overemphasised. It is true that the novel is much more than a parody travel-book; and we should always be cautious lest we explain away creative invention by finding a 'real' correlative for imaginary events. Nevertheless, the subject-matter of *Robinson Crusoe* does include many elements which (*differently handled*) were commonplace in travel literature, then one of the most widely read genres. To appreciate Defoe's achievement it is not sufficient to put his

book alongside Dampier, Rogers or Exquemelin; but it is desirable to
do so.

PIRATES AND PRIVATEERS

Piracy is only an incidental theme in *Robinson Crusoe*. But it does figure
in both the first two parts, and more prominently than we may realise
today. Captured by a Turkish rover in *RC1*, Crusoe twice compares his
treatment at the hands of his mutinous crew in *RC2* with the conduct of
pirates like Captain Kidd (pp. 357–8). Quite apart from Defoe's own
special interest in the topic, piracy was a basic fact of life. An age which
had not heard the phrase 'economic man' and had not learnt to talk of
the Protestant Ethic did have frequent recourse to the language of
buccaneers and privateers. Defoe's early experiences as a merchant had
given him good cause to be aware of the depredations the seamen
wrought; in his early twenties he was captured by Algerine pirates in the
North Sea, somewhere off Harwich, and must have been lucky to get
away without long servitude. It was not, however, until the last decade
of his life that he began to specialise in this subject in his own writing.

The major works directly concerned with piracy are led by *Captain
Singleton* (1720), published just before *RC3*, although a shorter fictional
treatment (*The King of Pirates*) appeared only four months after *RC2*
in December 1720. Thereafter six items in the *Checklist* may be said to
deal principally with the topic, although several other works on trade
have some bearing. These items are 458 (the two-volume *History of the
Pyrates*), 469 (the *New Voyage*), 474, 481, 483 and 511 (*Madagascar:
or, Robert Drury's Journal*). The *History*, attributed to 'Captain Charles
Johnson', was only recognised as Defoe's in the 1930s; it is, quite simply,
the most important work historically in the entire literature of piracy.
It incorporates a fictitious life, that of the resourceful Captain Misson,
in the second volume (1728); there is also a more or less factual account
of Thomas Avery in Volume I (1724), contrasting with the fanciful
version presented in *The King of Pirates*. In a host of minor works, as
well as in his huge journalistic output, Defoe turned again and again to
the subject. Piracy had complex economic, political and diplomatic
roots; it was twined around 'legal' trade like a climbing plant. Crusoe's
position in life – whether as seaman, as international trader or as
'governor' of a quasi-colony – can only be understood if the world of the
pirates is taken into proper consideration.[27]

Some definition of terms is appropriate. A privateer was, from the
point of view of his own countrymen, engaged in legal activities. The
British government would provide so-called letters of marque entitling
the holder to carry out harassing operations against the ships of a hostile
nation. In practice this usually meant either Spain or France, and for

this period it was overwhelmingly Spanish commercial fleets which were the objects of British attention. The considerable Dutch and Portuguese overseas empires, for various reasons, were seen to present less of a threat or an invitation. Privateering expeditions were not strictly confined to times of open warfare, though this was obviously the period when official support was most readily forthcoming. As Novak puts it:

> Privateering, although legal and practised by most nations, as Defoe noted, was nevertheless 'something like' piracy. It differed from piracy only in a few respects. The ship usually was owned by a group of investors rather than by the crew; the captain had more power; and the men received shares of the prizes taken instead of an equal division of the spoils. Whenever wars ceased, the sailors on privateers, rather than return to the stern discipline and hard life of merchant ships, often preferred to continue their careers of independence and prosperity as pirates. Sometimes they obtained commissions for privateering from the colonial governors even in periods of peace. But although they preferred the veneer of legality associated with privateering, few enterprising sailors rejected the opportunity to make their fortunes as pirates.[28]

The term *corsairs* was most frequently applied to the African and Mediterranean privateers who flourished for more than three centuries.[29] They were able to claim that a Holy War was continuously in progress and, even when they did not have the specific licence normally required, both Christian and pagan ships were treated with great tolerance by their own people. The Christian fleet was chiefly based in Malta; its adversaries operated from 'Barbary', that is, three north African regencies – Tunis, Algiers and Tripoli. The most important Moorish haven was Sallee, which of course figures directly in *Crusoe*. These corsairs in many respects preserved a separate identity, and their story is distinct from that of world piracy at large. They kept to their own waters and rarely strayed into the confrontations of major powers (unlike, say, the buccaneers of the Caribbean). Their doings had many links with the economy of Western Europe but the underlying rationale for these went back to the Christian–Moslem struggle.

Secord rightly stresses the relative familiarity of Crusoe's experience when he is caught by the Turkish rover:

> So great was the international jealousy that throughout the century the Barbary pirates were allowed to flourish, each nation deploring their shameful practice of subjecting Christian captives to the galleys and to other cruel forms of slavery, but each secretly glad for the damage done to the commerce of competitors. Events of which Defoe

must certainly have read were the expeditions fitted out by the English
government against the pirates of Salee, among whom Crusoe was to
spend two years of slavery. Lists of English seamen held at Salee were
published, as well as numerous accounts of individual experiences of
men who effected their escape.

The escape-story became a literary genre in its own right, if one with
strong links to other 'providential' narratives (see below, pp. 55–7).[30]
Crusoe's break for freedom is given less perfunctory treatment (*RC1*, pp.
19–34) than the period of captivity itself, but it is not a remarkably
circumstantial account. Defoe was employing a standard motif, and his
originality lay chiefly in the sustained fictional context into which he has
fitted the episode. In his youth Captain Singleton, too, found himself
taken by an Algerine rover (OEN, p. 3), although by chance the pirates
were themselves attacked by two Portuguese men-of-war who promptly
seized their prize. Defoe's fictional Captain Misson had an early
encounter with Sallee corsairs. A few years later Defoe returned to the
theme in his *Plan of the English Commerce* (1728), which contains 'A
Proposal for rooting out those Nests of Pyrates and Rovers, the *Turks*
and *Moors* of *Tunis*, *Tripoli*, *Algier*, and *Sallee*'. Typically the project
is coupled to a 'Scheme for the Improvement of Trade, by restoring and
establishing the ancient Commerce on the North and North West Coast
of *Africa*'. Crusoe will keep bumping into the obsessive places in Defoe's
imagination.

   Our image of pirates today is probably rather that of the men who
flourished during the seventeenth century in the vicinity of the West
Indies. This is the era of the swashbuckling Errol Flynn figure, to whom
Henry Morgan approximates less vaguely than most of his kind. It saw
many brutal and violent episodes, with the centre of piracy located first
in Hispaniola and then at Port Royal in Jamaica. The unwieldy Spanish
treasure-ships were a major target, even more so after an overland route
across the isthmus of Panama gave easier access to the Pacific. But
pirates were likely to regard any vulnerable object (floating or otherwise)
at fair game. By the 1690s, when Captain Kidd began his brief and
unlovely career – he, too, was a licensed privateer by origin – the pirate
was already a figure of legend, associated in the public mind with
extravagant daring and also extravagant wealth. The classic account was
certainly known to Defoe, who uses it in *Captain Singleton* and the *New
Voyage*: Alexandre Olivier Exquemelin's *Bucaniers of America* (English
translation 1684). As we have seen, there may be a momentary debt to
this work at the start of *RC1*.

   But by 1719 this was ancient history. During the War of the Spanish
Succession the British government offered a pardon to those of the
Caribbean buccaneers who would help in the war effort. Both France

and England made immense depredations upon the shipping of their enemy (this was the occasion of Defoe's first bankruptcy, when he unwisely entered marine insurance). When the war came to an end in 1713 the fleets found themselves all dressed out for privateering expeditions and with nowhere to go. There ensued what has been described as 'the greatest decade of pirate activity in modern history'.[31] Eventually things reached such a pitch that the traditional non-interventionist policy of governments had to be revised. A royal proclamation was issued and Woodes Rogers sent out as Governor of the Bahamas; indemnity was granted to pirates who surrendered within a set term to the new governor, whilst those who failed to do so were to be pursued and brought to trial.

In July 1718, Rogers reached New Providence, which was now the chief base for piracy. He began to fulfil his commission with his usual energy, rebuilding Fort Nassau, setting men to work on construction projects, and administering the law in respect of those pirates who had not taken advantage of the pardon. Defoe's *History of the Pyrates* devotes an appendix to the trials and hangings which took place at the end of 1718.[32] But Rogers lacked moral and financial support from England, and he was unable to complete the task laid on him. He was back in Bristol by 1721, and spent the next few years in dire poverty. He actually found himself in the debtor's prison, as Defoe had thirty years before. Finally Rogers returned to Nassau, where he died in 1732. He had been only partially successful in extirpating piracy from the Caribbean, but things were never to be as bad as they had been at the time of his arrival.[33]

In the meantime another major base had been established. This was in Madagascar, where there was 'no government, native or European, capable of driving [the pirates] out'.[34] Henry Avery had settled the first strong contingent there, around 1694, and since that time more and more had been heard of the fabulous riches amassed on the island. 'Colonies of retired pirates were established, intermarrying with the local population and even founding dynasties and minute states.'[35] A few half-hearted attempts were made to root out the pirates, but none had much effect. It seems that the Madagascar pirates only died out – some time after Defoe had gone to his own rest – from what might be termed natural causes: tropical disease principally. Defoe wrote about the colony on numerous occasions, for example, *Captain Singleton*, *A New Voyage* and *Robert Drury's Journal*. It is therefore perhaps a matter for surprise that Crusoe encounters only the native population during his visit to Madagascar (*RC2*, pp. 345–54). The pirate base had not attained its full strength at the supposed date of this visit, that is, the later 1690s, but that is not the sort of consideration which always weighed heavily with Defoe.

A little later in *RC2* Crusoe fears that he had been taken for a pirate
and 'should now come to be hang'd in [his] old age . . . for a crime [he]
was not in the least inclin'd to' (p. 247). Piracy in the eastern waters
contributed less to legend, but it was extensive throughout the seventeenth and early eighteenth centuries. There was, needless to say, no
certain method of recognising a pirate when one met an unknown
ship – it was normal for captains to carry 'a wide selection of flags and
pennants so that they could fly what appeared to be the most politic at
any given time'.[36] The incidence of piratical activity on Crusoe's travels
by no means exaggerates the scale of the problem. Wherever trade
by sea was prosperous, legitimate operators would be pursued by their
predators. The spice islands in the East Indies or the oceanic routes of
the silver galleons – it made no difference.

In fact Defoe gives a reasonably fair picture of the hazards men ran
when they went to sea. Crusoe's two years as a slave at Sallee could be
paralleled by hundreds of well-authenticated instances; escape was not
unknown but often it took the captive more than two years. As for the
general conditions of life at sea, any sailor could expect long periods of
tedium and sometimes enforced inaction (when the winds failed to
oblige), interspersed with dangerous storms and the passage through
uncharted reefs. Hunger and thirst were common attendants of a long
journey; medical care almost always inadequate. Navigation made only
slow progress, charts were poor. 'Harbours were more dangerous than
the sea itself.'[37] Crusoe is prone to lament his ill luck in the matter of
storms, but in fact he has average good fortune. It might be added that
one consequence of defective navigation – in particular, the lack of a
reliable means of determining the longitude – was that ships were forced
to sail along very predictable routes, often sticking tightly to a given
latitude until the expected land was sighted. This made life much easier
for pirates. In Defoe's time hydrography was advanced by Dampier's
work on wind systems, and a generation after his death John Harrison
finally produced a dependable chronometer to satisfy the Board of
Longitude. But Crusoe could have profited from neither development.
In the circumstances he coped well enough with the hurricane which
blew him in the direction of his island.

The adventure which lies at the heart of *RC1* was plausibly based on
a real set of conditions which mariners were liable to face every time
they left port for the great sea-routes. Crusoe may be right to blame
himself for his imprudence, but there was nothing specially baleful about
his being wrecked. We must look for the hand of Providence, not in the
wreck itself, but in the fact of his delivery.

THE COLONIAL THEME

Defoe was a prophet of empire before Britain had fully acquired an empire. For two hundred years Europe had thrust out into the remotest corners of the earth, with first Spain and Portugal, then Holland, leading the other nations. England and France were slower to establish a strong footing overseas, and it indeed was in the eighteenth century that their struggle for dominance (culminating in the Seven Years War of 1756–63) overshadowed the older imperial rivalries.[38] Defoe witnessed the beginnings of this contest, and had his own ideas about the best way of reaching a successful outcome – for the English, that is.

Both the Spanish and the Portuguese empires were some way past their prime in 1719. Portugal, in particular, was finding her huge and far-spread territory an impossible burden; she was a small and poor country, and the effort of expansion in the sixteenth century had debilitated her scanty resources. Her naval power ebbed away, her administration became barnacled with complacent inefficiency, her commerce grew less and less dynamic. The Dutch drove Portugal from many of her eastern colonies, and those that remained (like Goa) underwent what C. R. Boxer calls 'stagnation and contraction'.[39] By the time of Crusoe's oriental adventures, it was the Dutch who had taken over as the major power east of Suez. Brazil did remain to Portugal, and Crusoe's period as a tobacco-planter (*RC1*, pp. 34–9) gave him firsthand knowledge of her empire – he even learnt the Portuguese language (p. 38). He settled in the region of '*St Salvadore*', that is, Bahia, an important settlement since the middle of the seventeenth century; Dampier described it as 'a place of great trade'.[40] Around this time (the 1690s) gold was discovered, and the Brazilian economy enjoyed a dramatic upsurge. The dissension and breakdown of confidence which were ultimately to open the way for Portugal's loss of Brazil were still far into the future.

Spain retained the largest overseas empire, based on her extraordinary period of conquest during the early sixteenth century. The Pacific or 'South Sea' was long dominated by Spain, who possessed the important trading settlement of the Philippines. Then there was the whole of Mexico, most of South America (excepting Brazil, Guiana and small pockets elsewhere), and several West Indian islands – notably Cuba and Hispaniola. In theory Spain claimed areas of South America where her writ did not strictly apply, and it is Defoe's case that England could annex Chile and Patagonia with impunity because Spain would be unable to put up effective resistance on the confines of her empire. It is not that Spain was overstretched in the same way as Portugal; rather, a cumbrous bureaucracy, excessive centralisation and domestic weakness conspired to make her imperial pretensions outrun her ability to carry these through.[11] Intermarriage between native blacks, Indians and settlers produced a complex social hierarchy which in turn bred widespread resentment. Crusoe spends little time very close to Spanish possessions (Selkirk's island or, rather, archipelago was a Spanish discovery, although not properly settled); on the other hand, it is a Spanish ship, bound on a major trade-route from Buenos Aires to Havana, wrecked off his island, which first opens up the possibility of escape. The Spaniard whose life Crusoe had saved becomes the 'governor' of the island in his absence, and indeed Defoe takes a surprisingly soft line towards this papist state in *Crusoe*. Elsewhere he never tired of recommending an attack on the Spanish 'plate' fleet – that is, the convoys of ships carrying bullion – with the aim of weakening the Spanish economy; this would make easier his pet project of seizing land in South America to set up an English trading colony.

The Dutch had come to prominence in the seventeenth century, with a strong lead from the East India Company. They had established major bases at Batavia and Malacca, and rapidly became the most efficient of all the colonial powers. They made less headway in the Western hemisphere, although they did control a rich sugar-producing district of Brazil between 1630 and 1654 and in addition held New Netherland (around what is now New York) until the English seized this colony in 1664. For the most part the Dutch put more emphasis on trade pure and simple than their rivals, with less attempt to convert the heathen and less interbreeding with the native population.[42] The 'golden century' was just fading when Defoe came to maturity, and though he had political sympathies with the Dutch (especially when they fought as England's allies in the War of the Spanish Succession) he was anxious to see British traders outdo them in the sphere of international commerce. Crusoe's main contacts occur in the China Sea, where he spends six years in a region dominated by the Dutch spice trade (*RC2*, pp. 361–2).

The French were the most recent inheritors of colonial power. Their first important settlements had been established in the early 1600s: Quebec, which remained in French hands until Wolfe's victory over Montcalm in 1759, and Acadia – what we know as Nova Scotia – which was ceded to England as part of the Treaty of Utrecht. (The Acadians drifted away to form French-speaking colonies elsewhere, notably in Louisiana.) Gradually the Quebec settlement spread, westwards and southwards; by Defoe's time serious efforts were being made to develop the Mississippi and Ohio valleys. England by now claimed most of the eastern seaboard of North America, though Spain controlled Florida (as well as modern Texas). The major confrontations over these possessions took place a generation after Defoe's death, but friction was already building up in the first quarter of the century.

As for the English, they had begun under the Stuarts to lay the foundations of empire. Most important were the American colonies, first Virginia, Maryland and the New England provinces, to be followed in the later seventeenth century by Pennsylvania and the Carolinas. New York and New Jersey were developed after Dutch influence had been eradicated. A number of Caribbean islands were annexed, of which the most important commercially and strategically were to be Jamaica and Barbados. Meanwhile the Hudson's Bay Company was established to exploit the fur trade, the East India Company to import coffee, tea, silks and cotton, and the Royal African Company to transport slaves from west Africa to America. Unlike some of Defoe's other heroes and heroines, Crusoe sees little of this dawning colonialism. Moll Flanders is transported to Virginia, and later moves to other states; Colonel Jack is sold into servitude in Virginia again, and after obtaining his freedom becomes a Maryland planter. Captain Singleton spends much of his time in the vicinity of Dutch strongholds such as the Malabar coast and Ceylon, but he passes two years in the Caribbean (the Quaker William is taken 'out of a Sloop bound from *Pensilvania* to *Berbadoes*', OEN, p. 143). Ultimately the pirates' depredations reach such a point that English men-of-war are dispatched to round them up. Crusoe is closest to British rule in his spell in Bengal, where England and Holland were active through their rival East India Companies.[43]

Competition for territories opened up by exploration was intense at all times. But during any war between the major powers the acquisition of new colonies attained a special prominence; peace negotiations invariably included prolonged haggling over this matter. The War of the Spanish Succession (1702–13), by origin a dynastic struggle, became as time elapsed more and more a contest over economic and commercial rights. The Treaty of Utrecht (1713) comprised a number of separate agreements, and settled a number of longstanding issues in the European theatre. However, there were important provisions relating to the wider world, strengthening England's position *vis-à-vis* France, particularly in North America. Additionally, the famous *Asiento*, a contract to supply the Spanish colonies with slaves, was granted to the newly formed South Sea Company.[44] All living and literate inhabitants of Britain were well aware of this momentous treaty, whose drafting had been the culmination of intense political activity. But Defoe had a unique involvement, by reason of his background and interests. He wrote several pamphlets during and after the period of negotiations, and in his works on economics published later he was often concerned with the opportunities opened up for English overseas trade. After Utrecht the old rivalries did not die out – indeed, England and Spain were three times at war, in 1719, 1727 and 1739 – and it was not until after the Seven Years' War and, indeed, the War of American Independence that the great British Empire of the nineteenth century took shape.

There were many reasons for the colonial drive, but the chief impulse came from the expectation of finding resources or a market. As one historian has put it:

> Among the varied motives which sent Europeans exploring unknown seas and settling distant lands, the most potent was the economic one. Missionary zeal, intellectual curiosity and flight from persecution all played a part; but none was as universal a force as the hope of profit and better standards of living. The determination of individuals, companies and nations to enrich themselves by overseas trade and settlement was the mainspring of European expansion, and deeply affected the economies of the homelands.[45]

This was assuredly the factor which loomed large in Defoe's mind. Intellectually curious as he was, he gives no sign of wishing to extend the frontiers of botanical knowledge, or to conduct experiments in translating a noble savage to 'civilisation', as did the later *philosophes*. (His own *Mere Nature Delineated*, 1726, sees the primitive man as a cripple denied opportunity for growth by lack of education.) Crusoe's attitude to savages is by later standards condescending; his long reflection after Friday's arrival (*RC1*, pp. 209–10) reaches some fairly comfortable conclusions, and his thoughts on cannibals (pp. 170–2, 197) are guided by the consideration that 'They do not know it to be an Offence . . .'. It is undeniable that black lives are held cheaper than white, especially in the skirmishes of *RC2*; and the benighted Tartars are treated with equal concern: 'We aim'd so true (or Providence directed our shot so sure) that we kill'd fourteen of them, and wounded several others' (*RC2*). Defoe does not harp on the theme of the natural supremacy of European races, but this is probably because (as Peter Earle remarks) he took it for granted.[46]

Slavery was a question less vexed in 1719 than it was to become, but by no means a non-issue. We even find Defoe's first effective critic, Charles Gildon (see below, pp. 129–31), taking Crusoe to task for his activity as a slaver. The episode in point is that preceding Crusoe's arrival on the island, when he leaves his Brazilian plantation in order to embark on a speculative voyage to Guinea. It emerges now for the first time that his earlier ventures in these regions, before his captivity in Sallee, had involved slave-trading:

> I had frequently given them an Account of my two Voyages to the Coast of *Guinea*, the manner of Trading with the *Negroes* there, and how easy it was to purchase upon the Coast, for Trifles, such as Beads, Toys, Knives, Scissars, Hatchets, bits of Glass, and the like; not only Gold Dust, *Guinea* Grains, Elephants Teeth, &c. but *Negroes* for the Service of the *Brasils*, in great Numbers. (pp. 38–9)

Crusoe's business partners are particularly struck with this last piece of information, because the *Asiento* monopoly has pushed the price of slaves very high. There ensues the fateful journey which results in Crusoe's island experiences. Elsewhere Defoe was insistent on the need for slave labour to keep the valuable West Indian sugar industry in being; he has less to say about the increasing importation of blacks to American tobacco plantations.

It is true that Defoe was among the first to complain about the harsh conditions which slaves had to endure: in his satire *Reformation of Manners* (1702) he wrote a particularly trenchant passage on the subject:

> Others seek out to *Africk's* Torrid Zone,
>   And search the burning Shores of *Serralone*:
>   [Sierra Leone]
> There in insufferable Heats *they fry*,
>   And run vast Risques to see the Gold, *and die.*
> The harmless Natives basely they trepan,
>   And barter Baubles for the *Souls of Men*;
> The Wretches they to Christian Climes bring o'er,
>   To serve worse Heathens than they did before.
> The Cruelties they suffer there are such,
>   *Amboyna's* nothing, they've out-done the *Dutch.*
>   [Amboina, in the East Indies]
>
> *Cortez, Pizarro, Guzman, Penaloe,*
> Who drank the Blood and Gold of *Mexico,*
> Who thirteen Millions of Souls destroy'd,
> And left one third of God's Creation void,
> By Birth for Nature's Butchery design'd,
> Compar'd to these are merciful and kind;
> Death could *their* cruellest Designs fulfil,
> Blood quench'd *their* Thirst, and it suffic'd to kill;
> But these the tender *Coup de Grace* deny,
> And make Men beg in vain for leave to die;
> To more than *Spanish* Cruelty inclin'd,
> Torment the Body, and debauch the Mind:
> The ling'ring Life of Slavery preserve,
> And vilely teach them both to Sin and serve. . . .
> Thus thousands to Religion are brought o'er,
> And made worse Devils than they were before.[47]

There is also a substantial treatment of the problem in *Colonel Jack* (OEN, pp. 127–47). Again, Defoe shows sympathy for the plight of slaves, but it is noticeable that Jack's aim is to find 'that happy Secret, to have good Order kept, the Business of the Plantation done, and that with Diligence, and Dispatch, and that the *Negroes* are kept in Awe, the natural Temper of them Subjected, and the Safety and Peace of [the owner's] Family secur'd'. He wishes simply to effect this 'as well by

gentle Means, as by Rough, by moderate Correction, as by Torture, and
Barbarity; by a due Awe of just Discipline, as by the Horror of unsuffer-
able Torments' (p. 134). The evidence supports Earle's view that outside
Reformation of Manners 'Defoe never attacks the institution, but confines
his criticism to attacks on the harsh treatment of slaves'.[48] Whatever
Crusoe's original sin may have been, it cannot (*pace* Gildon) have been
the decision to turn slave-dealer.

For Defoe, then, colonial development raised economic as much as
moral questions. He was interested in the changes which the American
plantations offered to the reformed wrongdoer: both *Moll Flanders* and
Colonel Jack illustrate this theme. But though this was a topical issue
(transportation to Virginia started up again in 1718, after a fifty-year
gap) the focus is personal rather than public: in his fiction Defoe does
not make much of religious persecution or other 'social' factors in the
escape to America. His emphasis lies on the individual's capacity to
achieve economic independence and a kind of security. Moll and Jack
exhibit none of the true frontier mentality; they simply want to get
ahead sufficiently to be able to return to England as free and solid
citizens. Here is Jack's lesson for young wrongdoers:

1.   That *Virginia*, and a State of Transportation, may be the happiest
     Place and Condition they were ever in, for this Life, as by a
     sincere Repentance, and a diligent Application to the Business
     they are put to; they are effectually deliver'd from a Life of a
     flagrant Wickedness, and put in a perfectly new Condition, in
     which they have no Temptation to the Crimes they formerly
     committed, and have a prospect of Advantage for the future.
2.   That in *Virginia*, the meanest, and most despicable Creature
     after his time of Servitude is expir'd, if he will but apply himself
     with Diligence and Industry to the Business of the Country, is
     sure (Life and Health suppos'd) both of living Well and growing
     Rich.   (OEN, p. 173)

In a sense, the American colonies represent what Crusoe, with his
wandering disposition, had never found: an education in diligence, thrift
and the value of steady accumulation. He, too, is put in a 'perfectly new
Condition' on his island.

It is in this light that we should consider Crusoe's increasing readiness
to see himself as 'Governour' (e.g. *RC1*, pp. 268*ff*.) or even as the
monarch of all he surveys:

My Island was now peopled, and I thought my self very rich in
Subjects; and it was a merry Reflection which I frequently made, How
like a King I look'd. First of all, the whole Country was my own meer

Property; so that I had an undoubted Right of Dominion. *2dly,* My People were perfectly subjected: I was absolute Lord and Law-giver; they all owed their Lives to me, and were ready to lay down their Lives, *if there had been Occasion for it,* for me. It was remark-able too, we had but three Subjects, and they were of three different Religions. My Man *Friday* was a Protestant, his Father was a *Pagan* and a *Cannibal,* and the *Spaniard* was a Papist: However, I allow'd Liberty of Conscience throughout my Dominions: But this is by the Way. (p. 241)

The word 'merry' carries with it the suggestion that we should not take Crusoe's daydreaming too seriously. But it is hard not to feel that Defoe was indulging at some level in a fantasy of himself as colonial proprietor. Woodes Rogers had recently become Governor of the Bahamas, just as years before his first patron, Dalby Thomas, had been appointed Agent-General of the African Company's settlement in Guinea.[49] Defoe had devised an elaborate scheme for planting a colony of Protestant refugees in the New Forest; he set out this plan more than once, with the zeal of an early New Town enthusiast like Ebenezer Howard.[50] There are, at the very least, buried sympathies for Crusoe's colonial experiment in the store of his creator's memories and desires.

Yet Crusoe is far from a success as governor, as the first part of *RC2* makes plain. A long flashback reveals a story of disunity and lack of purpose. When Crusoe leaves his island for the last time, he finds himself obliged to give up his intention of providing the inhabitants with a sloop and armaments:

For I found, at least at my first coming, such seeds of divisions among them, that I saw it plainly had I set up the sloop, and left it among them, they would, upon every light disgust, have separated, and gone away from one another; or perhaps have turned pirates, and so made the island a den of thieves, instead of a plantation of sober and religious people, so as I intended it; nor did I leave the two pieces of brass cannon that I had on board, or the two quarter-deck guns that my nephew took extraordinarily, for the same reason. (pp. 175–6)

Maximillian Novak says bluntly that the colony 'languishes and fails. Like the proprietors of Carolina, whom Defoe attacked, Crusoe is "not furnished with Affection of Love to the People" whom he rules. Crusoe's failure, caused by his unwillingness to lead a productive life as the patriarch of his people, might have been intended as a reflection on England's unwillingness to treat her colonies with kindness and respect.'[51] It is undeniable that the Crusoe colony is a poor advertisement for the ideology which imbued so much of Defoe's writing throughout his life.

His fictional left hand seems not to trust the aspirations of his polemical right hand.

Novak further remarks that 'Defoe regarded almost all the lands where Crusoe wandered as possible areas for colonization', pointing out that as well as the Guiana project Defoe submitted in his *Plan of English Commerce* plans for an expedition against the Moorish pirates and for a permanent base in west Africa.[52] The remark does not strictly apply to the later sections of *RC2*, for the great empires of Asia remained too strong for serious hopes of colonisation to exist. Nevertheless, Crusoe is, up to the very last years of his travels, sent to places which Defoe would regard as ripe for exploitation. And the fact that the one practical experiment turns out largely a failure illustrates the difficulty, rather than the unfeasibility, of the task.

Even in *RC3* 'Robinson Crusoe, grown old in affliction' (p. 234), has fresh ideas for extending European influence to the remotest corners of the globe. The sixth section considers the relative strength of Christian and pagan areas of the world, and contains a proposal for a joint European force to carry out a new crusade 'to beat paganism out of the world' (p. 225). A concerted missionary effort would accompany the conquest, together with 'a just and generous behaviour to the natives, or at least to such of them as should show themselves willing to submit' (p. 240). As we should expect, there are benefits to be drawn on the side:

> In point of the interfering interests, Europe ought to take possession of these shores, without which it is manifest her commerce is not secured; and indeed, while that part of Africa bordering on the sea is in the hands of robbers, pirates cannot be secured. Now, this is a point of undisputed right, for a war-trade claims the protection of the powers to whom it belongs, and we make no scruple to make war upon one another for the protection of our trade, and it is allowed to be a good reason why we should do so. Why, then, is it not a good reason to make war upon thieves and robbers? . . .
>
> But shall we do thus to Christians, and scruple to make an universal war for the rooting out of a race of pirates and rovers, who live by rapine, and are continually employed, like the lions and tygers of their own Lybia, in devouring their neighbours? This, I say, makes such a war not only just on a religious account, but both just and necessary upon a civil account.

At such moments it is easy to disregard the thin pretence that this is the voice of Crusoe, who had himself endured slavery at the hands of these corsairs. The accents are those of a colonial propagandist, ready to use the choicest casuistry in order to find grounds for further territorial expansion. This is not to impugn the religious sincerity of Defoe's proposal: it is simply to indicate that, in a mind like his, at a time like his, the course of empire was advanced by arguments drawn from many different spheres of life.[53] Crusoe himself is part missionary, part conquistador, part trader, part colonial administrator. The first was the highest calling, but none of the others was less than a useful and necessary task, with the world organised as it was – or so Defoe believed.

The full meaning for Defoe of travel and its associated cluster of ideas eludes brief summary. It now appears that earlier scholarship tended to overstate the importance of direct 'sources' in travel literature. This literalism produced statements like that of W. A. Eddy, analysing the fictional voyages which underlay *Gulliver*: 'The realistic narrative of Defoe, at its best, is not distinguishable from a book of authentic biography or travel. It is interesting to note that this is the achievement of the man who had failed signally to produce a *Fantastic Voyage* of merit.' (This last comment refers to Defoe's *Consolidator*.)[54] In the face of such readings it is easy to agree with J. Paul Hunter that 'the artistry of *Robinson Crusoe* is . . . seriously maligned by viewing the novel's parts as somehow dependent upon travel books [and still more] by considering its total form to be patterned on the travel tradition'.[55] Nevertheless, Hunter seems to me to go too far in the other direction, and his valuable corrective ends up by relegating travel and adventure into an almost invisible role. As later chapters will show, Defoe had many other intellectual models and literary forms to work upon. But we should be wrong to underestimate the strong hold which discovery and commercial expansion exercised on his imagination.[56] *Robinson Crusoe* is far more than the result of poring over maps and reconstructing journeys; but these things had their place in its genesis.

NOTES

1 There are many discussions of Defoe's knowledge of such matters as exploration, maritime affairs and piracy; but surprisingly no definitive treatment of any of these aspects of his mind. See *Citizen*, pp. 274–82; Sutherland, pp. 29, 240–1; *History of Pyrates*, pp. xxii–xxxi; Secord, *passim*.

2 Hints of Defoe's reading are scattered through his works, but it is, of course, his *Library* which supplies the most useful information. There is a difficulty arising from the fact that the sale of his books (by Olive Payne, just off the Strand), beginning on 15 November 1731, included also the collection of Phillips Farewell, D.D. Farewell was a Fellow of Trinity College, Cambridge, and a sound Anglican. The assumption has always been made that the bulk of the books dealing with navigation and discovery (as well as British topographical works) must have belonged to Defoe; and I think it is not incautious to make this supposition. See also the edition of this catalogue by H. Heidenreich (Berlin, 1970). Particularly relevant to *Crusoe*, among the items listed, are such works as Hakluyt's *Voyages*;

Different Views of Guinea; a *Description d'Ukraine* (1660); an account of the East Indies trade; and various narratives of embassies and providential escape-stories.

3   *The Compleat English Gentleman*, ed. K. D. Bülbring (London, 1890), p. 225.

4   For background to this chapter, see the excellent survey, 'The wider world', in Earle, pp. 45–74 (from which I have adapted the title to the first section).

5   See Geoffroy Atkinson's two standard surveys, *The Extraordinary Voyage in French Literature before 1700* (New York, 1920), and *The Extraordinary Voyage in French Literature from 1700 to 1720* (Paris, 1922). Relevant, too, are P. G. Adams, *Travellers and Travel Liars 1660–1800* (Berkeley, Calif., 1962), and P. B. Gove, *The Imaginary Voyage in Prose Fiction* (New York, 1941; rev. edn. 1961).

6   Another collection of journeys to the South Seas and the Arctic, published in 1694, was of use to Defoe in his *New Voyage*; but there seems to be no direct borrowing in *Crusoe*.

7   Earle, p. 52.

8   Burton J. Fishman, 'Defoe, Herman Moll and the geography of South America', *HLQ*, Vol. XXXVI (1973), pp. 227–38. I am grateful to Professor Fishman for information in this connection.

9   *Letters*, pp. 345–9.

10 *History of Pyrates*, pp. xxvii–xxviii.

11 *Historical Account of Ralegh*, p. 55; *Mercurius Politicus* (1719), p. 552; Ellis, p. 18.

12 In *Citizen*, p. 73, Moore claims that Defoe 'could speak a little Dutch', but in my view it was probably only a very little.

13 The major treatments are Robert Alter, *Rogue's Progress* (Cambridge, Mass., 1964), and A. A. Parker, *Literature and the Delinquent* (Edinburgh, 1967). See also Christine J. Whitbourn (ed.), *Knaves and Swindlers* (London, 1974). None of these works gives any support to the idea that *Crusoe* could be termed picaresque: they suggest a partial fitness in the case of *Moll Flanders*.

14 See Donald W. Ferguson, *Captain Robert Knox . . . Contributions towards a Biography* (Colombo and Croydon, privately printed, 1896–7). Secord was evidently unable to see a copy of this 'inaccessible' work (p. 40), but it would not materially have altered his conclusions if he had done so.

15 Secord, pp. 32–40. Knox's *Relation* was item 198 in the *Library*.

16 Secord, pp. 42–3, 44.

17 There is a modern edition by John Masefield (London, 1906). The *New Voyage* was edited by Sir Albert Gray (London, 1927), and the *Voyages and Discoveries* by Clennell Wilkinson (London, 1931).

18 See W. H. Bonner, *Captain William Dampier* (Stanford, Calif., 1934); and J. C. Shipman, *William Dampier: Seaman-Scientist* (Lawrence, Kans., 1962).

19 *The Prose Works of Jonathan Swift*, ed. Herbert Davis (Oxford, 1939–68), Vol. XI, p. 5; *The Works of Jonathan Swift, D.D.*, ed. Walter Scott (Edinburgh, 1814), quoted by Kathleen Williams (ed.), *Swift: The Critical Heritage* (London, 1970), p. 307.

20 Secord, pp. 49–53. For the bibliographical history of the *Voyages*, see N. M. Penzer's note in Gray's edition, pp. v–viii.

21 Secord, pp. 53–63. For the old view that Defoe had Tobago in mind when describing Crusoe's island, see p. 56.

22 E. A. Baker, *The History of the English Novel* (London, 1929; reprinted New York, 1950), Vol. 3, p. 155. Baker's summary of sources (pp. 143–74) is a good one.

23 Secord, pp. 63–8. P. Dottin, *De Foe et ses romans* (Paris, 1924), Vol. II, pp. 340–1, suggests as another source Jan Nieuhoff's *Ambassade de la Compagnie hollandaise des Indes Orientales au grand Khan de Tartarie* (1665), trans. John Ogilby, 1669.

24 Secord, pp. 68–74.

25 ibid., pp. 236–9. Besides Cooke's account, there is a fourth and more obscure narrative: a twelve-page pamphlet called *Providence Displayed* (1712). Rae Blanchard thinks this may have influenced Steele's account (*The Englishman* (Oxford, 1955), p. 423), but there is no obvious sign that it contributed directly to *Crusoe*.

26 J. R. Moore, 'The Tempest and *Robinson Crusoe*', *RES*, Vol. XXI (1945), pp. 52–6; Novak, *Nature*, pp. 52–63; Walter de la Mare, *Desert Islands and Robinson Crusoe* (London, 1930), p. 43.

27 A general survey of the subject is Philip Gosse, *The History of Piracy* (New York, 1932; reprinted 1968). See also *History of Pyrates*, pp. xvi–xxii; Earle, pp. 60–5; and Novak, *Economics*, pp. 103–27. A recent attempt to specify Defoe's debt is Maurice Wehrung's 'The literature of privateering and piracy as a source of the Defoean hero's personality', in *Tradition et innovation: littérature et paralittérature* (Paris, 1975), pp. 159–91.

28 Novak, *Economics*, pp. 104–5.

29 An excellent account is P. Earle, *Corsairs of Malta and Barbary* (London, 1970). Though this book deals with the Mediterranean sphere of operation, its description of conditions at sea, of captive experiences, and of the mercantile nexus underlying corsair activity provides essential background to Defoe's fiction.

30 Secord, p. 25. For the stories of slavery at the hands of the Moors, see G. A. Starr, 'Escape from Barbary', *HLQ*, Vol. XXIX (1965), pp. 35–52. For Defoe's view of the Barbary rovers, see also *A Plan of the English Commerce* (Oxford, 1928), pp. 234–45.

31 *History of Pyrates*, p. xxi. Other authorities concur with Schonhorn's view.

32 ibid., pp. 615–60.

33 Little, pp. 182–98, is the fullest treatment of Rogers's period as governor.

34 J. H. Parry, *Trade and Dominion: English Overseas Empires in the Eighteenth Century* (London, 1971; reprinted 1974), p. 82.

35 Earle, p. 64.

36 Earle, *Corsairs*, p. 147.

37 J. H. Parry, *The Spanish Seaborne Empire* (London, 1966; Harmondsworth, 1973), p. 250.

38 A clear outline is provided by Glyndwr Williams, *The Expansion of Europe in the Eighteenth Century: Overseas Rivalry, Discovery and Exploitation* (London, 1966), pp. 5–47.

39 C. R. Boxer, *The Portuguese Seaborne Empire 1415–1825* (London, 1969; Harmondsworth, 1973), pp. 130–51. I have derived many points from this readable and informative work.

40 See ibid., p. 157.

41 Two excellent chapters in Parry, *Spanish Empire*, pp. 249–93, provide an outstandingly well-shaped discussion of Spain as an imperial power in this era.

42 C. R. Boxer, *The Dutch Seaborne Empire 1600–1800* (London, 1965; Harmondsworth, 1973), pp. 126–72, discusses the connection between

Calvinism and Dutch commercial expansion, concluding that the link has often been exaggerated.

43 The French and English empires (particularly in North America) are well treated in Ralph Davis, *The Rise of the Atlantic Economies* (London, 1973), which centres on economic history but contains many illuminating passages on social and political issues.

44 Parry, *Spanish Empire,* pp. 267–8, 294–8, gives an excellent account of the *Asiento,* showing that England did less well out of its concession in 1713 than she had hoped. See also Crusoe's reference (*RCI*, p. 39).

45 Williams, *Expansion of Europe*, p. 5.

46 Earle, p. 65.

47 *A True Collection of the Writings of the Author of the True Born English-man* (2nd edn., 1705), pp. 77–8.

48 Earle, p. 70.

49 The best account of Defoe's dealings with Thomas, one of the most important influences in his life, can be found in *Citizen,* pp. 287–9. It might be added that Defoe himself invested in the African Company (*Citizen,* p. 86). For a general treatment, see K. G. Davies, *The Royal African Company* (London, 1957).

50 *Review,* Vol. VI, pp. 153–9: *Tour,* Vol. I, pp. 200–6.

51 Novak, *Economics,* pp. 143–4. Defoe's attack on the proprietors in Carolina came in *Party-Tyranny* (1705) (*Checklist,* 105).

52 Novak, *Economics,* p. 144.

53 It is worth recalling Parry's judgement (*Trade and Dominion,* p. 147) that 'Spain retained its colonial empire intact in 1713 because its chief enemies preferred an extension of their trade . . . to an extension of their territorial dominion, which might have involved more fighting'. When different interests seemed to be in conflict (political, diplomatic, naval and military, economic, religious) it was frequently the commercial considerations which prevailed. There was, of course, a strong lobby in Parliament representing the trading community, especially the rich 'West Indians' who were engaged in the most economically valuable area of commerce. Motives of aggrandisement and ideology were not absent from the colonial drive, but they were expressed in less full-hearted tones than those of the mercantile lobby.

54 W. A. Eddy, *Gulliver's Travels: A Critical Study* (Princeton, NJ, reprinted 1923, reprinted New York, 1963), p. 35. Eddy's book is now largely disregarded by Swiftian scholars, on account of its unsophisticated approach to questions of literary influence, but it does contain some useful information.

55 Hunter, p. 13. Hunter's discussion of the topic (pp. 1–22) is important and timely.

56 It may be worth adding that George Shelvocke's account of his voyage round the world, made in 1719–22, was published in 1726: it was this book which provided Coleridge with his theme for *The Ancient Mariner*. It existed in manuscript prior to publication and could conceivably have influenced Defoe's works from about 1723 onwards.

CHAPTER 3

Religion and Allegory

THE PURITAN INHERITANCE

The most striking single development in our recent understanding of the novel has lain in the rediscovery of a pervasive spiritual motif. In the nineteenth century *Crusoe* had been treated mainly as an adventure-story, characterised by intense 'realism' of presentation. Robinson himself had been viewed as an upright and manly Englishman, whose Broad Church piety did not get in the way of his real mission – survival and ultimate prosperity. Even as lately as the 1950s it was usual to dismiss Crusoe's religious reflections as not much more than *appliqué* on the surface of the narrative. In the 1860s Karl Marx wrote: 'Of his prayers and the like we take no account, since they are a source of pleasure to him, and he looks upon them as so much recreation.'[1] Almost a hundred years later Ian Watt was inclined to agree:

> Both Marx and Gildon were right in drawing attention to the discontinuity between the religious aspects of the book and its action: but their explanations do Defoe some injustice. His spiritual intentions were probably quite sincere, but they have the weakness of all 'Sunday religion' and manifest themselves in somewhat unconvincing periodical tributes to the transcendental at times when a respite from real action and practical intellectual effort is allowed or enforced.

Watt went on to assert that Defoe's 'religious upbringing forced him from time to time to hand over a brilliant piece of narrative by a star-reporter to a distant colleague on the religious page who could be relied on to supply suitable spiritual commentaries quickly out of stock. Puritanism made the editorial policy unalterable; but it was usually satisfied by a purely formal adherence.'[2]

These sentiments now have an extraordinarily dated look, because of the rapid transformation in our reading habits. Partly this is explicable by reason of a more sympathetic attitude towards the Puritan mind. Watt's book had its intellectual genesis at a time when R. H. Tawney and Max Weber dominated the general response to religious history. They are quoted comparatively infrequently by Watt, but it would not be straining the evidence to detect in his book a subterranean current of ideas deriving from this source. A representative passage in Tawney sums up the outlook:

> The distinctive note of Puritan teaching . . . was individual responsibility, not social obligation. Training its pupils to the mastery of others through the mastery of self, it prized as a crown of glory the qualities which arm the spiritual athlete for his solitary contest with a hostile world, and dismissed concern with the social order as the prop of weaklings and the Capua of the soul.[3]

Subsequent writers have criticised Tawney's general thesis, and have adopted a less jaundiced attitude towards the individualist ethic. It would not now be so readily taken for granted that 'concern with the social order' is always a more desirable or positive element in intellectual life than a concern for private spiritual values.

However, it was the appearance of two critical studies in the 1960s which dramatically reversed the position. Building on other explorations of the Puritan mind, and following up work on Milton and Bunyan in particular, these books set *Crusoe* in a wholly new light. George A. Starr published *Defoe and Spiritual Autobiography* in 1965. He argued that a well-marked cycle of sin and regeneration underlay Crusoe's experiences throughout the novel. There is, indeed, 'a conventional progression in sin' and an equally conventional pattern of redemption. Starr applied the same schemata to other novels (*Moll* and *Roxana*), but *Robinson Crusoe* is granted most space and proves the most amenable to this treatment. Another feature of the reading is the importance given to Crusoe's conversion of Friday, formerly regarded as marginal or even impertinent.[4]

Though the detailed emphases of J. Paul Hunter's *The Reluctant Pilgrim* (1966) are different, the main drift of the argument is remarkably similar. Hunter confines himself to *Crusoe* and examines a number of 'Puritan subliterary traditions' relevant to its making. (Where Starr had tended to stress general religious background, citing Anglican as well as Puritan sources, Hunter prefers to work from the dissenting models.) In his view the external narrative of travel and adventure has been allowed too prominent a place in our assessment of *Crusoe*. Typical of his argument are passages like this:

> What Defoe distills from desert island experience is not an 'agreeable Relation' at all, but rather a rigorous multilevel moral examination of life. . . . Unlike its [adventure-story] analogues, *Robinson Crusoe* derives dramatic power from its understanding of man's struggle against nature as both physical and metaphysical. . . . [It] embodies the Puritan view of man on a most profound level; it . . . portrays,

through the struggles of one man, the rebellion and punishment, repentance and deliverance, of all men, as they sojourn in a hostile world.

Or this:

> Throughout *Robinson Crusoe* physical events reflect Crusoe's spiritual state, for Crusoe is concerned with accommodating himself to his world spiritually and physically at the same time, and his efforts to come to terms with his physical environment parallel his efforts to find a proper relationship with his God. Ultimately, his physical activities become a metaphor for his spiritual aspirations.

What is most important here is the attempt to see *Crusoe* as a *coherent* and formally sophisticated narrative. Hunter, like Starr, divides the plot into clear-cut phases: rebellion and punishment, repentance and deliverance. He, too, pays attention to the 'saving' of Friday. But he goes further than Starr in detecting overall 'emblematic' or allegorical structure, using standard metaphors, parables and symbols to create a moral pilgrimage rather than a bare escape-story. He places particular stress on the biblical and typological allusions, looking for events with a meaning consecrated by their appearance (in identical or closely related terms) in scripture.[5]

Both these approaches show *Crusoe* as dependent on widely known techniques of popular devotional or didactic literature. They make it easier to relate the work to Defoe's vein of pious conduct-books, such as *The Family Instructor*. Moreover, they have in common a desire to emphasise the 'thematic' content of *Crusoe*, as opposed to the fictional rendering of exciting events. It is possible to feel that both critics overstate their case a little, and Hunter in particular is led by his thesis to play down every aspect of the work other than those which fit his case. Nevertheless, these readings have enriched our understanding to a remarkable degree, and in suggesting a new generic context for *Crusoe* they have provided an artistic justification for features and episodes which previously seemed hard to explain. Seen as a Puritan fable of spiritual life, the novel appears not only different but also, in crucial ways, a better book: more deeply imagined and more cunningly wrought.

The major forms lying behind such a version would be these:

(a) *Spiritual autobiography*. The best-known example today is Bunyan's *Grace Abounding* (1666). The keeping of a diary of one's own progress towards salvation was not, as Starr emphasises, confined to dissenting sects, although its most extreme manifestations are found there. The habit inculcated in pious individuals was to scrutinise their own life for signs of advancement or backsliding. In Starr's words, 'Since every man is responsible for the well-being of his own soul, he must mark with care each event or stage in its development. As his own spiritual physician, he must duly note every symptom of progress or relapse.' Another impetus to the composition of spiritual autobiography lay in the belief that 'there are universal and recurrent elements in human affairs, particularly in vicissitudes of the soul. History repeats itself . . . in the spiritual life of individuals.' This in turn connects with the habit of searching the Bible for parallels and portents, to find what were called 'Scripture Similitudes'. Certain biblical images came to have special meanings accredited to them; in this area of moral exegesis Defoe would have the example of innumerable sermons but also formal hand-books such as the *Tropologia* (1681) by a London Baptist preacher, Benjamin Keach (1640–1704), which gathers together many 'express' allegories found in the Bible. Key metaphors included those of pilgrimage, of seafaring, and warfare. Though surrounded in his youth by spiritual autobiographers, Defoe did not attempt the form himself; it is true, however, that his tributes to his family pastor, Dr Annesley (see below, p. 59), and his life of *Daniel Williams* (1718) have been seen as related to the tradition.[6]

Starr, as indicated, discerns a standard 'rhythm' of conversion. From his 'original sin' in running away to sea, through his early wanderings to his shipwreck and gradual restoration on the island, a direct allusion to this pattern can be traced. (For example, the early travels reflect estrangement and alienation from God.) Then on the island come stock episodes such as dreams and earthquakes. God's interposition finally brings Crusoe to a recognition of his errors, and his regeneration reaches a climax in his conversion of Friday – zeal in this direction was a well-understood mark of spiritual advancement. In spiritual biography 'the purposeful pattern of the subject's life is superimposed over the chronological record of events'; Crusoe has first to discover this purpose and then shape his narrative to show its accomplishment.[7]

(*b*) *The guide tradition.* This is a branch of popular homiletic literature concerned with warning the reader against the perils of moral existence, and designed to offer a ready-to-hand hortatory or consolatory body of instruction. There were many general guides, but also specialised manuals directed towards a group or calling (seamen, tradesmen, farmers, etc.). A major sub-division was that of the guide to young persons, in which Timothy Cruso (see below, p. 60) was a practitioner. Perhaps the best-known of all works in this genre were Arthur Dent's *Plain Mans Pathway to Heaven* (1601) and Lewis Bayly's *Practice of Piety* (1613); the equally popular *Whole Duty of Man* (1658) has its roots in this tradition. Tracts and sermons not specifically organised as a 'guide' drew upon the same habit of advice. Even as late a work as William Law's *A Serious Call to a Devout and Holy Life* (1728) shows some impress; the penultimate chapter, for instance, is set out very much on the 'guide' formula: 'Of evening prayer. Of the nature and necessity of examination. How we are to be particular in the confession of all our sins. How we are to fill our minds with a just horror and of all sin.' Law, of course, was a High Churchman. But Defoe the dissenter would be exposed to many such manuals on practical living, conceived from a religious standpoint. Indeed, his own conduct-books, from *The Family Instructor* through to *The Compleat English Gentleman*, are secularised or dramatised variants of the guide. Hunter is surely justified in saying that *Crusoe* deals 'with the problems which the guide tradition had previously faced' – the nature of a calling, filial obedience, resistance to temptation. As Hunter goes on to remark, '*Robinson Crusoe* ultimately is much more complex than any of the traditions which nourish it, but the complexity should not obscure the ancestry'.[8]

(c) *The 'Providence' tradition.* This is Hunter's term for a widely employed technique (found in sermons, guides, biographies and elsewhere), showing the intervention of God in the affairs of man. All the forms discussed here were likely to interpret natural phenomena as marks of divine approval or disapproval, as reward for merit or punishment for evil. The specific tradition relates to explicit or extended use of this notion, especially the recital of extraordinary events which are carefully explicated in the light of their providential bearings. A prominent and still highly readable example is the work of an Anglican clergyman, William Turner (1653–1701); it is called *A Compleat History of the Most Remarkable Providences, Both of Judgment and Mercy, Which have Hapned in this Present Age* (1697). Bitty and uneven though it is, this book provides one of the clearest introductions we have to the mental world in which *Robinson Crusoe* came to birth. In a way it is literature of the 'Strange News from . . .' variety; but for contemporaries the over-riding interest undoubtedly lay in the interpretations rather than the events themselves – Turner divides his stories into categories, each illustrating particular modes of divine judgement. It should be added that the pamphlet version of Selkirk's story, *Providence Displayed* (see above, p. 49), is in essentials a reworking of Woodes Rogers towards providential ends.[9]

Defoe's awareness of this tradition is quite unmistakable. Even if he had not used as his theme delivery from shipwreck (and, incidentally, escape from Barbary) – standard providential material – and even if he had not stated in his preface (*RC1*, p. 1) that his aim was 'to justify and honour the Wisdom of Providence in all the Variety of our Circumstances', we should still have external evidence. In *RC3* a chapter is devoted to the subject of 'Listening to the Voice of Providence'. In this Defoe offers a definition of Providence ('the operation of the power, wisdom, justice, and goodness of God by which He influences, governs,

and directs not only the means, but the events, of all things which
concern us in this world', p. 187). He has Crusoe explain that 'by
listening to the voice of Providence, I mean to study its meaning in every
circumstance of life'; this should be 'our business and our interest' (p.
189). Crusoe's habit of noting dates, coincidences and significant con-
junctions is illuminated by his observation here, 'The concurrence of
events is a light to their causes, and the methods of Heaven, in some
things, are a happy guide to us to make a judgment in others; he that is
deaf to these things shuts his ears to instruction, and, like Solomon's fool,
hates knowledge' (p. 195). And at the end of this section:

> To listen to the voice of Providence, is to take strict notice of all the
> remarkable steps of Providence which relate to us in particular, to
> observe if there is nothing in them instructing to our conduct, no
> warning to us for avoiding some danger, no direction for the taking
> some particular steps for our safety or advantage, no hint to remind
> of such and such things omitted, no conviction of something com-
> mitted, no vindictive step, by way of retaliation, marking out the
> crime in the punishment. (p. 213)

It would be exceedingly rash to assume that this is simply an importunate
moral thrust on the self-sufficient narrative, an *ex post facto* signal by
Defoe behind the back of his creation Robinson. All the signs are that
Defoe, from the very beginning, meant his novel to bear these monitory
functions.

A significant clue here lies in a book published fifteen years earlier.
All his life Defoe was fascinated by natural disasters, whether volcanic
eruptions, earthquakes, fires, or epidemics. One of his most characteristic
early works is *The Storm* (1704), assembling reports on the great
'dreadful Tempest' which had struck Britain on 26–27 November 1703.
At least 8,000 people are believed to have perished in the savage wind
and floods: Eddystone lighthouse was destroyed, men-of-war lost while
at anchor, the Bishop of Bath and Wells killed with his wife as they lay
in bed. Defoe's compilation is, following the practice of the time, a
rambling affair: it moves from Ralph Bohen's theories on the causes
of wind through earlier hurricanes to the present storm, with a pastoral
elegy sent in by an unnamed contributor. The main part of the book is
taken up with eye-witness accounts from all over southern Britain. In his
preface Defoe spells out the providential implications, and challenges
freethinkers to examine their position: 'I cannot believe any Man so
rooted in Atheistical Opinions, as not to find some Cause whether he was
not in the Wrong, and a little to apprehend the Possibility of a Supreme
Being, when he felt the terrible blasts of this Tempest.' Indeed, Defoe

had originally intended to supply an account of 'some unthinking Wretches, who pass'd over this dreadful Judgment with Banter, Scoffing, and Contempt'; but he decided it would be charitable to omit this.[10]

A sceptic might ask whether Defoe would have had one of his early books strongly present in his mind when some 330 items separate this from *Crusoe* in the *Checklist*. But there is separate evidence that *The Storm* had a part to play in the genesis of the novel. As Secord demonstrated at length,[11] the account of the storm off Yarmouth roads (*RC1*, pp. 10–14) has strong affinities with various parts of *The Storm*, besides a connection with a passage on the Norfolk coast published in the *Tour* (1724).[12] The most direct parallel concerns the very last report inserted in *The Storm*, which carries the dateline, '*From on board* the John *and* Mary, *riding in* Yarmouth *Roads during the great Storm, but now in the River of* Thames'.[13] Secord itemised a number of closely similar features in the two books, showing a correspondence both in the materials of the description and in their ordering. Some aspects of the account in *Crusoe*, however, find their parallels in other reports included in *The Storm*. In addition, Secord briefly indicated a possible link between the Yarmouth narrative of 1704 and Crusoe's final shipwreck, that is, the one in the mouth of the Orinoco which results in his island captivity. There are occasional verbal parallels: 'the Sea went too high for any Boat to live' (*Storm*, pp. 268–9), 'the Sea went so high, that the Boat could not live' (*RC1*, p. 43). In both narratives a boat 'staves' to pieces when dashed against the ship; and other expressions recur ('abate', 'drive', as well as technical terms such as 'cable'). The resemblances are certainly greater than one would expect from two accounts of a storm chosen at random; and, while it would be going too far to list the 1704 description as an immediate 'source' of the 1719 wreck, some imaginative continuity may well be present. We do not know if Defoe himself wrote the relations of 'strange Deliverances' in *The Storm* – he may very easily have done so. In any case, the material stayed in his head for the rest of his life. There are several allusions to this national disaster in his *Tour* (1724–6): it rivals the Plague and the South Sea Bubble as an emblem of catastrophe.

It is probably unnecessary to emphasise here the fact that one of Defoe's later fictions, *A Journal of the Plague Year*, where the narrator refers to the plague as 'a particular Season of Divine Vengeance', is centrally concerned with natural events as a sign of God's wrath. H.F. sees the plague as occurring by 'the Appointment and Direction of Providence';[14] as usual Defoe makes it plain that divine will is expressed through second causes and only exceptionally through direct intervention outside the ordinary processes of nature. *Robinson Crusoe* is shot through with the same inclination to read providential meanings into occurrences both remarkable and humdrum. This proceeds from no eccentric or radical enthusiasm; it was a way of interpreting events and a way of

telling stories thoroughly acceptable to readers of the day, whatever
their particular shade of religious belief.

(*d*) *Other contexts.* Hunter describes a more generalised form, that is,
the 'pilgrim' allegory present in Bunyan's masterpiece and sketched less
memorably in a thousand sermons or tracts. The abstract scheme is set
out by Hunter in these terms:

> A man first sails away from the Home appointed for him (instead of
> proceeding toward it) and then becomes isolated from God as a result
> of discontent and selfish pride. Ultimately, however, God intervenes
> to deliver him from destruction, and the direction of his life is altered
> to a course pleasing to God and leading at last to the man's ultimate
> Home. The man, however, still must undergo numerous battles with
> evil before he can rest content at the end of the journey.

This scenario would also fit many spiritual biographies. The fact that
Crusoe emerges with much more concrete life and individuality than the
scheme allows for does not make the correspondences wholly irrelevant.[15]

In a separate article Hunter draws attention to the many seventeenth-
century accounts of missions among the American Indians. The missionaries were largely supported by New England Puritans, like Defoe's early
tutor, Charles Morton. In fact a major collection of such accounts, *A
Brief Narrative of the Success [of the] Gospel among the Indians in
New-England* (1694), was dedicated by its compiler, Matthew Mayhew,
to Morton amongst others. Hunter's main purpose on this occasion is to
show how the descriptions of native converts square with Defoe's picture
of Friday; but his article indicates another kind of work, straddling
devotional and 'discovery' themes, which must have lain at the back of
the novelist's mind.[16] So, of course, did innumerable sermons and
religious tracts; their influence may not be directly felt at any given
point in *Crusoe*, but they were abroad in the general imagination as
surely as the images of popular television programmes inhabit our
consciousness today. In 1719 no living Englishman (or woman) could
have escaped the power of the religious word; it was the stuff of his
culture.

EDUCATION IN DISSENT

The last comment would apply to any contemporary. But Defoe was
marked off by the fact that he had been intended for the nonconformist
ministry. His formative years were spent in a highly purposive environment, with a distinct aim in view. He grew up conscious of a special
destiny in store and, although he relinquished the calling, he retained
the sense of a personal fate. Whether or not *Crusoe* can be read as an

allegory of his private experience, he had a vein of self-pity which commonly expressed itself in laments at the 'afflictions' he was forced to endure. In the nearest he came to an autobiography, *An Appeal to Honour and Justice* (1715), he claimed that he alone had been 'silent under the infinite Clamours and Reproaches, causeless Curses, unusual Threatnings, and the most unjust and injurious Treatment in the World'.[17] Defoe had a profound consciousness of having been cheated somewhere along the line. Whether it was his abandoned career in the ministry, his failed business ventures, his allegiance to fallen ministers, the loss of his royal patron, William III, or a combination of these things – he felt he had not had his deserts. Crusoe and his other highly successful heroes and heroines may involve a compensatory fantasy.

Young Daniel Foe was only 2 years old when the Act of Uniformity passed through Parliament.[18] It meant that ministers were obliged to accept the new Book of Common Prayer, drawn up by a High Church convocation in 1661. In addition they had to submit to episcopal ordination. The vicar of St Giles, Cripplegate (the parish church, one might say, of Grub Street) was Samuel Annesley (?1620–96). He refused the new tests and was duly ejected. He took with him into the Presbyterian Church many parishioners; among these was the tallow-chandler of Fore Street, James Foe, together with his wife Alice and three children. In 1665, during the Plague, the Oxford Parliament passed the so-called Five Mile Act which strengthened the test and drove Annesley farther afield. After the Declaration of Indulgence in 1672 he was licensed to preach again, in Little St Helen's, off the lower end of Bishopsgate, opposite Gresham College. There he remained until his death in 1696, an event prompting Defoe to produce a verse elegy on his character – this stresses Annesley's loyalty to his parents, his piety from childhood on, and his qualities of calm, patience and fortitude in adversity.[19] Another strong link with nonconformity to come was forged by the marriage of his daughter to Samuel Wesley, the father of Charles and John. Moore is justified in saying that, through his association with Annesley, Defoe 'grew up near the center of Presbyterian worship in London'.[20]

Around 1668 Daniel lost his mother, and he was sent to a boarding school for dissenters near Dorking in Surrey. The master, James Fisher, was another ejected minister, although a man of lesser stature than Annesley. He was a Congregationalist, that is, a member of a less tightly organised sect than the Presbyterians. Defoe left school about 1674, and that should have been the end of his formal education. But instead he went on to study under yet another ejected minister, Charles Morton, at the famous Newington Green academy. This indicates that he was by now a candidate for the ministry. Much has been written about Morton (1627–98) and his possible influence upon Defoe. The basic facts are, first, that he, too, was a Congregationalist; secondly, that he was a widely cultivated man, a graduate of Oxford who had been incorporated at Cambridge and who was ultimately to become Vice-President of Harvard; thirdly, that his special interests were scientific and mathematical (thus reinforcing the bias towards practical subjects which dissenting academies developed in reaction against the obscurantist pedantry – as they saw it – of the universities). Defoe was proud of his association with the man and with the school, and at the end of his life was still propagating the values he had imbibed during this period. It should be added that Morton taught through the medium of English – an act of rebellion in itself – and his own spare prose may possibly have influenced his pupil's style.

A pupil of the academy at just about the same time was a young man some four years senior to Defoe. This was Timothy Cruso (?1656–97), who went on to become a Presbyterian minister and well-known preacher. He wrote some of the popular 'guides', including *God the Guide of Youth* (1695); but he would probably not be associated with Defoe today but for his surname. Since the nineteenth century biographers have speculated on the possibility that this is where the curious name derives. (Other theories would relate it to a Caribbean island, Curaçao, where pirates gathered; or to a Cruso family in King's Lynn; or to German words such as *kreutzen*, 'to cross or cruise', and *Kreutz*, 'a cross'.) Recently Hunter has revived the Timothy Cruso connection, arguing that Defoe employs an allusive mode to alert readers familiar with the career of this dissenting teacher. It is not a matter on which a definitive answer is likely to emerge.[21]

In any case Defoe left the academy about 1679. He made transcripts of sermons delivered by a former Congregationalist, John Collins (?1632–87), who also had Harvard connections. Collins, like Timothy Cruso later, was chosen as Merchant's Lecturer at Pinner's Hall (a major centre of dissent, in Broad Street, halfway between St Giles's and Little St Helen's). Defoe composed at this time some verse meditations which were first published in 1946. They have been described as 'confessional' poetry, but they do not really explain why Defoe should, very soon afterwards, turn his back on the ministry and enter trade. We are left with a long preparation for the role of a pastor; a boyhood and youth spent under the influence of enlightened dissenters like Annesley, Fisher and Morton; and then the sudden *volte-face*. Many 'personal' readings of literature are unconvincing, not least the highly biographic interpretations of *Crusoe* itself. But if it is accepted that Robinson Crusoe is haunted throughout by an early misjudgement, then the possibility that Defoe's switch of career has some deep-level connection with the issue cannot be regarded as implausible.

CRUSOE'S ORIGINAL SIN

In the middle of *RC1*, Crusoe reflects on his condition in the period between his discovery of the Spanish wreck and his meeting with Friday – he has spent some twenty-three years on the island:

> I have been in all my Circumstances a *Memento* to those who are touch'd with the general Plague of Mankind, whence, for ought I know, one half of their Miseries flow; I mean, that of not being satisfy'd with the Station wherein God and Nature has plac'd them; for not to look back upon my primitive Condition, and the excellent Advice of my Father, the Opposition to which, was, *as I may call it*, my *ORIGINAL SIN*; my subsequent Mistakes of the same kind had been the Means of my coming into this miserable Condition; for had that Providence, which so happily had seated me at the *Brasils*, as a Planter, bless'd me with confin'd Desires, and I could have been contented to have gone on gradually, I might have been by this Time; I *mean, in the Time of my being in this Island*, one of the most considerable Planters in the *Brasils*. . . .

Nor do the self-reproaches stop there:

> But as this is ordinarily the Fate of young Heads, so Reflection upon the Folly of it, is as ordinarily the Exercise of more Years, or of the dear bought Experience of Time; and so it was with me now; and yet so deep had the Mistake taken root in my Temper, that I could not satisfy myself in my Station, but was continually poring upon the Means, and Possibility of my Escape from this Place. . . . (pp. 194–5)

What precisely *was* this original sin? As the passage makes clear, it refers to Crusoe's first act of disobedience in leaving home to follow a seafaring life, rather than the legal career marked out for him. But this is only to shift the question back one stage. What kind of error does the 19-year-old Robinson commit? And is the root of his disobedience to be explained in religious, moral or psychological terms? No issue has more exercised recent commentators.

One remarkably clear-cut solution was proposed by Ian Watt. In his view, 'the argument between [Crusoe's] parents and himself is a debate, not about filial duty or religion, but about whether going or staying is likely to be the most advantageous course materially. . . . And, of course, Crusoe actually gains by his "original sin", and becomes richer than his father was.' Consequently, on this showing, 'Crusoe's "original sin" is really the dynamic tendency of capitalism itself, whose aim is never merely to maintain the *status quo*, but to transform it incessantly. Leaving home, improving on the lot one was born to, is a vital feature of the individualist pattern of life'.[22] Watt's verdict has been repeated by some later critics, including John J. Richetti, who locates Crusoe's urges still more precisely within the 'dangerously dynamic aspect of capitalist ideology which must in the context of the early eighteenth century be denied and suppressed'. Richetti suggests that Crusoe has to do more than merely repudiate his father: 'The destruction of the father . . . seems to be what lies behind Crusoe's desire to go to sea, that is, to become rich above his father's station. To surpass him economically is in a real sense to destroy him.' There is at the start 'a dance among various sorts of explanations – social, moral, and psycho-religious – for Crusoe's desire to roam'. An implied emphasis on 'mysterious internal impulse' is at odds with Crusoe's calculating nature.[23]

A modified and more elaborate version of the economic case was made by Maximillian E. Novak. The central proposition is announced with admirable directness: 'I suggest that Crusoe's sin is his refusal to follow the "calling" chosen for him by his father, and that the rationale for this action may be found in Crusoe's personal characteristics: his lack of economic prudence, his inability to follow a steady profession, his indifference to a calm bourgeois life, and his love of travel.' To buttress this argument Novak brings a variety of evidence. He reviews Crusoe's personal traits, observing that 'When he created the character of Crusoe, Defoe certainly had more empathy with the concept of the colonist than with that of the capitalist'. (Novak has in mind contemporaneous works like the life of Ralegh; see above, p. 27.) Defoe 'admired the merchant, but not the capitalist or even the tradesman who made excessive profits'. An 'excellent sketch' of Crusoe's own character is quoted from *RC2* (p. 216), where the narrator refers to himself as 'a mad rambling Boy'. Crusoe is 'a prototype of Shaw's Bluntschli – the hero raised as a trades-man but with a romantic temperament'. Novak then investigates the concept of 'calling', as evolving from Luther and modified by subsequent Protestant theology. Weber and Tawney again come much into the argument. Perceptively Novak remarks that 'Defoe's hero is not a hermit by nature; he survives his solitude, but he does not enjoy it' – this in itself throws some light on the thesis of Watt and Richetti. The conclusion is that 'Crusoe does not disobey his parents in the name of free enterprise or economic freedom, but for a strangely adventurous, romantic, and unprofitable desire to see foreign lands. If any economic moral can be drawn from Crusoe's narrative, it is a conservative warning that English-men about to embark on the economic disaster of the South Sea Bubble should mind their callings and stick to the sure road of trade.'[24]

This reading was quickly challenged by G. A. Starr, who contended that it demanded a 'more individualized portrait than Defoe actually gives us at [the start] of the book'. Starr cites *The Family Instructor* amongst other works to indicate the orthodoxy of Defoe's ideas at this point: 'That man is naturally subject to rebellious impulse is a principle he frequently asserts, and it would appear to provide a sufficient "rationale" for Crusoe's behavior on this occasion. Indeed the episode seems to rest on an orthodox Calvinistic conception of man's innate waywardness and obstinacy.' What we have is simply 'a generalized portrait of the young man'. Starr's counter-suggestion is that 'implicit in Defoe's treatment of the episode is a conventional identification of family, social and divine order, all of which are flouted by Crusoe's deed'. In a sense, Crusoe's act of disobedience 'is merely the first overt expression of a more fundamental source of trouble: the natural waywardness of every unregenerate man'. Its function is to 'initiate a pattern of wrongdoing'. The parallel with the story of Jonah mentioned by Crusoe's shipmate on his first voyage from Hull (*RC1*, p. 15) is seen as a close one: in both episodes the narrative provides 'a kind of "objective correlative" for the hero's turbulent, unruly spirit'. (The story of Jonah, located neither by Starr nor the OEN editor, is found, of course, in the book of Jonah, 1-2; it may be added that Hunter shows it to be a common emblem in providential works.) For Starr, who emphasises the 'special fondness' shown by Providence for the middle station, Crusoe 'like the Prodigal Son before him' displays not just a lack of economic prudence but 'a radical perversity and impiety'.[25]

All these readings have points of interest in them. If Starr seems to me the most convincing overall, this is chiefly on two counts. First, his view of the episode fits more snugly into a general sense of the way the book works: the opening episode contributes to the total pattern without altogether controlling later developments. Secondly, he gives to the phrase 'original sin' the primary acceptation it must have had for most readers, and not only those with a Calvinist background, in Defoe's time. By metaphor the phrase could no doubt be extended to social or economic areas of life, but its prime *theological* cast could never be dispelled. When we find Crusoe making explicit reference to St Luke's parable of the prodigal (*RC1*, pp. 8, 14) as well as to the Jonah story – the standard types of rebellion and disobedience in Puritan homiletics – we are pushed closer to the underlying allegory of the Fall itself, for so long the crucial datum in man's understanding of his own spiritual condition. As Hunter suggests, Crusoe's rejection of his parents 'takes its ultimate mythic dimension' from this source.[26] No interpretation of the opening of *Robinson Crusoe* which ignores this dimension of meaning will disclose the point of this episode in the full trajectory of Crusoe's career.

On the other hand it is possible to make the correspondences too strict and to drown the text in scriptural allusions of doubtful relevance.

Robert W. Ayers's typological reading does not altogether avoid this pitfall; building upon the fundamental analogical identity of Crusoe's father as God and the hero himself as Adam, he discovers emblems of all known temptations within the text. A new etymology for the name 'Crusoe' relates it to *crusader*. Ayers sees a metaphysical overtone in the phrase 'middle State' (*RC1*, p. 4), which makes the father's speech a proleptic hint of Pope's lines in the *Essay on Man*:

> Plac'd on this isthmus of a middle state,
> A being darkly wise, and rudely great.
> (Epistle II, pp. 3–4)

Ayers finds sacramental symbols thickly strewn about the island (caves, grapes, etc.), and is even able to identify the boy Xury as a Christ figure 'to some degree'.[27] It is not very obvious how one can be Christ to some degree.

But this is at worst an overstatement of genuine elements in the book. Whether we can discern the things detected by Watt and Richetti is a matter of taste and judgement: in general, those who dislike capitalism as a historical phenomenon are the readiest to suppose that Defoe sensed by intuition failings in its effects on the human spirit and that he chose to dramatise these through Crusoe. One of the difficulties in seeing the novel as a work which 'drew attention to the . . . need of building up a network of personal relationships on a new and conscious pattern' is that it neglects a key aspect of the plot: Crusoe achieves salvation, and over-comes his existential isolation, *without* any 'network of personal relation-ships' – Friday comes late on the scene and is a dependant rather than a friend. This is apart from the awkward fact that Defoe shows Crusoe's 'Island of Despair' as a Godless, not a manless, world; he is reconciled to his condition by solitary devotions (which go on while his capital is accreting), not by healthy interpersonal contacts.[28] True, many modern critics dislike Crusoe even at the end, and find something suspect (if not downright disreputable) in his accumulative habits; but it is far from clear that Defoe meant us to share this disapproval. As for Richetti, he requires us to believe that Crusoe destroys his father, not just symbolic-ally but 'in a real sense'.[29] In that case Defoe badly mismanaged things, for we have no idea how and when the father died. Crusoe simply learns on his return that his parents are dead and almost 'all the Family extinct' (*RC1*, p. 278). I hope it is not being too literal-minded to observe that he has been away from Yorkshire for nearly thirty-six years; his father was described as 'very ancient' when Crusoe was growing up – he had retired even before marrying. In such circumstances the hero's direct responsibility for his parent's demise looks a little blurred.

The fact is that Crusoe is allotted 'something fatal in that Propension

of Nature tending directly to the Life of Misery which was to befal me'
(*RC1*, p. 3). At the heart of this stands the 'meer wandering Inclination'
(p. 4) rightly emphasised by Novak; but it transcends the simple
ambition to travel as it does the mere pursuit of monetary gain. He is
not deflected by his experiences in the storm off Yarmouth, though the
portents are clear enough to him; nor by his captivity at Sallee, though
he again recalls his father's 'prophetick Discourse' (p. 19); nor by his
early struggles in Brazil, where he sees himself as 'just like a Man cast
away upon some desolate Island' (p. 35); nor by his later prosperity
there:

> Had I continued in the Station I was now in, I had room for all the
> happy things to have yet befallen me, for which my Father so
> earnestly recommended a quiet retired Life, and of which he had so
> sensibly describ'd the middle Station of Life to be full of; but other
> things attended me, and I was still to be the wilful Agent of all my
> own Miseries; and particularly to encrease my Fault and double the
> Reflections upon my self, which in my future Sorrows I should have
> leisure to make; all these Miscarriages were procured by my apparent
> obstinate adhering to my foolish inclination of wandring abroad and
> pursuing that Inclination, in contradiction to the clearest Views of
> doing my self good in a fair and plain pursuit of those Prospects and
> those measures of Life, which Nature and Providence concurred to
> present me with, and to make my Duty. (p. 38)

Crusoe does indeed have abundant leisure on his island to reflect upon
his past mistakes. Filial disobedience was followed by blind obstinacy –
a refusal to learn from the past which is not just imprudent but against
nature, perverse and, as it were, self-renewing.

Even in *RC2*, after he has grown rich, Crusoe finds the same
'distemper of wandering' (p. 8) overtaking him: he persuades himself
'it would be a kind of resisting Providence' if he were to reject his
nephew's offer of a new journey (p. 11). This is not the calculating
language of a self-aggrandising manipulator: it has the air of someone
possessed by an obscure private fantasy. At the very end of the second
part, Crusoe tells us he is finally stifling the demon within:

> And here resolving to harass myself no more, I am preparing for a
> longer journey than all these, having lived seventy-two years a life of
> infinite variety, and learnt sufficiently to know the value of retirement,
> and the blessing of ending our days in peace. (p. 323)

An unconvincing litany to go out upon, some would think; but in my
view a truly organic conclusion. The restlessness which drives Crusoe is

the very spirit of his being. It will be extirpated not by the end of his actual travels, or by the accomplishment of any economic goal; it is part of man's fallen nature, and will survive until he achieves salvation in death. Christian was freed of his burden of guilt at the foot of the Cross, although it was not until he crossed the River of Death that he put off his mortal garments.[30] For Crusoe the act of conversion brings insight, joy and a reanimated energy born of self-acceptance; but full release from the innate contradictions of his nature will come only with the 'longer journey' out of mortal existence.

ALLEGORY

It was the unfriendly critic Charles Gildon who first raised the issue of an allegorical component in the novel. His satiric dialogue (see below, pp. 129–31) includes an admission by Defoe that Crusoe is but 'the true Allegorick Image of [his] tender Father D——*I*'.[31] In *RC3* the following year Defoe chose to don this evidently well-fitting cap; Crusoe's preface contains these passages:

> There is a man alive, and well known too, the actions of whose life are the just subject of these volumes, and to whom all or most part of the story most directly alludes; this may be depended upon for truth, and to this I set my name.
>
> . . . In a word, the 'Adventures of Robinson Crusoe' are one whole scheme of a real life of eight and twenty years, spent in the most wandering, desolate and afflicting circumstances that ever man went through, and in which I have lived so long in a life of wonders, in continued storms, fought with the worst kind of savages and man-eaters; by unaccountable surprising incidents, fed by miracles greater than that of ravens; suffered all manner of violences and oppression, injurious reproaches, contempt of men, attacks of devils, corrections from Heaven, and oppositions on earth; have had innumerable ups and downs in matters of fortune, been in slavery worse than Turkish, escaped by exquisite management, as that in the story of Xury, and the boat at Sallee; been taken up at sea in distress, raised again and depressed again, and that oftener perhaps in one man's life than ever was known before; shipwrecked often, though more by land than by sea. In a word, there is not a circumstance in the imaginary story but has its just allusion to a real story, and chimes part for part and step for step with the inimitable Life of Robinson Crusoe. (pp. ix–xi.)

Crusoe goes on to explain that his references in the *Serious Reflections* observe the same code: 'All these reflections are just history of a state of forced confinement, which in my real history is represented by a confined retreat in an island; and it is as reasonable to represent one kind of imprisonment by another, as it is to represent anything that really exists by that which exists not.' As a final justification, he declares that 'here is the just and only good end of all parable or allegoric history brought to pass, viz., for moral and religious improvement' (p. xii).

The preface is signed 'Rob. Crusoe', but no one has ever doubted that Defoe was referring to himself as the 'man alive'. Difficulties arise because: (1) it is not certain whether he had such an intention all along, or was simply making opportunistic use of Gildon's idea; (2) we do not know how explicit and detailed the supposed allegory is meant to be; (3) Defoe seems confused in his attitude, claiming that the story, 'though allegorical, is also historical' (p. ix) – many commentators see the entire preface as seeking to have it both ways; and (4) we cannot be sure why Defoe should have chosen thus to reveal all at this particular juncture. It can hardly be doubted that Defoe was attempting to deflect the criticism of Gildon, who had asserted that 'The Christian Religion and the Doctrines of Providence are too Sacred to be deliver'd in Fictions and Lies',[32] a technique he associates with papist legends of the saints. It was vital for Defoe's purposes that the imputation of mere 'romance' status should be discounted. However, the manner in which he chose to combat the accusation has puzzled readers ever since. Comparison with *An Appeal to Honour and Justice* indicates that Defoe was attempting to vindicate his position by a more oblique means; but, again, we cannot be sure how active a concern this was during the composition of *RC1* and *RC2*.

Most of those who have tried to discover a close-knit personal allegory in *Crusoe* have confined themselves to the first part, and a frustrating task they have found it. Among these cryptographers was the biographer Thomas Wright (see below, pp. 139–40), although he subsequently modified his views. His original study was built on the theory that Defoe took a vow of silence on 30 September 1686, which he maintained until his illness in December 1714 (19 December, Wright says). This in turn rests on an anecdote in *RC3* (pp. 6–7) concerning a man who refused to speak for a period of almost twenty-nine years. Wright worked out that Crusoe's twenty-eight years, two months and nineteen days on the island (*RC1*, p. 278) matched Defoe's speechlessness. Crusoe's leaving home is identified with his leaving Newington academy and abandoning the ministry. Wright supposed that Defoe was born in 1659, which made the figures square more easily. A few other events are allotted allegorical meaning (for example, the coming of the savages to the island is obscurely connected with Defoe's peril at the time of the Sacheverell riots in 1710), but for the most part Wright discreetly avoided excessive particularity. Nobody to my knowledge has ever accepted this theory, although one or two other allegorists have made separate attempts.[33]

The commonest explanation has the shipwreck corresponding to Defoe's bankruptcy (that is, the first, or perhaps both); in that event it is difficult to see what the earlier portents – the Yarmouth storm and Sallee captivity – could consistently represent. A less personal interpretation would equate the twenty-eight years on the island with the period in the wilderness experienced by the dissenting community between 1660 and 1688. More than one attempt has been made to find a plausible Friday figure in Defoe's life but, as Sutherland says, 'There would be more justification for identifying Crusoe with Robert Harley, and the faithful Friday with Defoe'. The matter seems to me not finally closed; surrogates of Defoe do keep appearing in his novels (the gentleman tradesman in *Moll Flanders*, OEN, pp. 60–3; the mysterious Englishman in the African interior in *Captain Singleton*, OEN, pp. 121–37), and Moore may be right in detecting echoes of Defoe's own Newgate experiences.[34] I might add that the allegorists have yet to catch up with the discovery that Defoe was actually captured during the Monmouth rebellion and only escaped with his life by virtue of a royal pardon. We also know that Defoe was in the Fleet prison at least twice during his early financial difficulties.[35] These facts increase the allegorical range of that 'state of enforced confinement, which in my real history is represented by a confined retreat in an island'. Conceivably the Sallee episode relates to the Western Rising, although Defoe was about 25 whereas Crusoe was only 20 to 22 at the relevant dates. It would be rash to assume that we shall never unravel genuine bits of biographic allegory entwined in the novel.

But this would affect our estimate of its literary merits only in a marginal respect. The main importance of the 'captivity' theme is surely its underpinning of the basic Christian metaphor: the crucial imaginative process is the one suggested by Crusoe himself.

Now I began to construe the Words . . . *Call on me, and I will deliver you*; for then I had no Notion of any thing being call'd Deliverance, but my being deliver'd from the Captivity I was in; for tho' I was indeed at large in the Place, yet the Island was certainly a Prison to me, and that in the worst Sense in the World; but now I learn'd to take it in another Sense: Now I look'd back upon my past Life with such Horrour, and my Sins appear'd so dreadful, that my Soul sought nothing of God, but Deliverance of the Load of Guilt that bore down all my Comfort: As for my solitary Life it was nothing; I did not so much as pray to be deliver'd from it, or think of it; It was all of no Consideration in Comparison to this: And I add this Part here, to hint to whoever shall read it, that whenever they come to a true Sense of things, they will find Deliverance from Sin a much greater Blessing, than Deliverance from Affliction. (*RC1*, pp. 96–7)

What is rendered explicitly here opens out elsewhere in the book through allusion, parable and other dark conceits. Whether or not Defoe had his own experiences of privation in mind, the ultimate significance of captivity and deliverance in the imaginative fabric of *Robinson Crusoe* belongs to a universal realm of spiritual existence. Hunter does not exceed the truth when he writes of Crusoe as an Everyman figure, beginning as an aimless wanderer, nor when he adds that the hero 'ends as a pilgrim, crossing a final mountain to enter the promised land'.[36] A sustained religious image, one with scriptural roots and ubiquitous in Christian (especially Puritan) apologetics, gives body to the entire story of Crusoe – his rebellion, his drifting, his shipwreck, his castaway life, his conversion and ultimate deliverance. Having seen himself on the island as 'a Prisoner, lock'd up with the eternal Bars and Bolts of the Ocean, in an uninhabited Wilderness, without Redemption' (p. 113), he comes to find redemption in a fuller sense than he at first could have conceived.

There is much less to say about the religious content of the remaining parts. *RC2* gives us Crusoe's views on Christian marriage in the section describing his return to the island (pp. 136–62); some of this is close to the conduct-books, such as *Conjugal Lewdness*, but it is assimilated into the novel with awkward and laboured results. We see Crusoe pushing his faith into remote corners of the globe; he even blows up an idol in a village on the borders of Tartary and Muscovy, though we may fairly suspect that Defoe wanted an excuse to work in some of his favourite pyrotechnics (*RC2*, pp. 284–97). There is a surprisingly favourable picture of a French priest, which led Gildon to argue that Crusoe was trying to 'smooth the Way, as far as his little Abilities can do it, for the Popish Superstition to enter these Kingdoms'. For Gildon, the aim of Jesuit and other missionaries was 'to carry on a private interloping Trade, by which they bring in vast Treasures into their particular Orders'.[37]

As for *RC3*, it is straightforward and pious; the separate essays are only loosely tied to Crusoe's past history, and they lack any clear-cut organising principle. The chapters on solitude and on Providence are the most directly apposite to Crusoe as he appears in the first part. The 'Vision of the Angelick World' is notable for its treatment of apparitions and ghostly phenomena, which were to take a prominent place in Defoe's later writings. Crusoe's dream, at the time of his fever during his first summer on the island, is the most closely related episode in *RC1*, along with the passage on the 'Converse of the Spirits' (pp. 175–6) which follows his discovery of the remains of a cannibal feast. To sum up, there are plenty of explicit references to religion in the later parts, which square easily enough with the theological assumptions of *RC1*; but only the original story injects real conviction and dynamism into this theology.

By way of conclusion, it is worth recalling that in the Book of Common Prayer, as in the scriptures, the perils of the sea are often in evidence. The prayer-book contains a special form of service to be used at sea; there are particular prayers to be said during a storm and prior to a sea-battle; thanksgiving after a storm is expressed through collects and psalms, namely, Psalms 66 and 107. The latter includes a famous section concerning those who 'go down to the sea in ships' and 'do business in great waters' (verses 23–32); earlier sections of the psalm employ imagery of escape from solitude in the wilderness (verses 4–7), and of imprisonment and delivery (verses 10–16). Unlike Psalm 50, to which Defoe makes extended reference (*RC1*, pp. 94–7, 157), these poems of spiritual release are not quoted in the text; but the accents of a *Te Deum* 'after a dangerous tempest' (to quote the prayer-book again) underlie much of the island section. In the service for use at sea, there is provision for a situation of imminent danger; those on board are enjoined to make their confession, and it is laid down that 'every one ought *seriously* to *reflect* upon those particular sins of which his conscience shall accuse him' (my italics).[38]

NOTES

1 Quoted in *CH*, pp. 166–7.

2 Watt, p. 84. The argument that Defoe's secularised Puritanism produced 'the relative impotence of religion' in his novels (pp. 83–5) contains many provocative observations, but it also leaves many handles for rejoinder. For example, the statement that Crusoe must 'make his own way along a path no longer clearly illumined by God's particular providences' seems contradictory in view of Crusoe's own statements after his conversion. See for instance *RC1*, pp. 175–6, on the 'secret Intimations of Providence'. Similarly Crusoe speaks of 'a special Providence' that he was cast away on the side of the island (as he then supposed) where savages did not come (p. 164).

3 R. H. Tawney, *Religion and the Rise of Capitalism* (London, 1926; Harmondsworth, 1938), p. 212.

4 Starr, pp. 74–125. For another view of these matters, see Martin J. Greif, 'The conversion of Crusoe', *SEL*, Vol. VI (1966), pp. 551–74. Greif sees the book as 'the record of a notable spiritual pilgrimage across the sea of life, from a lawless course of living to true Christian repentance: a symbolic voyage from sin and folly to the gift of God's grace attained through sincere belief in Jesus Christ' (pp. 551–2). He sets out the 'Protestant scheme of salvation', stressing two primary motives to repentance – love of God and fear of His wrath. Like Hunter, Greif detects a number of 'Christian metaphors pervasively present in homiletic literature' (p. 555), mostly concerned with the sea and storms. He identifies caves as (typologically) the home of thieves and robbers (p. 567) and sheep as symbols of sanctification (p. 574). Less persuasive in detail than Starr or Hunter, Greif presents a sound overall case in harmony with theirs.

5 Hunter, *passim* (quotations from pp. 126, 189). For the conversion of Friday to Christianity, see pp. 184–6.

6   Starr, pp. 3–50; Hunter, pp. 76–92.

7   Starr, pp. 81–125; Hunter, pp. 88, 185.

8   ibid., pp 23–50.

9   ibid., pp. 51–75. The Presbyterian minister John Flavell (?1630–91) contributed both to the guide and the Providence traditions, as defined by Hunter; his *Seaman's Companion* is a good example of the guide aimed specifically at mariners.

10 *The Storm* (London, 1704), sig. A6r, p. 271.

11 Secord, pp. 78–85.

12 *Tour*, Vol. I, pp. 69–72.

13 *The Storm*, pp. 266–70.

14 See the comments of Louis A. Landa in the OEN edn (London, 1969), p. xxiii.

15 Hunter, pp. 105–24 (quotation from p. 123).

16 J. Paul Hunter, 'Friday as a convert', *RES*, Vol. XIV (1963), pp. 243–8.

17 *Daniel Defoe*, ed. J. T. Boulton (London, 1965), p. 166.

18 This and the following paragraphs draw on Sutherland, pp. 1–25; *Citizen*, pp. 1–43; and Shinagel, pp. 1–22. See also Lew Girdler, 'Defoe's education at Newington Green', *SP*, Vol. L (1953), pp. 573–91; and J. R. Moore, 'Defoe's religious sect', *RES*, Vol. XVII (1941), pp. 461–7.

19 *A True Collection of the Writings of the Author of the True Born English-man* (2nd edn, London, 1705), pp. 110–18.

20 *Citizen*, p. 19.

21 ibid., pp. 224–5; Hunter, pp. 47–9, 204–7.

22 Watt, pp. 67–8.

23 J. J. Richetti, *Defoe's Narratives* (Oxford, 1975), pp. 26–7.

24 Novak, *Economics*, pp. 32–48. Defoe was certainly deeply affected by the Bubble, as his later works show (it may even be a concealed metaphor in *A Journal of the Plague Year*); but to speak of the nation 'embarking' on the Bubble makes it a strangely purposeful brand of catastrophe.

25 Starr, pp. 74–81. For the Jonah emblem, see Hunter, p. 68; for a brief consideration of the 'original sin', ibid., pp. 128–33.

26 See ibid., pp. 133–43.

27 R. W. Ayers, '*Robinson Crusoe*: "allusive allegorick history" ', *PMLA*, Vol. LXXXII (1967), pp. 399–407.

28 Watt, p. 96. Watt's reading of Crusoe's experience as one of spiritual alienation, mirroring the isolated state of capitalist man, would ideally require the hero's misery and loneliness to be coterminous with his sojourn by himself on the island. But, as the narrator repeatedly makes clear, his sense of desolation belonged to his Godless rather than his unaccompanied condition.

29 Richetti, *Defoe's Narratives*, p. 26.

30 Hunter supplies no direct parallel between *Crusoe* and *The Pilgrim's Progress*, though their comparability lies at the heart of his case. Quite particular links can be discerned, e.g. the pilgrim's imperfect sight of the Celestial City through the shepherd's perspective glass as against Crusoe's vague sight of land to the west of his island (*RC1* p. 108). Both perhaps are variants of the typological Pisgah vision.

31 Gildon, p. x. Also cited in *CH*, p. 42.

32 Gildon, p. 47.

33 Thomas Wright, *The Life of Daniel Defoe* (London, 1894), pp. 23–30, 150–1, 234. A more recent attempt is by G. Parker, in *History*, Vol. X (1925), pp. 11–25, who argues that Defoe 'merely antedates every event

in his life 29 years'. Xury is Timothy Cruso; the cannibal feast, Sacheverell's impeachment.

34   Sutherland, p. 233; *Citizen*, p. 225; see also Hunter, pp. 120–1.
35   *Calendar of State Papers Domestic Series 1686/87* (London, 1964), p. 440; P. Rogers, 'Defoe in the Fleet prison', *RES*, Vol. XXH (1971), pp. 451–5.
36   Hunter, p. 201. For ambiguities surrounding 'deliverance', see E. Anthony James, *Daniel Defoe's Many Voices* (Amsterdam, 1972), pp. 182–7.
37   Gildon, pp. 42–3.
38   It is possible that there is a concealed allusion, not observed as far as I am aware, in the episode describing Crusoe's procedures to make contact with the captain of the mutinous ship. He makes a sudden and carefully staged entrance as a '*Spectre*-like Figure', having come 'as near [the three men] undiscovered as I could', and asks them '*What are ye Gentlemen?*' Not surprisingly the startled captain wonders if Crusoe is a real man or an angel; the hero replies, 'If God had sent an Angel to relieve you, he would have come better Cloath'd, and Arm'd after another manner than you see me in' (p. 254). Compare with this St Luke's account of the way in which Christ drew near two apostles on the road to Emmaus, with the questioning and talk of angels which ensues (Luke, 24: 13–31). I do not suggest that Crusoe is an exact 'typological' equivalent for Christ; but the saviour-like overtones of his mysterious appearance are unmistakable.

CHAPTER 4

Social and Philosophic Themes

THE MIDDLE STATION

The very first paragraph of the novel tells us that Robinson Crusoe was the son of an *émigré* businessman. Soon afterwards we learn that he was 'not bred to any Trade' but 'design'd . . . for the Law' (*RC1*, p. 3). There follows the famous passage in which Crusoe's father sets out the advantages of the 'middle State' in society or, more exactly, 'what might be called the upper Station of *Low Life*'. The tone is fervent in places, with 'true Felicity' attributed only to those 'placed in the Middle of the two Extremes'. Then comes one of the most characteristic things Defoe ever wrote, a warning against the 'Calamities' and 'Vicissitudes' endured by other strata of society – Defoe's prose is never more energetic than when he contemplates ruin or sudden reversals of fortune. The extreme ranks in the population face 'Distempers and Uneasinesses', whereas 'the middle Station of Life [is] calculated for all kind of vertues and all kinds of Enjoyment'. Crusoe's father wishes to point out the moral dignity of this condition, but it is principally the relief from anxiety which surfaces in his advice: 'this Way Men went silently and smoothly thro' the World, and comfortably out of it . . . in easy Circumstances sliding gently thro' the World'. Young Robinson, of course, will not listen; although 'sincerely affected' by what he hears, he remains 'obstinately deaf to all Proposals of settling to Business' and finally – with typically masked calculation – finds an opportunity to run away while visiting Hull for casual reasons (pp. 4–7).

The passage encapsulates many of the leading ideas in the book, and has naturally provoked a considerable body of commentary. It lies behind most accounts which treat the novel as an 'epic of the middle class', and dominates the view for those who wish to produce a socio-economic explanation of Crusoe's 'original sin' (see above, pp. 61–6). It is also the most convenient pretext for any attempt to locate *Crusoe* in the social and political ideology of the age. Not all readings pay careful attention to every detail of the passage: for example, few critics have noted that Crusoe's eldest brother, killed in the Spanish war, received the same advice and likewise ignored it. 'Young Desires' (p. 6) are clearly more extensive than the mere wish to break away from parents or the ambition to grow rich. Moreover, the characteristic note of the encounter is sometimes missed. Throughout, the idiom is one of desperate self-preservation rather than complacence; Crusoe's father constructs his admonitions around the idiom of bare survival in the face of threats of violent upheaval – 'not sold to the Life of Slavery for daily Bread, or harrast with perplex'd Circumstances, which rob the Soul of Peace, and the Body of Rest; not enrag'd with the Passion of Envy, or secret burning Lust of Ambition for great things' (p. 5). To put it another way, the language is closer to that of a revivalist preacher than to that of a careers adviser. Crusoe rejects more than bare prudence in disregarding this advice.

Despite such reservations, it must be admitted that the elder Crusoe reflects both Defoe's own attitudes, as visible elsewhere, and some of the dominant ideologies of the age. Perhaps the most sophisticated interpretation of Defoe as spokesman for a rising class comes in Isaac Kramnick's book on the 'politics of nostalgia' in early eighteenth-century England. According to Kramnick, 'Defoe's attitudes perfectly embodied all that Bolingbroke and his circle found distasteful in the age of Walpole' (for the relation to Scriblerian cultural values, see below, p. 105). He describes *A Journal of the Plague Year* as 'obvious political propaganda' for Walpole. Defoe is seen as the populariser of Locke's ideas on political authority; *Jure Divino* (1706) is used to show Defoe's sympathy with the Hobbesian psychology of self-love as fundamental in human relations. *Crusoe* itself is 'certainly an articulate and lyrical rendering of Locke's ideas. The isolated individual is depicted free of society, history and tradition.' Similarly, 'Hobbes's influence is also detected in Robinson Crusoe. After discovering the savages, Defoe's isolated individual is obsessed by fear of sudden destruction.' At the end Crusoe establishes civil society on his island, when 'the anarchy of the state of nature is ended'.

However, for Kramnick, this explicit use of Hobbes and Locke was not Defoe's major contribution 'to the new social order in Augustan England'. He contends that 'in no book is the spirit of this age better captured than in Defoe's *Essay on Projects*'. Defoe is 'the unabashed modern'; his possible links with the foundation of the Bank of England and with the establishment of the South Sea Company are stressed; he is said to embody 'the projecting spirit – the restless and optimistic desire to tinker with and change society and nature'.

Tradition, the inherited social order, and nature ceased to be sacred before the projector and tinkerer. His wholly progressive spirit gloried in inventions and newness, in solving traditional problems, in conquering new worlds. His practical and utilitarian spirit enshrined the useful, the handy, the profitable; his was the spirit of self-interest, avarice, and individualism. Projecting man, free of any functional duty to any organic social structure, stood alone, creating and shaping his own world and his own destiny. His was the spirit of Locke's man, of Robinson Crusoe, a necessary ingredient of the capitalist creed. How apt, then, that Defoe's *Essay on Projects* should have profoundly impressed . . . Benjamin Franklin.

Not surprisingly, this outlook is linked to Defoe's paeans upon the rising mercantile community, his approval of increased social mobility, his scorn for the presumptions of older gentry, his preoccupation with the theme of colonisation. 'Middle class readers in Augustan England could find their values and aspirations accurately rendered in Defoe's long string of successful novels where birth and ancestry mattered little.' Crusoe rejects his father's advice to stay in his place, and thus we see that 'Walpole's men and Defoe's heroes cheerfully cast off obsolete social encumbrances of class, place and station, when a world was to be won for the asking'. The message is that Crusoe *does* 'move up' – and this would not be lost on 'middle-class readers who shared Defoe's aspirations to gentility'. The novel thus reinforces the impression we gain from the non-fictional works of the 1720s, like the *Tour* and *The Complete English Tradesman*: Defoe endorses unhesitatingly the shift of power towards the business community, as a 'self-proclaimed apologist for the rising middle class'.[1]

This analysis seems to me to hold together only at the cost of some violence to the dialectic of *Robinson Crusoe*. Crusoe's fears are not just Hobbesian; they are existential as well as commonsensical. To speak of Crusoe's *cheerfully* casting off his allotted role in life is to miss an entire thread of guilt, self-examination and recrimination within the book. And to see Crusoe as enacting a pure success-story, happily overturning the values of his father's generation whilst Defoe applauds his effrontery, is to vulgarise the fictional meanings and to impair the whole moral texture. Crusoe does, it is true, prosper, and does achieve a strange kind of gentility even whilst on the island; but if he is a symbol of social mobility, then the book is far from avouching unalloyed confidence about the legitimacy of such expectations.

The theme of the search for social respectability is considered by Michael Shinagel in a useful book published in the same year as Kramnick's. Shinagel argues that Defoe's characters 'do not pursue wealth so much as they pursue gentility, which they know wealth can buy them'. He relates Crusoe's foreign origins to the Dutch background of Defoe's much-admired William III, and also to his own Flemish family roots. (Defoe himself, of course, had genteelised his own surname, without exactly anglicising it.) Shinagel makes the interesting point that 'Defoe underscores the basic difference between Crusoe *père* and *fils* in their approach to their callings by having young Crusoe set sail on his first voyage from Hull, the very town where his father had made his fortune by "merchandise" a generation before'. Like Kramnick, Shinagel sees Crusoe as occupying 'a new and challenging world', but he has a better sense of the mixed feelings about these things displayed in the novel. He realises, too, that *The Complete English Tradesman* was 'not only a practical manual on how to succeed in business but also a conduct book designed to dignify the profession and to polish the men who practise it'.

Two small riders might be added. First, it is possible that York and Hull are symbolic locations, shadowing forth a major aspect of the generation gap. The father has retired to York, seen in Defoe's *Tour* as notable for 'Antiquity', where Hull (now left to his son) has 'more Business done there than in any Town of its Bigness in Europe' – these are the opening phrases in the index entries, drawing on descriptions within the text. In York the city is 'laid open', spacious and leisured; in Hull the town is 'exceeding close built' and 'extraordinary populous, even to an inconvenience'. Secondly, *Crusoe* itself is a variant of the conduct-book. It deals with ambition and the rewards of ambition; but also with concepts such as filial obedience, the conversion of heathens, the uses of solitude.[2]

Later sections in this chapter will attempt some assessment of Defoe's moral philosophy; at this stage I wish only to stress that the over-whelming majority of 'middle-class' guides at this period were designed to show the reader how to fulfil his role decently, now how to escape it. Many critics want to define Crusoe as the representative bourgeois, whilst his story is clearly that of an adventurer *rejecting* the bourgeois comforts held out to him by his father. The orthodox middle-class pieties belong to the elder, not the younger, Crusoe. Though repeatedly convinced by adversity that his father was right, Crusoe never properly manages to become an active convert. His thrift is imposed by circumstances; his capital accumulates without his active surveillance (indeed, the Portuguese captain acts as a kind of portfolio manager for him); and he returns to his wayward and ecccentric pattern of living after the death of his wife. Marriage, for him, is just a short experiment in curbing natural instinct.

Finally, it should be recalled that projectors were, in contemporary estimation, dangerous and disruptive people. In Defoe's formative years they were represented by men like Thomas Neale (d.1699), an associate of Dalby Thomas in promoting wild schemes as well as the lottery that gave Defoe an official post; by Nicholas Barbon (d.1698), speculative builder and monetary theorist; and by Charles Povey (?1652–1743), writer and floater of insurance schemes. A group less in tune with the homekeeping Protestant Ethic can scarcely be imagined. It was men of this stamp who were blamed for the South Sea Bubble – not only by the Tory satirists – and even Defoe added his fulminations against the villainy of stock-jobbers, that is, projectors in the financial world.[3] To say with Kramnick that Defoe embodied 'the projecting spirit' is to identify him with Crusoe's restless temperament, the very thing that makes him hugely untypical of middle-class morals and habits.

ECONOMIC IDEAS

Ian Watt has remarked that the myth of Robinson Crusoe 'as it has taken shape in our minds is surely not primarily about religious or psychological alienation, nor even about solitude as such. Crusoe lives in the imagination mainly as a triumph of human achievement and enterprise, and as a favourite example of the elementary processes of political economy.'[4] Leaving aside the question as to whether this falsifies the novel in its deepest imaginative implications, we must agree that the popular image of Crusoe is of a highly secular creature. Few things are more celebrated about him than his excellent book-keeping. His fondness for quoting precise monetary figures leads him both to itemise the 'Thirty-six Pounds value in Money' he takes from the wreck (*RC1*, p. 57) and to specify the exact state of his accounts when he gets to Lisbon after rescue (pp. 282–5). He gives receipts promptly, and uses the double-entry system of accounts to draw up a balance-sheet of moral credit and debit on his island (p. 66). But does this concern with financial accuracy mean that he is centrally or even importantly an economic case-study?

In distinction to Watt and others who have found the use of Crusoe as economic man to be a plausible reading, Diana Spearman has concluded that this is wildly unlikely.

> It cannot possibly be true on the conscious level. No one in his senses would choose the story of a man cast alone on an uninhabited island to illustrate a theory which only applies to the exchange of goods and services. The essence of economic individualism is the view that a better result will be attained by leaving economic decisions to individuals than by any kind of centralized plan or governmental intervention. It is not at all easy to be sure what Defoe thought about this.

Defoe, according to Mrs Spearman, had 'no original general theory' about economic policy. She thinks that *Crusoe* serves only to illustrate 'the nature of some economic behaviour, for example saving, which would, in their simpler forms, be much the same for a solitary individual as for an individual in society'. Mrs Spearman departs from other commentators in believing that the interest in economic affairs apparent in the *Essay on Projects* or *The Complete English Tradesman* finds little by way of direct expression in the novels. 'Only one book, *Robinson Crusoe*, is about a merchant or trader. His commercial activities are, however, in the first part only a means of getting him on to the island. While in the second, which is concerned with his activities as a merchant, the inspiration has clearly failed.' And again:

> Robinson Crusoe is indeed a merchant, and in the latter part of the book his trading activities seem to be regarded as praiseworthy, but anyone who seeks to find in the book a reflection of the prevailing ideas about trading activities is faced with a difficulty at the beginning. If there were nothing left but *Robinson Crusoe* as a source for the contemporary view one would suppose that public opinion regarded trade, at least trade carried on in ships, as somehow wicked or unlawful.

Mrs Spearman decides that Defoe, writing for 'honest Dick and Moll', and blissfully unaware that he would be read 'by Pope and Swift, by Coleridge and Karl Marx', was just trying to get Crusoe on to the island and did not consider the nature of the 'original sin' too closely. She concludes that the novel is 'neither an allegory of capitalism nor of Defoe's own life. Fundamentally, it is a story of man against nature.'[5]

The fullest examination of the problem has been conducted by Maximillian E. Novak. His analysis of 'The Economic Meaning of *Robinson Crusoe*' puts special weight on the quality of fable in the book. Novak believes that Defoe was a conservative economic thinker, prizing the older mercantilist views above the growing movement towards *laissez-faire* and individualism. He sees *Crusoe* as in part a fictional rendering of ideas expressed in *A General History of Trade* (1713). The hero is 'driven to invention both by necessity and by a desire for conveniences'.

> Through diligence, ingenuity, and invention he duplicates all the branches of the arts of agriculture and manufacturing. By parsimony and by refusing to consume his products he is able to increase his wealth. Crusoe's aim in all this activity is to re-create upon the microcosm of his island the standard of existence of Western civilization in his day – to duplicate in the existence of one man all the useful products required by the human race for comfort and convenience.

Novak goes on to consider the conditions which would allow this plan to be realised. He shows how Locke's account of the division of labour, in the *Two Treatises on Government* (1960), is filled out in Crusoe's operations as a bread-maker and the like. He argues that the island episode may have been based partly on the attempt to establish a commonwealth in Bermuda; apart from the older sources, Defoe could have got ideas here from a book like John Oldmixon's *British Empire in America* (1708). A further revealing observation is this: 'When Crusoe decides to settle the colony along permanent lines, he does not give the land away to the colonists, but following closely Defoe's plan for a colony of Palatine immigrants in the forested areas of England, he rents his property with long leases and deferred payment' (see above, p. 22).

The final statement is in accord with Novak's account of the 'original sin':

> Crusoe does not fulfill his promise as a colonizer. Like Raleigh with his Virginia plantation, he leaves his colony and allows it to languish. The cause lies once more in Crusoe's urge to travel and his unwillingness to labour in his calling. . . . He is a shrewd merchant, a skilled craftsman, and a tough-minded colonizer, but as a 'True Born Englishman' in the age of voyaging and exploration, Crusoe prefers to wander.

Novak contends elsewhere in his book that 'there is no reason to assume that he gains materially by his wandering. There is . . . no question that he loses money by his stay on his island.' Had he remained in Brazil, he would have amassed a much more considerable fortune, perhaps 'an hundred thousand *Moydors*' (*RC1*, p. 195) – Novak estimates this value as £137,500 at current values. He adds that it is 'futile to speculate on Crusoe's possible success as a lawyer or tradesman in England', but it can be safely asserted that few such men reached so vast a fortune.[6] Even if they got to the top and became 'the rich, who live very plentifully' (to adopt the classification Defoe uses in a famous *Review* paper),[7] then we are still talking in terms of an income of around £2,000 a year. Perhaps one or two crooked attorneys like Peter Walter attained the huge sums Crusoe envisaged, but only a handful of merchant princes could hope to do as well.[8] The clear implication of the narrative is that, if Crusoe had stuck to his last in Brazil, he would have become a very rich man indeed.

Crusoe's successive 'mechanick operations' also figure in a valuable study by William H. Halewood, tracing 'contradictory impulses' within Crusoe. This sees the hero as 'divided between earth and heaven, between accumulation and renunciation, action and contemplation'. He is thus 'not merely the symbol of *homo economicus* . . . but of *homo* in general'. Halewood thinks that Crusoe himself recognises the discontinuities 'between his religious attitudes and his practical behaviour', and that the book dramatises this clash in a whole series of rises and falls (see below, p. 81).[9] Halewood devotes a certain amount of space to the 'money' episode, to which I shall turn shortly.

Most recently the economic historian Peter Earle has allotted two chapters of his book on Defoe respectively to financial and social matters. He reaches an opposite conclusion to Mrs Spearman's in detecting a more or less coherent (though in some ways unoriginal) body of economic theory. Earle stresses the novelty of Defoe's ideas in some areas, thus departing from Novak's broadly traditional thinker. He does not apply this analysis to *Crusoe* directly, except in so far as he considers the 'middle sort of people' as members of a new reading public: 'Now they could sit back in comfort and take a vicarious delight in the adventurous life of a man like Robinson Crusoe who had been so foolish as to give up the advantages of the middle station. As they slid gently through their world they could only marvel at the desperate straits of those so unfortunate as not to belong to it.'[10] I think we may legitimately doubt whether *Crusoe* would serve as a cautionary tale if it is an *economic* fable, except for fairly prosperous members of the trading classes; not everyone could aspire to the Brazilian riches Crusoe cast aside, and most would have been happy enough to come away with the capital and income Crusoe inherits on his return. The homekeeping reader would be glad to avoid Crusoe's perilous adventures, and his spiritual anxieties; his worldly success is another matter.

I mentioned just now the famous moment when Crusoe finds the money, hidden in a locker drawer, on his twelfth sortie to the ship. The passage which follows, with Crusoe thinking aloud, is – along with that of the footprint – the most celebrated in all Defoe's millions of words (*RC1*, p. 57). It was Coleridge who first drew particular attention to it, with his comment, 'Worthy of Shakespeare; and yet the simple semi-colon after it ['I took it away'], the instant passing on without the least pause of reflex consciousness is more exquisite and masterlike than the touch itself'.[11] More sceptical is Ian Watt, who wonders whether the apparent irony regarding Crusoe's 'second thoughts' may not be accidental. He suggests it is 'merely the result of the extreme insouciance with which Defoe the publicist jerks himself back to his role as novelist, and hastens to tell us what he knows Crusoe, and indeed anyone else, would actually do in the circumstances'. Watt also rightly warns us to remember: (1) that the original edition had a comma, not a semi-colon; and (2) that there are 'lots of others' as the sentence rambles on – actually fifteen more commas plus two other stops, by my calculation. 'This seems to be hiding the effect a little too much,' Watt drily observes. Elsewhere he defined the implication of the passage as 'the irrationality of the goals which shape the character of economic man and which affect his actions more powerfully than his own understanding of his real needs'.[12] If the myth embodies a 'metaphor of human solitude', then Crusoe's money presumably stands for the cash nexus, false and delusive modes of human interconnection.

Maximillian Novak takes a different position. He thinks that the speech is more in character than Ian Watt would allow: 'If the romantic in Crusoe can condemn the money, the prudent streak in his nature cannot resist the temptation to take it away. There can be no question that Defoe was being ironic about his hero's pretensions, although Defoe probably shared Crusoe's wavering feelings toward the gold.' Not all readers share Novak's confidence in attributing ironic intent to Defoe, and this passage remains an interpretative crux. Nevertheless, Novak performed a valuable service in aligning Crusoe's reflections on the uselessness of gold on his island (e.g. *RC1*, p. 129) with his expressed views on the theory of value.[13] Subsequently, William H. Halewood has analysed the passage to show 'the comic grandiloquence of the apostrophe and its low-spoken conclusion'. He describes the language as exhibiting an 'over-inflation' which prepares us for the second thoughts. Moreover, Halewood argues, Crusoe's care later on to look after his money well indicates that his revulsion was conventional and insincere. The passage thus 'concentrates in a little space the central irony of the book', that is, the confused state of the hero, torn between religious and secular urges.[14]

In my opinion the presence of conscious irony cannot certainly be determined. On the other hand, there is a splendid little reversal in the construction of the scene; a miniaturised peripeteia, if the term is not itself a form of inflation. Crusoe has been making repeated voyages, as he calls them, to the ship. It is lucky that he survived the wreck at all; even luckier that the ship should have been driven to its convenient resting-place within a mile of the shore. The expeditions have proved successful, only one ending in the loss of his cargo when his raft overturns. Crusoe had some time ago decided that he had 'nothing more to expect from the Ship' and yet he persists. Returning to the cabin, which he thought he had adequately searched, he finds on the twelfth trip an unopened locker. There is a characteristic Defovian order to what follows:

> Tho' I thought I had rumag'd the Cabbin so effectually, as that nothing more could be found, yet I discover'd a Locker with Drawers in it, in one of which I found two or three Razors, and one Pair of large Sizzers, with some ten or a Dozen of good Knives and Forks; in another I found about Thirty-six Pounds value in Money, some *European* Coin, some *Brasil*, some Pieces of Eight, some Gold, some Silver. (p. 57)

The itemising technique renders a particular way of apprehending reality. There are three 'approximating' terms (see below, p. 122); Crusoe tells us first the value, then the component coins with their denominations, as though he had a pocket calculator to count as quickly as he can see the objects. There is a kind of patient scrupulosity in telling us of the

contents of the first drawer before springing the more spectacular find
on us. The language enacts the process of rummaging about in one place
then another: it refuses to concentrate on the *finds* but reduplicates the
search.

Overnight the ship breaks up, and afterwards only odd fragments are
driven ashore, 'of small use' to Crusoe. He congratulates himself on
having lost no time 'nor abated no Dilligence' in salvaging the wreck.
It is made transparently clear that he only got the money because he
persisted and did not allow his settling-in to deflect him from the task
in hand. He did not waste time attempting to make another raft, which
might again have been overturned. Prudence and discipline have
triumphed, as they will generally (but not always) on the island.
The money is a kind of reward. Seen in this light, the momentary
lapse into rhapsodic denunciation becomes a resistance to providential
aid. To leave the gold as 'a Creature whose Life is not worth
saving' is to invoke a hint of gratuitous cruelty; at the moment of
abandoning his 'drug' Crusoe is acknowledging its vitality. When he
compares it with the knives, there is a paradox in that even Crusoe is
unlikely to wear out implements fast enough to require a dozen knives
and forks for many years to come (at this stage, the effective time-scale
is captivity of weeks or months, for nothing like twenty-eight years is
envisaged). But the money has a fiduciary rather than a practical value:
if Crusoe is ever going to be rescued, its utility will be unimpaired by
the wait. As soon as he utters the apostrophe, Crusoe realises that he
cannot be sure what is 'not worth saving'. Taking the money is his way
of accepting his fate: it acknowledges the dimension beyond immediate
necessity (hatchets and crowbars), the fact that civilisation is going on
although Crusoe is condemned to a bare island where gold is a superfluous commodity.

SELF-PRESERVATION AND SELF-HELP

In his poem *Jure Divino* (1706) Defoe had set out a Hobbesian theory
of self-interest as the basic psychological drive underlying men's relations
with one another. Government is at bottom a device for protecting people
against violent and lawless anarchy, for 'Power United, Power Expos'd
Protects'. And God works through the laws of nature:

> *Self-Preservation* is the only Law,
> That does *Involuntary Duty* Draw;
> It serves for Reason and Authority,
> And they'll defend themselves, *that know not why.*[15]

At a political level, this fundamental urge justifies non-resistance, as in
the constitutional crisis of 1688. In personal terms it validates the quest

for an inviolate private existence – we should say 'identity' – which dominates the life of Moll, Colonel Jack, Roxana and even Crusoe. Where the others are threatened by gaol, bankruptcy or seduction (the downward pressure exerted in organised society), Robinson Crusoe struggles against solitude, fear and his own despair.

Defoe's attitude towards the moral problems of self and society has been most fully explored by Novak in his book *Defoe and the Nature of Man*. The entire study casts light on *Crusoe*, but one chapter has special relevance. Taking up Crusoe's reference to his having been 'reduced to a meer State of Nature' (*RC1*, p. 118), Novak considers the implication of this phrase in the context of eighteenth-century ethics. He shows that Crusoe's isolation 'identifies him with the state of nature which precedes society, a condition in which man could not live alone not because he was godlike, but because he was bestial'. (Similarly Crusoe was at first 'meerly thoughtless of a God, or a Providence; [and] acted like a meer Brute from the Principles of Nature', p. 88.) Novak emphasises, too, that Crusoe never develops any Rousseauesque desire to return to the state of nature: 'Crusoe's real life was to be lived in the world, following his calling.' But, lacking security on his island, he is forced to spend much of his time protecting himself against real or imagined enemies.

Having conquered the worst of his original fears, he is thrust back by his discovery of the footprint into the perpetual anxiety which is the condition of isolated natural man. Later on he has cannibals and pirates to deal with; the desert island is no paradise but a place of edgy and unrelenting vigilance. At least, with the coming of Friday, there is for Crusoe 'the comparative security of the social state of nature'. The unconverted savage, though sometimes capable of a pristine moral innocence, is bereft of all the advantages of civilisation; for Defoe the natural man was not so much prelapsarian as brutal and incomplete until he had been tamed by religion and reason. (His reading would have included the Puritan accounts of American Indians, which portray the savage as treacherous and inconstant.) Towards the end of *RC1*, and on his return to the island in *RC2*, Crusoe struggles to rescue his self-created dominion from an anarchic state of nature. True social intercourse demands the restraints imposed by reason and authority; the articles of agreement to which Crusoe is so addicted represent a voluntary contract by which men submit to law and abandon destructive 'nature'. Potentially flawed by their original sin, men can only live harmoniously by abnegation of their aggressive desires.[16]

But self-defence and self-help were not numbered among the destructive impulses. As Crusoe's struggle to make himself a secure dwelling indicates, the individual's first task is to cling on to existence. His solitude dramatises the need to look after one's own fate: before this is an allegory of Puritan spirituality (if it *is* that), it is a statement of practical ethics. And beyond bare survival the individual should use the resources of civilisation to improve his own lot, since it will be of no benefit to society – according to this way of thinking – if he skulks around in primitive conditions. Of course, Crusoe has relatively few implements with which to shape his environment; but those he has he uses, and wherever possible he improvises an alternative technology, as with his bread-making techniques. Crusoe is far from an unqualified success as an inventor and craftsman. His most famous lapse concerns boat-building: in his fourth year he devotes almost six months to making a piragua from a cedar-tree, only to find he cannot get the vessel to the nearest water. But there are many minor setbacks apart from this: Crusoe produces only crude workmanship as a potter and as a tailor. However, he manages to get by even in these activities, and is able to reflect on his good fortune in rescuing tools from the wreck – for without them 'I should have liv'd, if I had not perish'd, like a meer Savage' (p. 130). Again and again the emphasis is put on the power of man to harness his environment granted the right implements. This is not a fashionable message in our anti-technological age; but Defoe was no friend of the earth. He believed that man was the dominant species, and the only one who had been granted revelation of God's purposes; it was man's prerogative to bend nature to his will.

Crusoe's considerable energy has led commentators to examine the implicit attitude to industry. For Ian Watt, Rousseau was right to see the book as 'an object lesson in the educational virtues of manual labour'. The novel's power as a myth is connected with the 'character-forming satisfactions' of Crusoe's unintellectual activity. Watt goes so far as to speculate on the influence this myth might have had on the development of the arts and crafts movement. In various ways the quest for 'dignity of labour' in Marx, William Morris, Samuel Smiles and Carlyle is part of the legacy of the myth. The dogma of the uplifting effect of work 'finds its supreme narrative realization on Crusoe's island'. We observe that the arrival of Friday is 'a signal, not for increased leisure, but for expanded production'. Although Defoe knew very well the harshness of everyday labour for most men and women of his age, his book manages to conceal this fact in its potent evocation of 'Crusoe's lonely and triumphant struggle'.[17]

For Novak, labour serves as a way of hanging on to selfhood. 'Crusoe's tools not only make it possible to create a new life, but they also provide an escape from lassitude or madness.' Further, Defoe 'seems to have believed that most men had a drive to work, or an "instinct of workmanship" accompanied by a hatred of idleness'. Elsewhere Defoe wrote that the only means of living comfortably was through diligence, 'for a Life of Sloth and Idleness is not Happiness or Comfort; Employment is

Life, Sloth and Indolence is Death'. What marks off Crusoe, in Novak's judgement, is 'his willingness to labor and his joy in invention. Refusing to succumb to despair, Crusoe utilizes his "instinct of workmanship" to re-create on his island the economic level of existence which he had known in England and Brazil.' Reversing the tide of history, Crusoe showed the life of the Jack-of-all-trades as a successful challenge to the division of labour.[18]

One thing should be added to these accounts. Crusoe's concern for his own 'preservation' (for example, 'I took all the Measures humane Prudence could suggest for my own Preservation', p. 162) is counter-pointed against God's care for the preservation of his soul. 'Human prudence', self-help, labour are all essential for survival; but after his conversion Crusoe is equally insistent that 'the merciful Dispositions of Heaven' provide 'secret Hints' which enable man to fulfil his destiny (p. 175). The ethic of work is powerfully present in *Crusoe*, but so is the insistence that in all the operations of life we are in the hands of God. For some critics this level of meaning remains on the level of intention rather than achievement; but if we miss the intention we shall falsify the nature of that struggle for survival. The hazards of Crusoe's solitary life are perhaps submerged metaphors for the calamities of mercantile life, but they are also images of the snares of the soul – into which, unprotected by God, every sinful man will inevitably fall. The vigilance of Crusoe the self-preserver is an emblem of that spiritual awareness which guards man from eternal damnation.

SOLITUDE AND RETIREMENT

'I have often looked back', writes Crusoe at the start of *RC3*, 'upon the notions of a long tedious life of solitude, which I have represented to the world, and of which you must have formed some ideas, from the life of a man in an island' (p. 3). His 'serious reflections' begin with a meditation on solitude, which reaches the conclusion that 'the business is to get a retired soul, a frame of mind truly elevated above the world, and then we may be alone whenever we please, in the greatest apparent hurry of business or company' (p. 9). Again, 'that man can never want conversation who is company for himself' (p. 5). The truth is, in Crusoe's formu-lation, 'that all those religious hermit-like solitudes, which men value themselves so much upon, are but an acknowledgment of the defect or imperfection of our resolutions, our incapacity to bind ourselves to needful restraints, or rigorously to observe the limitations we have vowed ourselves to observe' (p. 8). And by way of summary:

> Solitude, therefore, as I understand by it, a retreat from human society, on a religious or philosophical account, is a mere cheat. . . .

Let the man that would reap the advantage of solitude, and that understands the meaning of the word, learn to retire into himself. (pp. 12–13)

The reflection concludes with a reiteration of its theme, that complete solitude can be found in the midst of society, just as well as 'in the deserts of Arabia and Lybia, or in the desolate life of an uninhabited island' (p. 18).

Yet it is this desolate life which has excited the imagination of generations of readers. We think of *Crusoe* as a study in isolation. Throughout all his adventures Crusoe is what we now describe as a loner – from the moment of his break with his father (and characteristic effort to get his mother's quiet complicity) to the Asian travels of *RC2*. His marriage is brief, his business partnerships generally short-lived (associates may be loyal to him in his absence, but there is no real co-operative activity portrayed in the text). Having found himself the sole survivor of a wreck in *RC1*, Crusoe is forced in the second part to abandon ship at an unspecified port in Bengal. The echoes of his earlier experience are unmistakable: he fears that his mutinous crew will run away with the ship, 'and then I had been stripped naked, in a remote country, and nothing to help myself; in short, I had been in a worse case than when I was all alone in the island' (p. 211). He is duly put down on shore, and reflects, 'I was now alone in the remotest part of the world, as I think I may call it, for I was near three thousand leagues, by sea, further off from England than I was at my island' (p. 212). Again, Crusoe is fortunately provided with a useful stock, this time of trading capital. He accedes to a suggestion from his fellow-lodger, an English merchant, that they should make a commercial voyage to China. Crusoe explains his willingness in his habitual terms: 'I might, perhaps, say with some truth, that if trade was not my element, rambling was; and no proposal for seeing any part of the world which I had not seen before, could possibly come amiss to me' (p. 214). He once more moves from solitude and remoteness to achievement, gain and mastery of others.

The crucial period of isolation is obviously the twenty-eight years on the island or, more strictly, the twenty-four years that precede Friday's arrival. It is this lone struggle which represents for most of the older critics, along with some of the modern commentators, the heart of *Robinson Crusoe*. To take a single example, James Sutherland (who views Crusoe as 'a self-made man . . . the sober industrious Englishman, hardened by difficulties but not overwhelmed by them') believes that 'in his story of a shipwrecked mariner Defoe had succeeded in touching some of the most powerful chords in the human heart'. In particular, 'It is his isolation which gives him his hold upon the imagination . . . he is the ordinary decent man triumphing over circumstances, and making such a remarkable job of it that we are sorry in the end that he has to be rescued and sent back to a world of ease and plenty'. Sutherland concludes:

> To read *Robinson Crusoe* is to be compelled to face up to all sorts of physical problems that civilized man has long since forgotten. It is in some sense to retrace the history of the human race; it is certainly to look again with the unspoilt eyes of childhood on many things that one had long since ceased to notice at all.[19]

Similarly John Robert Moore says that

> it is in the island episode, in which Crusoe comes face to face with the problems of mankind, that we have the supreme achievement. . . . Nowhere in all literature before Defoe could one anticipate the cry of the Ancient Mariner,

> > Alone, alone, all, all alone,
> > Alone on a wide, wide, sea!

The bare fact of survival in solitude constitutes the power of the myth. We admire Crusoe for what he achieves *in spite of* loneliness.[20]

But, like everything else in the book, isolation can be allotted any number of symbolic functions. If we accept the idea of an autobiographic allegory then Defoe's own exposed position, as a dissenter employed by the Anglican establishment, can be read into the island experience – or, indeed, his friendless condition after the death or eclipse of his patrons. Sentimental Victorian readers could easily identify Crusoe in his cast-away state with Defoe *in tenebris* at the end of his life, hiding from a creditor and cut off from his family:

> It is not possible for me to come to Enfield, unless you could find a retired Lodging for me, where I might not be known, and might have the Comfort of seeing you both [his daughter and son-in-law] now and then; Upon such a circumstance, I could gladly give the days to Solitude, to have the Comfort of half an Hour now and then, with you both, for two or three Weeks. But just to come and look at you, and retire immediately, 'tis a Burden too heavy. The Parting will be a Price beyond the Enjoyment.[21]

On the other hand, those who see the book as an embodiment of secularised Puritanism or the capitalist ethic can easily regard the isolation as dramatising Crusoe's 'radical egocentricity'. For Ian Watt, solitude is the 'universal image of individualist experience'. Crusoe's 'exceptional prowess' (*pace* Coleridge) lies in his capacity to 'manage quite on his own'. Watt believes that the 'realities of absolute solitude', as found in true-life castaway-stories, were far less comforting: prolonged lack of human society induced psychological tensions not apparent in Crusoe. In fact 'Defoe departs from psychological probability in order to redeem his picture of man's inexorable solitariness'.[22] Watt's estimate of psychological needs is not one everybody will share, but his eloquent and provocative discussion contains the most searching analysis we have of the issue.

A related concept is that of retirement. Eighteenth-century writers inherited from classical, mediaeval and Renaissance sources a strong pre-occupation with the clash of active and contemplative ways of life. In the age of Defoe this was most powerfully expressed in pleas for a Horatian retreat away from the corruption of cities and courts, though it turns up in other forms. An excellent study by Maren-Sofie Røstvig, *The Happy Man*, shows some of the Augustan uses to which this traditional motif was put: in poets like James Thomson the petition for an absolute retreat comes to be associated with the artist's need to withdraw from society.[23] On an earlier occasion I have argued that Crusoe has important resemblances to 'The Happy Gardener' and other exemplars of the retirement theme. Over the course of his first decade or so on the island, Crusoe becomes a landscape gardener and estate manager. His 'country seat' on the west side of the island figures itself in his imagination as a kind of weekend cottage, where he can escape from the 'cares' of his domestic employments. It is a 'Bower' (p. 108), and the scenery round about resembles 'a planted Garden' (p. 99). His original dwelling is a place of fortification, where arts and crafts are practised, goods are kept in store, and day-to-day living goes on its busy way. His second home is situated in a fruitful valley, with a pleasant situation and secure from bad weather. This 'delicious Vale' (*RC1*, p. 100) is reserved for relaxation and enjoyment; it stands, on this reading, for the contemplative rather than the active hero.[24]

It is worth adding here that other critics have detected a different pattern of symbol. E. B. Benjamin regards the geography of the island in another set of moral terms. The far side of the island (where the bower is located) is interpreted as 'like Egypt to the Israelites on the march to Canaan, a temptation to be resisted'. The extensive flora and fauna on the other part of the island symbolise an illusory and slothful world – one might almost say (though Benjamin resists it) a bower of bliss.[25] I find this unconvincing to the extent that Crusoe's moments of lethargy and despair take place at his original home. He refuses to shift his dwelling not because of the *accidia* which may descend upon him in the golden valley, but because he will not be able to sight any ship that may pass close to the island (p. 101). J. J. Richetti sees Crusoe's trips across the island as part of an effort to 'leave his paranoid seclusion and to convert his island from a prison into a garden'. He finds 'an equivocal paradise' where he must himself refine nature into that which will sustain his own existence.[26] Michael Shinagel discusses the same language of proprietorial estates as I consider in my article, but he sees this as a betraying lapse where I argue that the idiom suits Crusoe's role as (so far as possible) Horatian country gentleman.[27] Where other commentators have emphasised Crusoe's pretensions to lordly possession, my essay draws attention to his *domestic* occupations and his longing for a modest place of his own – the primal urge in the literature of retirement.

A final topic which might be ranged under the heading of this section is sex – or, rather, the absence of it. The aspect of Crusoe's isolation which has most concerned some readers is his womanless condition. And, indeed, there is no denying Ian Watt's ultimate conclusion:

> Crusoe's attitude to women is also marked by an extreme inhibition of what we now consider to be normal human feelings. There are, of course, none on the island, and their absence is not deplored. When Crusoe does notice the lack of 'society', he prays for company, but it is for that of a male slave. With Friday, he is fully satisfied by an idyll without benefit of woman. It is an interesting break from the traditional expectations aroused by desert islands, from the *Odyssey* to the *New Yorker*.[28]

We can hardly deflect this point by asserting that Crusoe eventually does get married, since the relationship lasts only a few years (six at most) and four pages. There are three children, but we do not know their ultimate fate. And, for all the anxious arrangements surrounding the sex life of his new colonists in *RC2*, Crusoe remains sternly aloof from all the pairing-off. The sequel declines to imitate· the second part of *The Pilgrim's Progress* and give us the female path to salvation. Somehow the childless Augustans left women out of their fantasies as they did (officially, anyway) keep them apart from their lives. It is a bachelor culture, built around male clubs and coffee-house chumminess. Its representative men, like the Spectator and Gulliver, are in flight from domesticity. There is a huge irony here. Defoe was to pioneer a form in which women's feelings were to be given fuller expression than in any other literary genre, and in which women writers were to take a pre-dominant role. But his greatest single work, *RC1*, ignores sexual as it does social relations – the stuff of later fiction.

The most illuminating discussion of the issues raised here – loneliness, retreat, secretion – is to be found in a valuable and original article by Homer O. Brown. He points out that the central episode is 'based on the etymological metaphor "islanded" – isolated'. Starting from Defoe's fondness for false names, or no names at all (see above, p. 5), Brown goes on to explore *Crusoe* as 'a kind of myth to explain the fear of exposure'. Like other critics, he finds the hero's worry lest he be devoured by wild beasts full of psychological charge; it is, he thinks, another way of rendering Crusoe's fear that he will be exposed or forced to reveal himself. At the heart of the novel lies a desire to conceal the self, to erase traces of one's being. Brown brilliantly shows how Defoe's novels enact this process of deflecting or averting selfhood. Through Crusoe, he argues, Defoe was himself impersonating a kind of unseen Providence; like his hero in the fortress, he could live in the open yet 'unseen and unmolested'. It is impossible to read Brown's essay without a richer sense of the novel's workings, even though he perhaps merges Crusoe's strategies for survival too easily with Defoe's literary proclivities. This is a particularly imaginative study, which detects in the intense privacy of Crusoe's existence a statement of its author's own need for subterfuge, withdrawal and what might be called psychological distance from his art.[29]

Still, a less particularised conclusion is possible. According to Hunter, 'Crusoe's isolation epitomises the Puritan version of the plight of man. Fallen man is alienated from God. . . . He is lonely and isolated in a world for which he was not in the first place intended, but into which he is cast as a result of sin.'[30] But the metaphor has an intense worldly vehicle to accompany the spiritual tenor: Crusoe finds himself during his isolation, and solitude breeds initiative and invention along with grace.

NOTES

1   I. Kramnick, *Bolingbroke and His Circle* (Cambridge, Mass., 1968), pp. 188–200. In his next section, pp. 201–4, Kramnick considers Mandeville as another representative of Walpole's England in the world of literature.

2   Shinagel, pp. 122–41, 211: *Tour*, Vol. II, pp. 635, 651–3, 849, 858.

3   Relevant here is Howard Erskine-Hill's excellent chapter on Sir John Blunt in *The Social Milieu of Alexander Pope* (New Haven, Conn., 1975), pp. 166–203. It is foolish to suppose that Defoe was as favourably disposed towards the projector in 1719 as he had been in 1697: quite apart from his own disasters, and the eclipse of the Darien scheme launched by his friend William Paterson, the auguries were already visible. In *The Anatomy of Exchange-Alley*, published only five weeks after the appearance of *RC1*, Defoe complained of the arts used by stock-jobbers 'to draw Innocent Families into their Snares' (cf. *Checklist*, 414).

4   Ian Watt, 'Robinson Crusoe as a myth', *EIC*, Vol. I (1951), pp. 95–119; reprinted in *Eighteenth Century English Literature: Modern Essays in Criticism*, ed. J. L. Clifford (New York, 1959), pp. 158–79 (quotation from p. 159). It is fair to state that many of Watt's best-known observations regarding *Crusoe* apply to the myth rather than to the novel as such – a fact his critics often forget.

5   Diana Spearman, *The Novel and Society* (London, 1966), pp. 154–72.
6   Novak, *Economics*, pp. 49–62, 163n.
7   *Review*, Vol. VI, p. 142.
8   Erskine-Hill, *Social Milieu*, p. 130.
9   W. H. Halewood, 'Religion and invention in *Robinson Crusoe*', *EIC*, Vol. XIV (1964), pp. 339–51 (reprinted in Ellis, pp. 79–89).
10 Earle, pp. 107–201 (quotation from p. 166).
11 Quoted in *CH*, p. 82.
12 Watt, pp. 124–5; '*Robinson Crusoe* as a myth', p. 174.
13 Novak, *Economics*, pp. 58–62 (quotation from p. 60).
14 Cited in Ellis, pp. 88–9.
15 *Jure Divino. A Satyr* (London, 1706) [II], p. 4 [III], p. 10.
16 Novak, *Nature*, pp. 22–64. See also pp. 144–5 for a good discussion of Crusoe's passive courage.
17 Watt, '*Robinson Crusoe* as a myth', pp. 163–7. Watt makes the excellent point that classical myths typically 'are inspired by the prospect of never having to work again' (p. 165).
18 Novak, *Economics*, pp. 52–5; *A Plan of the English Commerce* (Oxford, 1928), p. 52.
19 Sutherland, pp. 231–4. Sutherland sees Crusoe as 'like his creator, a practical, level-headed, intelligent and resolute Englishman who has inherited the sterling qualities of the middle class into which he was born'.
20 *Citizen*, p. 227.
21 *Letters*, p. 475. Note the alternative expression, 'two or three Weeks'.
22 Watt, pp. 89–92; see also '*Robinson Crusoe* as a myth', pp. 167–8. Another critic to find a degree of psychological implausibility is J. J. Richetti, *Defoe's Narratives* (Oxford, 1975), p. 54: 'It is a curiously unreal dream in which Crusoe does not really participate but simply watches action with a cool detachment totally foreign to normal dream experience.' I can only say that my notions of psychological reality correspond more closely with Defoe's than those of his critics.
23 Maren-Sofie Røstvig, *The Happy Man: Studies in the Metamorphoses of a Classical Ideal* (Oslo, 1954–8; 2nd edn 1971).
24 P. Rogers, 'Crusoe's home', *EIC*, Vol. XXIV (1974), pp. 375–90.
25 E. B. Benjamin, 'Symbolic elements in *Robinson Crusoe*', *PQ*, XXX (1951), pp. 206–11; reprinted in Ellis, pp. 34–8.
26 Richetti, *Defoe's Narratives*, p. 46.
27 Shinagel, p. 130.
28 Watt, '*Robinson Crusoe* as a myth', p. 173.
29 Homer O. Brown, 'The displaced self in the novels of Daniel Defoe', *ELH*, Vol. XXXVIII (1971), pp. 562–90.
30 Hunter, p. 142.

CHAPTER 5

Literary Background

APPROPRIATE FORMS

One of the most amazing things about *Robinson Crusoe* is the way in which it makes capital of some dubious literary precedents. It cannot be said that there were no fictional models available to Defoe, but they offered little promise of high creative achievement. Indeed, the English novel, as a serious artistic endeavour, might have got started more quickly if there had been *no* prose fiction about the place, rather than the medley of semi-literary genres which existed in 1700. As for non-fiction, the great modes (historiography, for instance) were ill-adapted to the task of presenting the daily experiences of ordinary men and women. There were, as we shall see, varieties of popular biography and many sorts of traveller's tale. But it took the peculiar genius of Defoe to invent the chemistry which would combine these elements in a unified work of art.

The most widely cultivated branch of fiction was the romance, generally a domesticised and cheerful version of the grand French model. In 1718, for example, Mary Hearne brought out *The Lover's Week, or the Six Days Adventures of Philander and Amaryllis*, an amiable chronicle of amours amid the card-tables and milliners' shops, with intermittent pauses for a dish of bohea tea.[1] More common was the epistolary mode practised in *Passionate Love-Letters between a Certain Chevalier* (1719); the chevalier, as might have been guessed, is the Pretender. Real-life scandal was often retailed through this method, and 'secret history' became a well-recognised genre, allegorising the true or invented escapades of high-society figures. It is unlikely that Mrs Manley, a specialist in this last mode, had much direct effect on Defoe, but *Roxana* borrows a few of the features of melodramatic romance as practised by Mrs Haywood or Mrs Aubin, who liked to build her plots around abduction, Turkish captivity, Barbary pirates and the like. Some readers at least must have come to *Robinson Crusoe* expecting the strange surprising adventures to move in the direction of a sultan's harem or a Portuguese nunnery. *That* was what adventure meant to the devotee of popular fiction.

The suggestion has been offered that Defoe incurred a particular debt to one celebrated *ur*-novel. According to this theory, *Crusoe* draws elements from Mrs Aphra Behn's *Oroonoko: or the Royal Slave* (1688).

The book is set in Surinam (Guiana), where Mrs Behn (1640–89) claimed to have been an eye-witness of the events described. Unfortunately, it is by no means certain that she ever set foot in South America, although the possibility cannot be ruled out. This matter aside, the parallels discovered between her creation and Defoe's are somewhat vague. It is contended that the noble savage in *Oroonoko* prefigures a similar aspect of Friday's quality, with the added feature that the two men were related in their physical appearance.[2] *Oroonoko* was an exceedingly popular production, as it deserved to be, and the theme found dramatic expression in a tragedy by Thomas Southerne (1696). Defoe must, then, have known about it. But his own artistic idiom lies at the opposite pole to the intense, extravagant and rapid narrative of *Oroonoko*. The suggestion lies, as it were, on the table; it requires fuller evidence to be generally accepted.

A diverse collection of literature is generally classified under the heading of rogues' biographies. Some of these were unblushingly fabricated – and, indeed, *The English Rogue* is simply the best the British could do by way of rivalling picaresque novels like *Lazarillo de Tormes* or *El Buscón*. Few people now believe that *Crusoe* has anything to do with picaresque as such; but the native tradition of cony-catching, gulls and cutpurses survived its birth in the Elizabethan underworld. Long after Nashe, Dekker and Deloney there were stories of ingenious low-life characters, ambitious apprentices, charlatans like Bampfylde-Moore-Carew, based indifferently on real or invented characters. Closer to actuality were the lives of prominent criminals, notably highwaymen – although the last speeches and dying confessions generally embody much sententious moralising and a little flimsy narrative. Defoe became a specialist in Newgate memoirs when he worked on Applebee's *Weekly Journal*, between roughly 1720 and 1725; John Applebee was a kind of early cheque-book journalist, who would buy the rights to a dying speech, and may even have gone so far as to supply Jack Sheppard – that noted escapologist who wished to avoid the anatomists at Surgeon's Hall – with a hearse and a strong coffin. So it came about that Defoe contributed two lives, at least, to the flood of obituary material on Sheppard in 1724; as well as three (probably) to the even greater flow of Jonathan Wild biographies the following year.[3]

Allied forms were memoirs of pirates, gamesters and prostitutes. The courtesy title of 'Captain' was often adopted by authors; Defoe himself became 'Captain Charles Johnson' for the purposes of the *History of Pyrates*. A celebrated courtesan like Sally Salisbury (see below, p. 128) would find her name used in all kinds of scabrous pamphlets, rather as innuendo concerning the principal persons involved pervaded British television at the time of the Profumo affair in 1963, or as Watergate infiltrated comedy ten years later. Not much straight biography is found in these pamphlets, and the same tricks are shamelessly transferred from one criminal to another. Only a very exceptional figure acquires any individuality in their pages; it happens with Wild, cold, self-enclosed and anxious, obsessively methodical like his later embodiment, Peachum; or with Colonel Charteris, rapist, adventurer, con-man and profligate, a man of joyless mirth. Again, the links are stronger in the case of Defoe's later fiction than with *Crusoe*, whose hero practises his cunning on renegade seamen rather than on the forces of the law.

An interesting analysis of these sub-literary kinds as they may have affected Defoe has been made by John J. Richetti. He discusses some of the early Robinsonades as well as *Crusoe* itself, seeking in the stories of 'Travellers, Pirates and Pilgrims' a kind of dialectical model for the book.[4] The pirate, he contends, is a personification of 'radical isolation'; the genre occupied by the doings of such men is built around a clash of passive (religious) and active (secular) values in the eighteenth century. 'The secular energies required to survive in the world necessarily involve destructive competition with others. Crusoe contends with nature pure and simple, and his exertions thus take place in a moral vacuum.' For Richetti, the hero is the embodiment of secular energies 'which chafe under the traditional system of social and moral limitations and their religious foundations'.[5] Because of Crusoe's unique location, Defoe was able to have it both ways. Some readers may feel that Richetti overstates the connection between Crusoe and pirate heroes (even Defoe's own characters, like Captain Misson); he does not perhaps distinguish sharply enough between what might be termed the 'career' adventurers – like buccaneers and corsairs – and such people as castaways, lost travellers and abducted seamen. However, his study has the considerable merit of putting *Crusoe* into a context of popular adventure-stories. (Richetti also gives some attention to the lives of 'Rogues and Whores', a section with closer relevance to other novels by Defoe.)[6] He offers a salutary reminder that Crusoe was not the only hero to undergo desparate mishaps on the high seas or to find himself cut adrift from normal civilisation.

Whether any of these narrative forms echoed as clearly in Defoe's imagination as did the sermons he had heard, and read, from his youth we may well doubt. There were devotional tracts, too, and the guides to spiritual living already considered in Chapter 3. Broader modes of didacticism included the conduct-books to which Defoe had made a startlingly successful contribution with *The Family Instructor* (1715–18). Bonamy Dobrée saw the importance of these books in the fact that Defoe here combined dialogue and narrative effectively for the first time – and also in the appearance of characteristic 'themes' such as the monitory voices of *Crusoe*.[7] As several critics have pointed out, the issue of filial obedience is common to *Crusoe* and the *Instructor*: the perils of ingratitude are starkly presented in the latter. Sometimes the rebellion of childhood takes forms that even the unpuritanical Gildon might have acknowledged as undesirable (gaming, for instance); usually it is on the level of playgoing, the reading of 'foolish Romances' or going to the park on Sundays. Parents, to be sure, have their own obligations; but Defoe appears to think that they need fewer reminders.

Then we cannot avoid the possible relevance of journalism. This element in Defoe's literary background was exaggerated in the nineteenth and early twentieth centuries, and we need to handle the concept with care. Defoe's *Review* in its nine-year span was, as had been said, a journal of opinion rather than a newspaper. Defoe was not a reporter in the sense of a man who habitually writes up his 'stories' from first-person observation. He was an essayist, a moralist and economic speculator *around* the news, a sub-editor processing narratives that arrived from all over the world. His work on Mist's *Weekly Journal* (from about 1717) equipped him to editorialise rather than to report. And this sorts with his novels where, in Sutherland's words, he preferred 'to embroider upon the actual rather than indulge in pure invention'. There is one classic case of embroidery in *Crusoe*: the episode in which the travellers cross the Pyrenees and are beset by wolves (*RC1*, pp. 290–302) is directly based on a story which had appeared in Mist's paper on 4 January 1718, though very much fleshed out in detail. Defoe probably wrote the original paragraph; either way he made it his own.[8]

From time to time in the columns of Mist or Applebee we encounter items, very likely from Defoe's pen, which suggest interesting links with *Robinson Crusoe*. They come often in the shape of analogues rather than sources. Thus, on 9 December 1721, Applebee's *Weekly Journal* printed a brief account of the release of 280 English captives 'redeemed by the late Treaty made with the King of Fez and Morocco', and who 'marched in their Moorish Habits in good Order' through London to St. Paul's, for a service of thanksgiving. If this had occurred in time for *Crusoe* or *Captain Singleton*, Defoe might have been able to work something appropriate into his novel. The month of April in 1719, momentous above all others in Defoe's writing career, shows the newspapers full of stories concerning pirate attacks off Virginia; a sea-fight between an English letter-of-mark ship and a Spanish privateer; reflections on the meaning of the 'great meteor' recently observed ('Must God's Goodness and Mercy any more than his Vengeance and Justice be tied up, so that he cannot make use of such Things as these when he thinks fit, as well to warn and foretell what the World are to expect from Him if they change not their wicked courses?'); and similar items. Only the moralising on the subject of Providence, set off by the meteor, bears very closely on *Crusoe*; but all these news-stories are indicative of the intellectual matrix in which the novel is embedded. Mist and Applebee render in a direct

and literal way matters which, transmuted and refracted, become
constituent parts of the fiction.[9]

There remains the question of 'truth' in these narratives. It has
generally been argued that Defoe saw no real distinction between his
accounts of Jack Sheppard, a real person, and of Moll Flanders, an
invented character. There is certainly some evidence for this view. When
the eccentric writer and bookseller John Dunton died in 1733, his books
were sold in the same manner as those of Defoe (whom he had known
well). Listed among the biographies, together with such an item as
Oldmixon's life of Arthur Maynwaring, we find *Colonel Jack*.[10] As is
well known, Dr Johnson was deceived into thinking the memoirs of
Captain Carleton an authentic narrative;[11] while many readers were
equally misled by *Memoirs of a Cavalier*. Although this does not prove
that Defoe himself did not know what he was about, it does suggest that
the line was one which tended to waver.

This affords an additional reason for Defoe's exaggerated protestations
concerning the truth of his fiction – whether by way of introductory
assertion ('The Editor believes the thing to be a just History of Fact;
neither is there any Appearance of Fiction in it', *RC1* p. 1) or by way
of later gloss ('All the endeavours of envious people to reproach it with
being a romance . . . have proved abortive', *RC2*, p. vii). The general
explanation for this strategy has been a Puritanical dislike of 'lying',
which made Defoe adopt any shift which would clear him of the imputation of telling imaginary stories. By the time of *RC3* this has been
converted into defence by allegory or parable. But it may well be that
Defoe knew he was entering an ambiguous area. His own works of
biography prior to 1719 covered figures such as a statesman, the Duke
of Shrewsbury (*Checklist*, item 401), a dissenting minister, Daniel
Williams (389), and a great prince, Charles XII (322). He had also
produced bogus lives such as *Memoirs of John, Duke of Melfort* (272)
and *Memoirs of Major Alexander Ramkins* (408). This last, published
four months prior to *RC1*, describes twenty-eight years' service by a
Highland officer; it was reissued in December 1719 with a new title,
*The Life and Strange Surprising Adventures of Majr. Alexander
Ramkins*. In a corner of literature where fact and fantasy often became
blurred, Defoe was seeking by every means at his disposal to allocate
Crusoe to the non-fictional segment.[12] It would be more a matter of
literary appeal than one of conscientious scruple.

THE RISE OF THE NOVEL

Today, however, we read *Crusoe* in the light of what was to follow.
Whatever its background in rogues' tales, romance or popular biography,
it belongs for us at the start of a line stretching forward for two and a

half centuries. We make our adult acquaintance of Crusoe having been already introduced to *Middlemarch* and *The Portrait of a Lady*. Students encounter Defoe in courses that lead through Richardson and Fielding to Sterne and Jane Austen. Whether we like it or not, the operative frame of reference is the Novel, and that does not mean Mrs Haywood or *Lives of the Gamesters*. History has given *Robinson Crusoe* a role it could not have fulfilled for its original public in 1719.

We immediately arrive at an embarrassing fact. Defoe's later novels take up themes central to subsequent fiction – the search for gentility, the relations of the sexes, the effect of childhood experiences upon an adult individual. *Crusoe* seems obstinately to cut itself off from these favourite topics. The only personal relation studied at length is the paternalistic master-and-servant dealings of Crusoe and Friday; these are further inhibited under the aspect of psychological revelation by the crude dialogue technique and pidgin English which prevail in their conversations. However, on closer examination the inward drama of the hero's isolation, guilt and recovery enacts a process endemic to the genre – the crisis is more directly spiritual than it is in many subsequent novels, but the overall trajectory is similar. Consider, for instance, the parallel course of estrangement, confinement, despair and ultimate rescue in the life-history of Arthur Clennam, the hero of *Little Dorrit*. Characteristically, the ending of this work is altogether more muted than the close of *RC1*; but the main architecture of the case-study (as opposed to the precise moral and religious ideas underlying the psychological portrait) is comparable in its shaping and organisation. The *structure* of Clennam's narrative is close to that of Crusoe's, but the texture is quite different. This gap is partly a matter of individual authorship, partly a reflection of historical change – by the time of Dickens, novels no longer owed much allegiance to the Puritan homily.

Recent discussion of early fiction has been, of course, heavily influenced by Ian Watt's outstanding book, *The Rise of the Novel*. Central to this account is a perceptive chapter on a new mode of 'realism', identified not as literal photographic accuracy but as a fullness of presentation, a closeness to the 'immediate facts of consciousness', a readiness to include even 'the most ephemeral thoughts and actions'. Rejecting the notion of realism as simple concentration on the seamy side of life, Watt relates it instead to such things as the avoidance of accepted formal conventions, the abandonment of traditional plot-lines, and 'the exploration of the personality as it is defined in the interpenetration of its past and present self-awareness'. He puts special emphasis on the particularising bent of the novel, that is, its tendency to substitute highly individuated persons for the character-types of earlier times, and to deal in a carefully localised time and place. With these developments goes a new functionalism of style, which equally serves to bring experience closer to the reader;

'concrete particularity' becomes a goal, even if it results in verbosity or awkwardness in language.[13]

Watt then proceeded to develop a concept he termed 'formal realism', by which he meant the narrative consequences of the 'realistic' aim of producing 'a full and authentic report of human experience'.[14] He suggested that the growth of a middle-class reading public had important consequences for the way novels were written – and *by whom* they were written. Defoe and Richardson, above all, could scarcely have become writers at all in previous ages: they 'knew little or nothing of the "ancient laws" of literature'. Indeed, 'their ideas and training were such that they could hardly have hoped to appeal to the old arbiters of literary destiny'; thus, they naturally were drawn to the techniques of formal realism, to which the classical viewpoint was wholly 'adverse'. They broke with all the 'classical literary criteria' and techniques.[15] In another brilliant chapter, Watt considers the use of 'private experience' in the novel. He argues that Richardson's narrative mode may be regarded as 'a reflection of a much larger change in outlook – the transition from the objective, social, and public orientation of the classical world to the subjective, individualist, and private orientation of the life and literature of the last two hundred years'. At this point, Watt has Richardson chiefly in mind, with epistolary fiction the relevant technique; but he also takes account of the 'private and egocentric mental life we find in Defoe's heroes'.[16]

Watt is unique in the clarity, depth and liveliness with which he explores this phase in literary history. He is particularly successful in describing the achievement of Defoe and Richardson; towards Fielding he seems a shade unsympathetic. But there have naturally been objections raised to some features of his argument. The assault is conducted on the broadest front by Diana Spearman, who questions the whole theory of a middle-class novel. She contends that the surviving legacy of mediaeval romance was larger than has been allowed; that the middle class had not achieved anything like the prominence which some readings would demand (here Watt is less vulnerable than certain other critics quoted by Mrs Spearman); and that allied fictional modes have grown up in very different social circumstances. Especially valuable is her emphasis on fantasy and make-believe in eighteenth-century fiction, as opposed to mere reportage. And Mrs Spearman is alive, as many writers are not, to the *unique* features of Daniel Defoe, the things that set him apart from other men of his time and his class. She sees him as far from representative of Puritanism at large; his mind as 'not only original, but almost eccentric', and his opinions as exceedingly individualistic. Finally, she observes that 'in spite of the popularity of *Robinson Crusoe*, no novelist attempted to imitate Defoe's literary technique, as distinct from copying the plot of *Robinson Crusoe*, until the twentieth century'. This is perhaps an exaggeration – there are traces of Colonel Jack's boyhood in the Victorian novelists, to take one example. But Mrs Spearman makes invigorating reading. She gives back to Defoe some personal quiddity he was in danger of losing under the influence of social interpretations of the novel.[17]

On an earlier occasion I set out what seemed to me the true process of causation:

> As the inherited idiom came to seem obsolete – too ringing, declamatory, histrionic – a new medium of expression was required. It had to be able to focus more narrowly on individuals, to offer a close-up on experience, to take the reader into a situation rather than merely present happenings for him to gaze at. Nicholas Rowe, for one, attempted to bend the existing language of tragedy to such a purpose. But the aloofness of stage production defeated him. So it was in the sustained intimacy of the novel, with a single voice to direct the reader, commune with him, amuse him – it was here that an especially receptive instrument was devised. The novel worked on a new social 'register', a kind of communal whispering gallery. For this to take place, the middle class did not need to rise, fall or jump on the spot. It simply had to listen and learn.[18]

If there is anything in this theory of 'sustained intimacy', then *Robinson Crusoe* stands firmly at the head of the line. We can see what has happened if we contrast a passage of typical pre-Defoe fiction with a snatch of *Crusoe*: the first excerpt comes from William Congreve's *Incognita* (1692), sub-titled 'Love and Duty Reconcil'd'. It is a sort of novella with a double plot, set in a timeless but vaguely chivalric Florence:

> 'Tis strange now, but all Accounts agree, that just here Leonora who had run like a violent Stream against Aurelian hitherto, now retorted with as much precipitation in his Favour. I could never get any Body to give me a satisfactory reason, for her suddain and dextrous Change of Opinion just at that stop, which made me conclude she could not help it; and that Nature boil'd over in her at that time when it had so fair an Opportunity to show it self: For Leonora it seems was a Woman Beautiful, and otherwise of an excellent Disposition; but in the Bottom a very Woman. This last Objection, this Opportunity of perswading Man to Disobedience, determined the Matter in Favour of Aurelian, more than all his Excellencies and Qualifications, take him as Aurelian, or Hippolito, or both together.
> Well, the Spirit of Contradiction and of Eve was strong in her; and she was in a fair Way to Love Aurelian, for she lik'd him already;

that it was Aurelian she no longer doubted, for had it been a Villain, who had only taken his Name upon him for any ill Designs, he would never have slip'd so favourable an Opportunity as when they were alone, and in the Night coming through the Garden and broad Space before the Piazza.[19]

And this from quite near the end of *RC1*:

I had not kept my self long in this Posture, but I saw the Boat draw near the Shore, as if they look'd for a Creek to thrust in at for the Convenience of Landing; however, as they did not come quite far enough, they did not see the little Inlet where I formerly landed my Rafts; but run their Boat on Shore upon the Beach, at about half a Mile from me, which was very happy for me; for otherwise they would have landed just as I may say at my Door, and would soon have beaten me out of my Castle, and perhaps have plunder'd me of all I had.

When they were on Shore, I was fully satisfy'd that they were *English* Men; at least, most of them; one or two I thought were *Dutch*; but it did not prove so: There were in all eleven Men, whereof three of them I found unarm'd, and as I thought, bound; and when the first four or five of them were jump'd on Shore, they took those three out of the Boat as Prisoners: One of the three I could perceive using the most Passionate Gestures of Entreaty, Affliction and Despair, even to a Kind of Extravagance; the other two I could perceive lifted up their Hands sometimes, and appear'd concern'd indeed, but not to such a Degree as the first.

I was perfectly confounded at the Sight, and knew not what the Meaning of it should be. (pp. 250–1)

Congreve's narrator describes contradictory states of mind with an easy flow; the syntax is leisurely, the constructions work towards obvious climax ('but in the Bottom a very Woman'), the antitheses arrive in good order. The editorial epithets ('suddain and dextrous') give an effect of distance. The expressions of time and place are vague; there is little sense of an existence prior to the immediate adventures (in fact the plot is confined to forty-eight hours, and from this passage alone we might guess something of the sort). The narrator readily appeals to stock views of the female character: the conventional-sounding Leonora and Aurelian have the air of tactful *noms de guerre*. Everything conspires to make the episode a remote, stylised and public ('all Accounts agree') ritual.

The greater immediacy of the writing in *Crusoe* owes much, but not everything, to the first-person narration. Crusoe shares with us his secret knowledge of the inlet, denied to the English crew; he reminds us of his earlier life on the island; he tells us of his wrong conjectures which are subsequently to be corrected. We are given a strong sense of infiltrators arriving on an already occupied site; events do not strike up against a *tabula rasa* but bounce into a prepared surface at calculable angles. Not only Crusoe has the advantage of the newcomers; so do *we* as readers. His proprietorial phrases ('landed . . . at my Door', 'beaten me out of my Castle') allude to locations long familiar to us; the rhetoric encourages us to share the sentiment of disturbance, conveyed by images of thrusting *inwards*. Even when a puzzling detail emerges, we can hardly forget that Crusoe himself had made 'a Thousand Gestures and Motions' on the shore when he was cast up – expressing, like the captives now arrived, 'Entreaty, Affliction and Despair, even to a kind of Extravagance'. The topographical precision in this excerpt is matched by Crusoe's habitual 'approximating' (see below, p. 122), suggesting here that he did not have time or was not quite near enough to be sure of the figure.

Everything is rendered through the narrator's consciousness ('I was fully satisfy'd', 'as I thought', 'I could perceive', 'I was perfectly confounded'); the familiar redundancy ('whereof three of them') conveys an impression of words falling out where they will, as against the planned sequentiality in Congreve. Between *Incognita* and *Robinson Crusoe* the narrative mode has taken a sudden inward turn; the storyteller is still privileged, but he shares his confidences with us, and lets the tiny second-by-second data of his being control the pace of the story. We are *told* of competing feelings in Leonora; we are in there with Crusoe as he changes his mind in mid-sentence. One is a mode of demonstration, the other an act of complicity. In the end *Robinson Crusoe* contributed just as much to the mainstream of the novel as *Moll Flanders*; it helped to teach writers how to bring their characters (wherever they might be stranded) within the circle of our privacy.

THE READERS OF *ROBINSON CRUSOE*

About the audience of *Robinson Crusoe*, it would be rash to make very firm judgements. It is often supposed that Defoe was able to reach a wider social spectrum than most polite Augustan authors, and indeed that a substantial part of his readership was composed of people with background and interests similar to his own. Ian Watt is careful not to speculate in this area but, if such a view were true, it would plainly strengthen his conjectures regarding the 'new' reading public:

> By virtue of their multifarious contacts with printing, bookselling, and journalism, Defoe and Richardson were in very direct contact with the new interests and capacities of the reading public; but it is even more important that they themselves were wholly representative of the new centre of gravity of that public. As middle-class London trades-

men they had only to consult their own standards of form and content
to be sure that what they wrote would appeal to a wide audience.
This is probably the supremely important effect of the changed
composition of the reading public and the new dominance of the
booksellers upon the rise of the novel; not so much that Defoe and
Richardson responded to the new needs of their audience, but that
they were able to express those needs from the inside much more
freely than would previously have been possible.

Watt's own evidence suggests that until 1740 economic factors held back
'a substantial marginal section of the reading public' and that this group
'was largely composed of potential novel readers, many of them women'.
He concludes that the reading public early in the eighteenth century 'did
not normally extend much further down the social scale than to tradesmen and shopkeepers'. However, he believes that new recruits to this
public came chiefly from 'the increasingly prosperous and numerous
social groups concerned with commerce and manufacture'.[20] Defoe was
assuredly spokesman for just this class; but whether its members read
Crusoe remains a matter of guesswork.

It may well be that in the first instance the audience for novels would
overlap with the traditional literary public. One of the few early works
of fiction to appear by subscription was Eliza Haywood's *Letters from
a Lady of Quality to a Chevalier* (1724). This was actually a version of
a work by Edmé Boursault (1699), but it appeared in Mrs Haywood's
Works (1724) and was clearly thought of as hers. The 310 subscribers
contain the astonishing total of 125 women (40 per cent), the highest
proportion I have ever encountered. It is certainly a less aristocratic body
of readers than many ventures of the day attracted; and a handful of
men with City connections can be identified. But the feminine com-
plexion is much more evident than the class shift. Of course, subscribers
are not necessarily a trustworthy guide to readership at large; but they
do indicate the sort of person who was willing to be associated with a
particular variety of book.

Defoe's own major subscription venture was for *Jure Divino* (1706)
but he did not publish the names of his supporters. By contrast *Caledonia*
does contain in its London edition (1707) 'A List of Benefactors and
Subscribers to this Work', that is, subscribers to the Edinburgh edition
of 1706. There are eighty-four names headed by the leading figures in
the political world of Scotland (the Duke of Queensberry, the Earl of
Roxburgh, the Marquis of Tweeddale, the Duke of Argyll, the Earl of
Mar, Sir Hew Dalrymple, the Earl of Stair, the Earl of Seafield, George
Baillie, etc.). Every individual name is Scottish and every single one
male. There are thirty-three peers, including twenty-three earls, and a
large number of men who were elected to the new Parliament of Great

Britain. Over a third of those listed figure in the *Dictionary of National Biography*, a higher proportion than Pope, Gay or Prior achieved with their sumptuous subscription volumes in the next two decades. If we were to judge Defoe's public by this example, we should be forced to conclude that he aimed for a special and localised audience on each occasion. Most of his writing, in fact, must have sought a wider base of support; but the evidence should warn us not to imagine that he was always preaching to a converted middle class.

There are grounds for believing that Defoe's contacts were wider both socially and geographically than were those of (say) Dryden, Swift or Pope. On his travels for Harley in 1706 he had built up a network of local agents who helped in the distribution of a pro-government pamphlet. There are over sixty names, with a high proportion of dissenting ministers and a few other identifiable professions (bookseller, attorney, draper, even a country gentleman and MP).[21] We know that Defoe had extensive links with East Anglia, with Yorkshire and with the West Country. Whereas Pope's Homer subscription is overwhelmingly metropolitan in cast – probably 70 per cent had London connections, including landowners with a town house – Defoe could claim firsthand knowledge of some remote and rural parts of England.[22] This is, of course, without considering the acquaintance with Scottish men and affairs he built up during his service for Harley and Godolphin (1706–13). Since Defoe's works did not appear under his own name, or only very rarely, the point is not that his books would instantly reach a captive market (waiting for the latest Defoe, as though it were the latest Harold Robbins), but that he would have internalised the tastes and expectations of a wide segment of the nation. His training as a professional author would not allow him to neglect these presuppositions.

Much of Charles Gildon's criticism of *Robinson Crusoe* (below, p. 129) has been dismissed as envious sneering, but his suggestion that the book was avidly sought out below stairs is often seen as the highest kind of tribute – unconscious confirmation of Defoe's broad appeal. Seven years after Defoe's death, the anonymous author of *A Letter to the Society of Booksellers* equated *Crusoe* with the meanest 'common Trumpery' of the age:

> However, it is certain, that the Sale of a Book chiefly depends on the Universality of the Subject, and that the most excellent do not meet with the greatest Success; and accordingly we find, that *Robinson Crusoe* sells quicker than *Locke* on Human Understanding, and the Beggar's Opera than the best Comedy: nay, is it not sufficiently known, that some have acquired Estates, by printing Tom Thumb, Riddles, Songs, Fables, the Pilgrim's Progress, and such like common Trumpery?[23]

There are oddities here, even allowing for the fact that the author is disgruntled about booksellers (not writers) who strike it lucky. (He might almost be predicting the total commercial failure of Hume's *Treatise*, published the following year.) Even in 1738, 'Universality of the Subject' has an approbatory ring, which sounds through the author's gloomy distaste for anything popular, and the books he chose – immensely durable works by Defoe, Gay, Fielding and Bunyan – suggest that they had already detached themselves above the mass of ephemera. (Fielding's *Tom Thumb* was 'printed for' James Roberts, as were many of Defoe's books – he did not own copyrights but acted as a distributor – and in any case Roberts was not a great man for songs and riddles.)

Later in the century *Crusoe* became a target for chapbook compilers: when Parson Woodforde bought a copy from a travelling salesman, together with *The Complete Fortune Teller* and *Laugh and Grow Fat*, we may reasonably suspect that this was no full or authentic text.[24] But conversion into a cheap and easily digestible form, two or three generations on, does not establish the precise contemporary market for *Robinson Crusoe*. Even the abridgements and serialisations look to me to be intended for a reasonably literate audience. Pirates generally sought to cream the existing public, rather than to reach a wholly new class of readers: Cox, for example, aimed to make the book more 'portable'. If we consider the circumstances of publication (Taylor's involvement, the use of advertising, etc.), the likelihood must be that the work was a normal trade venture, which was aimed at a broad spectrum of readership, habituated to narratives of travel and biography (rather than 'low' fictional modes). In a loose sense this is a middle-class public: it certainly would not extend down as far as the least-educated sections of society.

The authorised editions of *Robinson Crusoe* never reached the scale of Bowyer's 2,500 or 2,000 copies for each printing of *Gulliver's Travels*. Moreover, the serialisation of the text was performed in a distinctly obscure journal with no discernible prestige or influence. Nevertheless, it cannot be doubted that *Crusoe* was a highly popular work, and from the very beginning a 'mythic' quality accreted round the first part. Around 1750, the very time when Defoe reached a predictable nadir in his reputation, the author of Cibber's *Lives* could still refer to it as having an immense currency (see below, p. 131). As late as 1770 a bookseller managed to acquire a job-lot of copyrights, including *Moll Flanders* and *Roxana*, for as little as 8 guineas;[25] but *Crusoe* was fought over by the trade, and there were rival London editions in the 1760s and 1770s. (The descendants of the authorised editions were put out by a consortium including Longman and Thomas Caslon; they were opposed by a version whose imprint carries twelve fictitious names including T. Clitch, F. Frithcet, J. Dwarf and J. Liblond.) By this date Rousseau had begun the process of elevating *Crusoe* in serious critical esteem, and the book was poised for its canonisation by the Romantics and its edition per year in the nineteenth century. It moved into the schoolroom, and spawned more and more adaptations. The ironies of history were working themselves out – what is popular (that is, low) in its own time may occasionally survive as popular (that is, of universal appeal) in later generations. A book that occupied no clear-cut position in the literary scheme of things, when it came out, endured until it served even to define a genre.

BATTLES OF THE BOOK

It has generally been thought that Defoe and the prominent group of Scriblerus satirists were ranged against one another, mighty opposites in a struggle over the direction which the English nation was taking. This view is succinctly expressed by George DeF. Lord:

> Thus the greatness of Dryden, Swift, and Pope has obscured or misrepresented what really happened in England between 1660 and 1714. 'The Peace of the Augustans' was not due to the triumph of traditional social standards or 'Tory values but to political stability engendered by the Whig magnates. In *Windsor Forest* Pope correctly predicted a period of peace and prosperity, starting with the Treaty of Utrecht (1713), but the architect of this unprecedented political stability was not to be his philosophical friend Bolingbroke and what Kramnick evocatively calls 'the politics of nostalgia', but the creative and unprincipled Walpole and political writers such as Marvell and Defoe.[26]

This is, perhaps, an unduly literary approach to a transformation with important constitutional, economic and social roots. But I think it also makes cut and dried a situation that, so far as Defoe was concerned, shifted with each vacillation in day-to-day politics. Though he was deeply conservative on many moral issues, Defoe was scarcely an apostle of political stability – which is a creature in large measure of infrequent elections, skilled borough-mongering, and the quiet elimination of minority viewpoints. Defoe's greatest political writing was elicited by moments of drama and crisis (Sacheverell, the Hanoverian accession, the Bubble). He was an ideologue of commercial prosperity, rather than an architect of Whig dynastic power in the eighteenth century.

Kramnick terms Defoe 'Walpole's Laureate', but he was this in a contingent way at most. The argument is that Defoe was used by Walpole to dispel 'with optimism the gloom purveyed by the Opposition'. I am doubtful if a fully fledged Opposition normally existed at the relevant period, that is, before Bolingbroke's return from exile in 1725;

when it did, during the ten years specified by Kramnick, Walpole was himself its instigator, as around 1717–18. The traditional 'gloom' of the Tory satirists turns up again in Kramnick's picture of 'Swift, the frustrated and gloomy aristocrat, and Defoe, the restless and optimistic bourgeois' (was Swift an aristocrat, and was not Defoe a deeply frustrated man?). 'Defoe accepted and rejoiced in the age of Walpole; Swift rejected it with satire, horror, and bitterness.' Perhaps, although there was much in Walpole's England which Defoe severely criticised, as a work like *Augusta Triumphans* (1728) amply displays. For Kramnick, the 'projecting spirit was particularly despised by Bolingbroke's circle'. He attributes this to their humanist outlook: 'Restlessness and eagerness to transform appalled classicists whose eyes were firmly fixed on the past. The words "project" and "scheme" were anathema to Walpole's Tory critics.' This is certainly correct, and Defoe's willingness, right to the end, to submit unironic Plans and Effectual Methods to achieve this or that is the most marked way in which he diverges from the Scriblerians. Finally, Kramnick contends that Defoe 'spoke for, and was read by a class totally alien to Bolingbroke, Swift, Pope, and Gay. [They] thought Defoe's work socially and intellectually inferior, a fact indicated by its success with the new and bourgeois reading public.' Kramnick then considers Steele, briefly, and Bernard Mandeville as other laureates of the new age, scornful of Tory nostalgia.[27]

Details aside, there is obviously a large element of truth in this contrast, which has always been the accepted view of the matter, though never drawn out so clearly as by Kramnick. There are, it seems to me, weaknesses in the case. One very strange omission is Joseph Addison, whose name does not once appear in Kramnick's entire book. It was Addison above all who dignified the merchant community in print; what Defoe struggled to do in hasty pamphlets or didactic manuals Addison achieved singlehanded in a few eloquent papers in the *Spectator*. I say this not to disparage Defoe, but to report the bare reality of cultural history: it was the *Spectator*, and not *A Plan of the English Commerce*, which generations of English men and women internalised as part of their understanding of the way society worked. Again, we have to cope with the facts that Pope admired much of Defoe's work, particularly the first part of *Crusoe*; that Swift, despite his barbed comment when the *Examiner* was countering the *Review*, was often on the same side of the fence as Defoe, and each enjoyed Harley's patronage; and finally that these man actually practised the same forms (satire, weekly journalism, political pamphlets, imaginary voyages) for what may well have been much the same audience. Their repertoire of literary resources – allegory, irony, unreliable narrators, etc. – is in large measure identical.

It would certainly be misleading to think of Defoe as a forlorn outsider, perpetually skulking in the shadows while the favoured

Augustans basked in patronage. Although he was a dissenter, Defoe made a propitious early marriage, prospered in trade for something like a decade, and had established fair claims to gentility well before the time of *Crusoe*. His inopportune support for Monmouth in 1685 did not lead him to the gallows or to transportation, as it well might have done; in 1688 he chose the right side and benefited through the king's friendship in the 1690s. In Scotland he came to know dukes, marquesses and earls. Unlike Swift, Pope and Gay, he died in a world closer to his ideals than the one into which he had been born. And, whilst it may be going too far to describe him as 'Walpole's laureate', he had no need to join factious opposition to the ministry. He was, in a sense, a Grub Street writer of genius – the only one, perhaps, in eighteenth-century England – but he inhabited the popular, successful and energetic end of the street, not the depressive garrets whose cracked skylights looked out on Bedlam.[28] He enjoyed controversy, and thrived in a polemical climate. We need not be sorry for him if he was a tourist rather than a house-guest at Blenheim or Chatsworth.

Comparisons have frequently been drawn between *Crusoe* and *Gulliver's Travels*.[29] Even though Gulliver did not make his appearance in the world until 1726, the book was undoubtedly under way some years earlier. Those who detect a sly current of allusion to Defoe on the first page of the *Travels* (the London hosier, city addresses like Old Jewry – where there was a Presbyterian meeting-house – and the Dampier parallel) may well have some right on their side. As the books develop, needless to say, the divergences are altogether more substantial than the similarities. 'The point is', as one critic quoted by Moore observes, 'that Gulliver took off his clothes while Crusoe put them on.'[30] Swift strips off the veneer of civilisation; Defoe just as carefully gives mankind a recoat. Gulliver visits populous nations and ends up estranged; Crusoe lives almost half a lifetime quite alone and replicates the corporate doings of the human race.

In some ways, as indicated, the contemporary writer closest to Defoe is Joseph Addison. He possessed the humanist training and social acceptability of the Scriblerian party: two years before *Crusoe* came out, he was Secretary of State, as high an office as Walpole (four years his junior) had yet held. Addison, however, shared many of Defoe's deeper urges and intuitions; this emerges in his famous setpiece in the *Spectator* no. 69 (9 May 1711) on the Royal Exchange.

It gives me a secret Satisfaction, and, in some measure, gratifies my Vanity, as I am an *Englishman*, to see so rich an Assembly of Country-men and Foreigners consulting together upon the private Business of Mankind, and making this Metropolis a kind of *Emporium* for the whole Earth. I must confess I look upon High-Change to be a great Council, in which all considerable Nations have their Representatives. Factors in the Trading World are what Ambassadors are in the Politick World; they negotiate Affairs, conclude Treaties, and maintain a good Correspondence between those wealthy Societies of Men that are divided from one another by Seas and Oceans, or live on the different Extremities of a Continent.

So Defoe was to welcome the variety of traders on the exchange at Hull, where Crusoe senior dealt on his arrival from overseas. Addison continues:

I am wonderfully delighted to see such a Body of Men thriving in their own private Fortunes, and at the same time promoting the Publick Stock; or in other Words, raising Estates for their own Families, by bringing into their Country whatever is wanting, and carrying out of it whatever is superfluous.

There are, the essay concludes, 'not more useful Members of a Commonwealth than Merchants. They knit Mankind together in a mutual Intercourse of good Offices, distribute the Gifts of Nature, find Work for the Poor, add Wealth to the Rich, and Magnificence to the Great.' How surprised one of the old kings whose effigies hang in the Exchange would be, the writer reflects, 'to see so many private Men, who in his Time would have been the Vassals of some powerful Baron, Negotiating like Princes for greater Sums of Mony than were formerly to be met with in the Royal Treasury!'[31] Defoe would have tagged on an elegiac side-note concerning those who had suffered ruin through trade, yet in the main the sentiments are his – behind the more elegantly poised phrasing. Addison was not a man of Defoe's kind, except in the broadest political sense, but the Spectator would delight to contemplate a world made free for Crusoes. In this, at least, they were ranged against the Scriblerians, not from class loyalties or specific Walpolian ideology but as men in tune with their own times.

NOTES

1 Reprinted in Natascha Würzbach, *The Novel in Letters: Epistolary Fiction in the Early English Novel 1678–1740* (London, 1969), pp. 67–90. The best guide to this field is provided by R. A. Day, *Told in Letters* (Ann Arbor, Mich., 1966). For the relation of *Crusoe* to romance, see also M. E. Novak, 'Defoe's theory of fiction', *MP* Vol. LXI (1964), pp. 650–68.

2 Edward D. Seeber, 'Oroonoko and Crusoe's Man Friday', *MLQ*, Vol. XII (1951), pp. 286–91. For a recent view of Mrs Behn, supporting her claims to firsthand knowledge of events in Surinam, see Maureen Duffy, *The Passionate Shepherdess* (London, 1977).

3 The criminal lives are discussed by Shinagel, pp. 168–70; for Sheppard's relations with Applebee, see Gerald Howson, *Thief-Taker General: The Rise and Fall of Jonathan Wild* (London, 1970), p. 221. Howson lists Wild pamphlets, pp. 318–20.

4 J. J. Richetti, *Popular Fiction before Richardson* (Oxford, 1969), pp. 60–118.
5 ibid., pp. 59, 95.
6 ibid., pp. 23–59.
7 Bonamy Dobrée, *English Literature in the Early Eighteenth Century* (Oxford, 1959), pp. 403–44. Dobrée's discussion of Defoe (pp. 395–431 cover this period) is amongst the best portions of his volume in the Oxford History of English Literature series. A relevant excerpt from *The Family Instructor* is reprinted by J. T. Boulton (ed.), *Daniel Defoe* (London, 1965), pp. 197–207.
8 See *Citizen*, pp. 225–6; Sutherland, p. 250.
9 The items described are found in Lee, Vol. II, pp. 118–24, 461. Whilst Lee's attributions are no more than intelligent guesswork, the majority are dependable enough for most purposes.
10 *Catalogue of the Libraries of the Eminent Mr John Dunton, and the Revd Mr Williams, both lately Deceased* (London, 1733), p. 17. Note that Dunton, unlike Defoe, had not acquired the rank of a gentleman.
11 *CH*, pp. 58–9.
12 In *Citizen*, p. 246, Moore shows the influence on Defoe of *Memoirs of the Count de Rochefort*, 3rd edn (London, 1705); but no direct link with *Crusoe* has been observed.
13 Watt, pp. 9–31. For a consideration of Watt's account and other estimates of the rise of the novel, see P. Rogers, *The Augustan Vision* (London, 1974), pp. 245–54.
14 Watt, pp. 31–5.
15 ibid., pp. 36–61 (quotations from p. 60).
16 ibid., pp. 180–215 (quotations from pp. 182–3).
17 Diana Spearman, *The Novel and Society* (London, 1966), *passim* (quotations from pp. 169, 172).
18 Rogers, *Augustan Vision*, pp. 253–4.
19 *Congreve: Incognita and The Way of the World*, ed. A. N. Jeffares (London, 1966), pp. 60–1.
20 Watt, pp. 44–5, 49, 60–1. *RC1*, in its first edition at 5 shillings, would have cost rather more than half the weekly wage of a labourer in country districts; even the élite London building-trade workers would have spent more than a day's wages on its purchase (assuming they could read, as some could).
21 *Letters*, pp. 115–18.
22 Data on subscriptions are based on unpublished findings and my article, 'Pope and his subscribers', *Publishing History*, Vol. III (1978), pp. 7–36.
23 Quoted by A. D. McKillop, *The Early Masters of English Fiction* (Lawrence, Kans., 1956), p. 44.
24 *Citizen*, p. 223.
25 For fuller details (the transaction is simplified here), consult *CH*, p. 8.
26 *Anthology of Poems on Affairs of State*, ed. G. DeF. Lord (New Haven, Conn., 1975), pp. xxix–xxx.
27 I. Kramnick, *Bolingbroke and his Circle* (Cambridge, Mass., 1968), pp. 188–9, 191, 194, 196, 201–4.
28 See P. Rogers, *Grub Street* (London, 1972), pp. 311–27.
29 An interesting early example is found in the *Gentleman's Magazine* for November 1785, reprinted in *CH*, p. 55.
30 *Citizen*, p. 226.
31 *The Spectator*, ed. D. F. Bond (Oxford, 1965), Vol. I, pp. 294–6.

CHAPTER 6

Structure and Style

STRUCTURE

The first question that arises in respect of the construction of *Robinson Crusoe* is the relation of the three parts one to another. Scarcely anyone has been able to allot the *Serious Reflections* an integral role in the design, although modern criticism has found it easier to read back its ideas into the fictive world of the earlier parts. As to *RC1* and *RC2*, the general view is that expressed by Hunter: 'The two ·sequels . . . were published later and seem, like *1 Henry IV* and *2 Henry IV*, to have been separately conceived.'[1] This view should perhaps be qualified in two particulars. Although published 'later', *RC2* followed within four months of the original volume. Only three short books intervened: we could reasonably suppose that Defoe was writing in the same flow of inspiration, even if the quality of his second performance prompts an opposite view. (Logically it is possible that he had composed some or all of *RC2* before April 1719, but I know of no reader who has reached such a conclusion.) The other fact we should bear in mind is that Crusoe rehearses the plot of his continuation at the end of *RC1* (pp. 305–6) – Defoe must therefore have had, at the very least, the outline of the sequel in his head. But *1 Henry IV* likewise signals forward to its successor – more, obliquely, it is true. Could one argue, however, that *RC1* is 'patently incomplete' by itself, as Tillyard said of *1 Henry IV*?[2] The fact surely is that the first part of *Crusoe* already has a decisive close – some might assert, a protracted Beethoven-like ending with false resolution followed by coda.

The nearest we can come to an organic two-part structure is by way of parallels and developments in *RC2* which reinforce motifs already visible in *RC1*. For example, the island still takes up almost a half of the sequel. But (*a*) much of this is flashback, a report of events transacted in Crusoe's *absence*; (*b*) the place is now teeming with a growing population; and (*c*) Crusoe goes there by his own volition and departs when he chooses. The contrast with his original isolated sojourn is complete. There is also a marked disjunction between Crusoe's earliest trading ventures (vague outward movements, seaborne, indecisively mounted) and his final purposeful homeward trek across Russia. And, thirdly, the virtual mutiny of his crew following their wild conduct in Madagascar serves to isolate Crusoe once more, this time in circumstances that do him credit (see also above, p. 86). Having been the sole proprietor of a remote island ('wholly owned' by its finder, as one might say), Crusoe now finds himself cut off in an equally distant – but thickly inhabited – part of the world. In *RC1* he had faced no serious competition; now he has to take on numerous trading rivals in a basically Dutch-controlled region. Instead of a crew of desperadoes arriving hapless on his well-charted home territory, Crusoe is himself taken for a pirate and forced to consider the prospect of being executed:

> How hard I thought it was that I, who had spent forty years in a life of continued difficulties, and was at last come, as it were, to the port or haven which all men drive at, viz., to have rest and plenty, should be a volunteer in new sorrows by my own unhappy choice; and that I, who escaped so many dangers in my youth, should now come to be hanged in my old age, and in so remote a place, for a crime I was not in the least inclined to, much less really guilty of; and in a place or circumstance, where innocence was not like to be any protection at all to me. (*RC2*, pp. 246–7)

He decides that Providence 'might justly inflict this punishment as a retribution; and that I ought to submit to this, just as I would to a shipwreck, if it had pleased God to have brought such a disaster upon me'. The attempt to yoke together the providential meanings of *RC1* and *RC2* is not altogether a happy one: the 'crimes' for which he was to be punished must principally be those recounted in the former part, but a shipwreck already *has* brought retribution there. After his conversion, Crusoe is not allowed to do anything really reprehensible; yet his creator wants to go on using him as a vessel of God's purposes. The consequence is that the second part depends for its *moral* content on narrative features of the first volume, which insensibly devalues the story we are actually following in *RC2*.

More rewarding is the structure of the *Strange and Surprizing Adventures*, considered as a separate unit. The most ambitious attempt to fit out *RC1* with a clean and significant organisation is that of Douglas Brooks, who approaches the work from the point of view of numerological criticism. The book would appear to suit this approach less than some of the other works considered by Brooks, for example *Tom Jones* and *Tristram Shandy*. Nevertheless, he is able to adapt the readings of Starr and Hunter to locate 'a symmetrical structural patterning which is itself Providential', with order in the fictive organisation emblematic of divine order. The book in this period, Brooks believes, 'was still, potentially at least, a cosmic model'. Taking up a hint of Tillyard, he suggests cross-references between the first (pre-island) portion and the last (post-island) phase, notably the howls of animals (*RC1*, p. 25) recalled during the Pyrenean crossing (p. 297). Brooks accepts also the reversing 'chiastic' scheme discerned by F. H. Ellis, that is, a pattern of (A) fear of being devoured (p. 23); (B) howlings and yellings of savages (p. 25); (C) the prospect of being eaten by these savages (p. 25); – followed by (C2) Friday's apprehension of being eaten by cannibals (p. 230); (B2) the howls of the wolves (p. 298); and (A2) Crusoe's fear that the wolves will devour him (pp. 299–300). One serious weakness of this scheme, it seems to me, is the long gap between what I have called C2 and B2 – a break that disturbs any sense of clear pattern. However, Brooks discovers another chiastic arrangement, that is, 'Adventures with Xury/Brazil//Island//Brazil/Adventures with Friday'. The last phrase must refer to the Pyrenean episode; what is more doubtful is the use of 'Brazil' to cover Crusoe's visit to *Lisbon* 'to find out about his Brazilian plantation'. If Defoe intended any symmetry here, he was astonishingly devious in his execution.[3]

Brooks rightly draws attention to the centrality of the footprint, occurring precisely halfway through the book (see the next section of this chapter). Across this particular divide Brooks traces a number of common motifs in Crusoe's experience, for example, the wrecked ship in each stage of his island life, and the canoes he constructs first unaided and later, more successfully, with Friday's help. There is also 'repetitive patterning' in the recurrence of certain elements in Crusoe's dream (p. 87), though this could be seen as not much more than the fulfilment of a prophecy. Altogether, Brooks discerns in the structural workings 'a paradigm of the ordered workings of providence'. He concludes:

> Finally, in view of the precision of the novel's chronology and the Puritan habit of regarding the date of one's conversion as one's new birthday, we are surely justified in interpreting the nine months which elapse from the moment of Crusoe's being cast away to that of his recovery from his illness and his spiritual conversion (30 September to 30 June) as a symbolic gestation period.

Without the aid of numerological tools I had myself reached this conclusion, and I believe Brooks has a valuable point here, even if we discount his faith in the 'regenerative 8' in this connection. It would be more of an implausible coincidence if Defoe had *not* meant this to be significant than if he had.[4]

Other minor symmetries have come to the surface now and then, as in Starr's observation of traditional seven-year 'ages' of man, found in spiritual biography[5] – he does not apply this directly to Crusoe, but the footprint introduces 'A New Scene of [his] Life' after fifteen years; the first invaders arrive after twenty-two (that is, fourteen and twenty-one after his conversion). The total island episode, of course, lasts twenty-eight years, making thirty-five years' absence from England – both facts reported by Crusoe (p. 278). This leads me to wonder whether Defoe's miscalculations regarding dates might not be better adjusted if we push *back* the date of the shipwreck to 1658 – this would preserve the twenty-eight year sojourn and leave a seven-year period of wandering and 'alienation' preceding it.

A more ingenious and elaborate explanation has been put forward by Dewey Genzel. He suggests that Defoe originally had in mind a spell of 27 + years on the island, but that in his revisions he adopted a scheme of 28 + years, and failed to make the necessary allowances. For Genzel, incidentally, this lapse is the 'one clear contradiction' in the chronology of *Robinson Crusoe*. He conjectures that a long section in the middle (pp. 194–222) was a later interpolation: this includes Crusoe's dream of the savages (pp. 198–9), as well as Friday's arrival and religious education. It is not clear precisely how Defoe would have introduced Friday on the older abandoned scheme; and, as Ellis remarks, if this is an interpolation it reinforces existing symmetries.[6] In the end all efforts to get round the chronological anomalies are likely to prove abortive: whether or not Defoe expanded Friday's role (and we have no means of reaching a definite view on this), the book as it stands must be our touchstone for any interpretation. My own view is that *Robinson Crusoe* contains some degree of patterning, though less than Brooks indicates; it is a work mixing symmetry and asymmetry, tidy and untidy by turns, planned and spontaneous in fits.[7] That there is an overall design in *RC1*, connected with the hero's misspent youth, his isolation, conversion and regeneration, followed by his return and coming into his kingdom, I am entirely persuaded. Just how shapely an organisation Defoe has fabricated to express this scheme is another matter.

THE MEANING OF THE FOOTPRINT

The most famous moment in the book, almost the most celebrated in fiction, is Crusoe's discovery of a man's footprint (*RC1*, p. 153). Structural accounts like that of Douglas Brooks, as much as the emblematic reading of Hunter, place special emphasis on this episode. And any interpretation which ignored the footprint would stand condemned by that very fact.

As most readers will have noticed, this crucial event is introduced with studied casualness. Richetti observes, 'There is no novelistic preparation for the footprint, no transition is offered, merely an abrupt new topic'. According to the same critic, this sudden quality is appropriate because it shows Crusoe facing his greatest danger when he had come to feel secure; and because the hero now has to 'repeat the stabilizing and possessive operation he has performed first upon himself and then upon his island' – but now he has to do this with others. What Crusoe really seeks is 'to re-enact the mastery he has already achieved'.[8] Certainly the footprint marks the moment of change from total isolation to a (potentially, and then actually) shared island existence. There is a clear irony, too: isolation, which had seemed at first so threatening and destructive, now appears reassuring to Crusoe. When first cast ashore, he had sought desperately for signs of life; the footprint induces terror that there *may* be someone else alive, after all.[9]

Crusoe's response is described as 'innumerable fluttering Thoughts, like a Man perfectly confus'd and out of my self' (p. 154); he flees to his cave like a 'Fox to Earth'. His collapsed state that night has odd parallels with his reaction in Lisbon, much later, when he finds how rich he has grown in his absence: 'It is impossible to express here the Flutterings of my very Heart, when I look'd over these Letters. . . . In a word, I turned pale, and grew sick; and had not the old Man run and fetch'd me a Cordial, I believe the sudden Surprize of Joy had overset Nature, and I had dy'd upon the Spot' (pp. 284–5). Partly the similarity may arise from the limited repertoire of physiological gesture which Defoe employs on all emotional occasions; but the shock of recognition has more particular points of comparison in these two cases. Crusoe had thought himself alone, and realises he may have had savages for company *all along*. It is three days before he will risk stirring abroad, a period he appears to spend mostly in bed. In the later instance he has to be bled by a physician after 'some Hours' of dangerous illness. He had believed himself an elderly adventurer, long given over for dead, without family or friends. In Lisbon he discovers he has money, an estate and surviving contacts, who have looked after his interests with particular diligence. In one case, Crusoe suffers a collapse because he may not be alone, and is thus threatened; in the other, he swoons away because he may not be alone, and is thus restored to the height of fortune.

The seemingly fortuitous circumstances in which Crusoe comes on the footprint ('It happen'd one Day about Noon going towards by Boat . . .') emphasise an unlooked-for quality in the event, and this in turn reinforces the slightly grotesque aspect of encountering a single print. Its perfectly defined contours ('Toes, Heel, and every Part of a Foot') suggest perhaps the deliberate gesture of an unknown adversary, some mysterious 'other' who shares Crusoe's human status and challenges his unquestioned title to the island. Crusoe has lost something of physical identity during his captivity; he is covered in coarse garments, never goes out without his hat on, frequently skulks behind his laboriously made 'Umbrella' (pp. 134–5). His time has been spent learning mechanic arts and generally recivilising himself after his original hapless arrival. Now the naked footprint appears to remind him of unaccommodated man – in fact that very state of nature he has been busy putting behind him. Of course, there is a direct threat to his life – he can only assume, rightly as it turns out, that it must be a cannibal race who visit the island, and so his fear of being devoured surfaces again. But there is also a kind of metaphysical dilemma raised, rather as though Ronald Knox's ineffable God had mischievously left tracks in the quad. To put it more seriously, the devout Puritan would certainly see in such a graphic 'sign' a clue to some divine purpose. This is strengthened by the fact that the print is found in a part of the island little frequented by Crusoe. Has he perhaps been missing God's signals as he occupies himself in his own quasi-domestic routine?

Another interpretation of the event stresses its function within the pattern of Crusoe's conversion. J. Paul Hunter, for example, argues that the discovery of the print 'temporarily disrupt[s] the newfound order of his existence and almost causes him to lose his spiritual foothold before he can understand the event and use it as an aid to ultimate deliverance'. But in the end Crusoe is able to overcome this relapse into fear and superstition, 'as the footprint materalizes into creatures who intrude upon his philosophy and force him to expand his Christianity from an individual level to a social one'.[10] Whether or not we accept so spiritualised a reading, it is undeniable that the episode prepares us for the arrival of Friday. In fact there is an interval of some eight years between the two occurrences, but the gradual acceleration in the narrative means that only forty pages have elapsed. Meanwhile there have been alarms or promises of human company for Crusoe (as he variously interprets them): the sight of the bones remaining from a cannibal feast, the goat in his cave among the woods, the nine savages on the shore, and finally the wrecked Spanish ship. As Ellis observes, the narrative of *RC1* is 'rich in suspense and surprise'.[11] Defoe constantly prepares us for one event (say, the reappearance of the savages) and then intercuts another (the Spanish wreck). What the footprint does is to set in motion a chain of events and reactions in Crusoe's mind. Until he comes on the print, the emphasis has been on spiritual and material regeneration: his task has been to learn to live with solitude. From that time forwards, there is always the hint of an escape route, but also the possibility that all his work will be undone and his advancement crushed. The episode shifts our attention from the present to the future.

Again the most fully worked-out structural account is that of Douglas Brooks. He sees the print as both thematically and structurally central, 'appearing, as it does, exactly halfway through the novel, that is, in the first edition, on pp. 81–2 out of a total of 364'. Defoe underlines this positioning by three references: (1) to the time of day ('about Noon'); (2) to 'the rising Ground'; (3) to the mid-point in the preceding paragraph ('about half Way between my other Habitation, and the Place where I had laid up my Boat'). This indicates in Brooks's judgement a debt to the iconographical tradition of 'elevation at the centre'. Likewise the temporal directive (noon) points to an 'identification of the midday sun with the *Sol iustitiae* and the consequent interpretation of noon as a time of trial and judgment'. There is confirmation for this view, Brooks contends, in Crusoe's poem upon the sun in *RC3* (pp. 133–4), which 'structurally affirms the sun's sovereignty in [a] centrally placed triplet'. Similarly the mid-point of *RC2* is marked by a special accent, the baptism of Will Atkins's wife and the Christian marriage ceremony (p. 161). Brooks goes on to argue that the footprint is a trial of Crusoe's spiritual strength and serves to define 'the beginnings of his re-education'. Round this axis Brooks detects a series of echoes and parallels between Crusoe's early life on the island and his later experiences there.[12]

As a whole this makes a coherent and intelligible view of the book, not fundamentally dissimilar from the orthodox reading but putting much more emphasis on planned symmetry. Most readers will probably share Brooks's impressions concerning the underlying meaning of the novel, although they may not all follow him in finding numerological causes for every effect. While it is interesting that the common device of 'elevation' should briefly enter the text at the central moment, and that there should be a reference to midday, the mode of allusion is certainly very oblique. Moreover, there are chance occurrences of such things elsewhere – on 1 January in his first year, Crusoe's journal tells us, he lay still 'in the Middle of the Day' – but he goes down in the valley instead of climbing a hill (p. 75). (Can the nadir of Crusoe's spiritual condition be expressed by a mid-point declination?) Defoe was sufficiently in contact with older habits of thought to make fitful use of the structural devices they supported; and his reading of providential literature would undoubtedly familiarise him with techniques aimed to reflect divine correspondences within the formal layout of a book. The question is whether *Crusoe* is constructed with enough architectonic concern to render its narrative emblematic even down to such tiny details. Brooks has certainly uncovered more symmetry than anyone before him; it remains open for others to confirm or rebut his particular findings.

EXPRESSIVE DEVICES

Defoe's use of first-person narration is a regular feature of his novels. Even in *Memoirs of a Cavalier* and *A New Voyage Round the World*, where the hero is not given a proper identity, the method is retained. As everyone knows, Defoe adopts a female guise in *Moll Flanders* and *Roxana*, though many people have felt that a masculine personality shows through. In my judgement Crusoe is the character most perfectly in tune with the given mode of narration, for reasons I have previously set out:

Defoe habitually employs a factual, literal, rather unvaried manner. Events succeed one another in an apparently routine way; there are not many signs of climax or emotional dynamics. Now it happens that Crusoe, by birth and training, is exactly suited to conveying this account of experience. A man of his upbringing at this date would be likely to display the literary (as well as personal) qualities with which the book endows him. He would be intent, not just on survival, but on coming through morally. He would enter a dogged journal of the most minute particulars (even if it meant telling us the same things twice). English puritanism of this era heavily endorsed a sort of spiritual book-keeping. And in any case Crusoe, with his mercantile background, would be likely to see his existence on the island as a series of day-to-day transactions with the environment. The flat style and cautious descriptions register precisely the right quantity of thoughts and feelings.

The conclusion reached was that 'the circumstantial, level-paced style beautifully registers this unending diurnal flow. Never again did Defoe find a subject so congenial to his own habits of composition.' The contrast might be drawn, say, with Moll: 'It was one thing for Crusoe, with his background, to be a devoted chronicler of his own sensations. It is quite another with Moll, who has lived life for the moment, yet tells her story with detached comprehension.'[13] I would add to this that the balance-sheet was a common motif in some modes of literature at this juncture – witness Swift's bills of gratitude comparing Marlborough with a Roman general.[14] For Crusoe to tot up the victims in his fight with the savages (*RC1*, p. 237) is similarly an extension of enumerating devices common in expository prose and particularly favoured by Defoe: many of his pamphlets and *Review* papers itemise facts in a seriatim manner, where modern literary decorum would prescribe a more discursive treatment. Defoe's innovation is perhaps to incorporate such lists in a fictional context.

The dialogue form employed during the education of Friday goes back to the question-and-answer mode of instruction popularised by John Dunton in the 1690s; it was Dunton who gave Defoe some of his first opportunities. By 1719, of course, books like *The Family Instructor* had made sustained use of quasi-dramatic writing; and, indeed, Defoe's anxieties regarding the morality of stage-plays are accompanied by a real interest in drama, something that was not true of all Jeremy Collier's adherents. Crude as the transition from straight narrative may appear to us, we must remember that different conventions operated, according to different psychological habits: Crusoe himself in *RC3* can suddenly launch into verse, and that would be impossibly self-conscious today. Yet film-makers are permitted to switch from colour into monochrome, for a particular effect, and television producers are seemingly compelled by some higher ordinance to present certain actions (high dives or car crashes) in slow motion. If the prolonged exchanges between Crusoe and Will Atkins (*RC2*, pp. 150–3) and then Atkins and his wife (pp. 154–9) seem lifeless, that is because Defoe has not imagined them with enough sharpness or intensity: the dialogue form itself is not to blame.

As for the journal in *RC1*, its most conspicuous feature is its strict redundance. Crusoe admits before he begins to quote from it that the foregoing particulars will be told all over again (p. 69). However, the journal is prolonged considerably beyond the point reached in the main narrative; and the crucial episode of his fever and impulse towards conversion is related in this way. After about a year the ink begins to run out, and Crusoe decides 'to write down only the most remarkable Events of my Life, without continuing daily *Memorandum* of other Things' (p. 104). This enables Defoe, first, to slide back into direct narrative; and, secondly, to give less detailed attention to his regular doings. In a way the journal serves to free the narration from direct dependence on chronology (when it is dropped, the time-scale can be slipped out of gear), and that is exactly what Tristram Shandy finds he cannot do. Had Tristram been on the island we should only have reached the nine-months 'awakening' sequence by the end of the book.

Other devices belong, arguably, to the repertoire of structural aids.[15] The framing technique, with a pre-island phase matched by a post-island segment, has already been mentioned. Despite the efforts of recent commentators to justify the Pyrenean journey (pp. 289–302), I doubt if many readers have ever been able to look on this as other than anticlimax. In *RC2* we have an early and rather hamhanded use of flashback: Crusoe awkwardly tries to creep out of a narrative he has dominated from the start.

> I shall no longer trouble the story with a relation in the first person, which will put me to the expense of ten thousand said I's, and said he's, and he told me's, and I told him's, and the like; but I shall collect the facts historically as near as I can gather them out of my memory from what they related to me, and from what I met with in my conversing with them, and with the place.
>
> In order to do this succinctly, and as intelligibly as I can, I must go back to the circumstance in which I left the island, and in which the persons were of whom I am to speak. And first it is necessary to repeat, that I had sent away Friday's father and the Spaniard, the two whose lives I had rescued from the savages: I say, I had sent them away in a large canoe to the main, as I then thought it. . . . (p. 38)

There may be people alive who will attribute the effects here to conscious artistry; but the bumbling syntax and overlapping time-scales are surely the kind of high incompetence to which Defoe was prone when he aimed to be skilful. Crusoe talks of making inquiries so that he might 'begin where [he] left off' (p. 39), an exact statement of Defoe's narrational imperative. Having issued his trailer at the end of *RC1* he has no room for plotting manœuvre. The result is a loss of momentum until he can get Crusoe away from the island a hundred pages later. It may be true of some writers that technique is vision, and certainly formal elaboration can enhance the revelatory power of fiction in the hands of a Fielding, a Dickens or a Joyce. With Defoe too much technique simply obstructed his vision.

On the analogy of the dog who did not bark, the chapter divisions which are not made merit brief scrutiny. Adaptations generally insert breaks of this kind, and even where that is not attempted reprints sometimes supply a kind of synopsis in place of the contents list. None of Defoe's fiction pure and simple uses chapters, although his didactic works (some containing fictional episodes) often do. *RC3* is, of course, set out in seven distinct sections. *Crusoe* would lose some of its relentless sense of one day on the island succeeding another, one year another, if breaks were introduced; but otherwise not much harm would be done.

STYLE

The earliest discussions of the language used in *Crusoe* were philological in nature. A characteristic undertaking is that of Gustaf L. Lannert, published in 1910: *The Language of Robinson Crusoe, Compared with that of Other 18th Century Works.* Lannert began by comparing the autograph manuscript of *The Compleat English Gentleman* with a proof-sheet that happens to survive; his aim was principally to reach a view on Defoe's orthographic habits. He concluded that the writer himself used little punctuation and that the printers had tidied up Defoe's spelling according to accepted norms, on the evidence of the sample from *The Compleat English Gentleman.* By extension he assumed this to have happened in the case of *Crusoe* also. Intending at the outset to 'call attention to the points in which the language of Robinson Crusoe deviates from present day standard English', Lannert widened his inquiry to consider the phonology and accidence of the book as they consorted with eighteenth-century habits. His judgement was that Defoe's style, contrary to an impression then prevailing, was *not* particularly archaic. However, Lannert stressed a predilection for long sentences which produce 'great verbosity' in the novel. He was followed four years later by Franz Horten, who conducted almost the same tests and reached similar conclusions.[16] Both critics were occupied by spelling to an extent which would now seem surprising. Their inquiries served to reinforce the orthodox Victorian opinion that Defoe wrote in a 'simple' and unsophisticated manner, without literary flourish and without great care.

Recent commentators have been prepared to give Defoe more credit for linguistic finesse. For example, James T. Boulton has examined rhetorical effect and dramatic skill in Defoe's prose; he stresses the proverbial element in much of the imagery and illustrates the quality of personal involvement which animates the style.[17] Following up Mrs Barbauld's description of 'minuteness', Ian Watt remarks that Defoe's writing

> obeys more fully than ever before the purpose of language as Locke redefined it: 'to convey knowledge of things'. Defoe concentrates his description on the primary qualities of objects as Locke saw them: especially solidity, extension, and number; and he gives them in the simplest language – Defoe's prose contains a higher percentage of words of Anglo-Saxon origin than that of any other well-known writer, except Bunyan. . . . The lack of strong pauses within the sentence gives his style an urgent, immediate, breathless quality; at the same time, his units of meaning are so small, and their relatedness is made so clear by frequent repetition and recapitulation, that he nevertheless gives the impression of perfectly simple lucidity.[18]

Some of these recapitulative formulas, along with typical devices such as 'economic statements' (for example, 'To bring the story short . . .') have been described by Arthur Sherbo. The same critic tabulates the imagery used in Defoe's novels, but the yield is predictably scanty – no one would be able to develop an approach to the inner meaning of these works based on the model of Shakespearian image-patterns.[19]

A most interesting recent discussion is that of George A. Starr, which raises a number of important historical issues. Starr justifiably questions the view that 'exact, objective description' is used – for example – to introduce Friday. Crusoe, as the critic sees it, 'endows Friday with his own humanity'; he projects his own feelings and values on to the newcomer. Starr disputes Watt's view that there is a 'wholly referential' quality in the language. He admits the strong element of *things* in Defoe's prose, but sees these as placed in psychological, aesthetic and moral terms by the narrator's intervention. In these novels the characters 'are not secure, detached observers of the world, but actors in it, vulnerable to it and intent on triumph over it'; the style reflects this buffeting relationship between speaker and external world, and brings 'human significance' to the bare material facts.[20]

The only book-length study of the topic in recent years is that of E. Anthony James, who conducts a 'rhetorical study of prose style and literary method'. He devotes a substantial chapter to *Crusoe* under the title 'Isolation Dramatized'. James argues that Defoe makes Crusoe 'a habitual semantic quibbler'; the hero's perplexity when cast away is 'nicely registered in his frequent inability to provide clear and concrete descriptions of the tasks he undertakes'. This is evident in the fuzzy pairings of synonyms and near-synonyms, the endless qualifications, and the 'agonizing uncertainties' of Crusoe's attempts to make sense of his unfamiliar surroundings. James goes on to explore some particular verbal techniques, that is, the use by Crusoe of grandiose terms to boost his own confidence (seeing himself as a 'Lord of the Manor', etc.), and his extensive use of 'providence' and 'delivery' as richly ambiguous co-ordinates of his moral dilemma on the island. James makes some sound discriminations and supplies a graphic account of the struggle to 'civilize the uncivilized'; he describes Crusoe's attempt to tot up the victims in his fight with the savages as written 'like an inventory of dry goods'. Overall James' treatment of the stylistic effects in *Crusoe* deserves fuller attention than it has received.[21]

Two particular features of the language seem to have been passed over by all commentators. One is the technique of what might be called 'false adversatives', that is, the attempt to impart drama to an event or tension to an internal debate by using expressions of contrariety where they were not necessary or logical. This occurs throughout the work, and a good sustained example can be found in *RC2* (pp. 225–6: in this case I quote from the Everyman text, which preserves the original sentence-structure).[22]

We call'd again to the foremost boat, and offer'd a truce to parley again, and to know what was her business with us; *but* had no answer, *only* she crowded close under our stern; upon this our gunner, who was a very dextrous fellow, run out his two chase-guns, and fired again at her; *but* the shot missing, the men in the boat shouted, wav'd their caps, and came on; *but* the gunner getting quickly ready again, fir'd among them the second time; one shot of which, *tho'* it miss'd the boat it self, *yet* fell in among the men, and we could easily see, had done a great deal of mischief among them; *but* we taking no notice of that, war'd the ship again, and brought our quarter to bear upon them; and firing three guns more, we found the boat was split almost to pieces; in particular, her rudder and a piece of her stern was shot quite away, so they handed their sail immediately, and were in great disorder; *but* to compleat their misfortune, our gunner let fly two guns at them again; where he hit them we could not tell, *but* we found the boat was sinking, and some of the men already in the water. . . . (italics mine)

It would make perfectly good sense to rewrite this passage inserting connectives like 'and' or 'so' in place of the words italicised. The adversative sense is very weak in most cases; in a phrase like 'but to compleat their misfortune' it is really a cumulative rather than a contradictory impression which Crusoe is supplying. Something of the same sort may be present in the 'money' passage (see above, p. 80); 'However' is used where an expression such as 'in the event' might do. Similarly in the middle of the 'footprint' paragraph Crusoe wheels about on a 'but' that reflects no change in understanding or reaction (p. 154); the sense is 'Well, faced with this, all I could do was to go home . . .'. Defoe the casuist inserts a measure of irresolution into the simplest acts. His adversative particles impart motion and conflict where there is only mild puzzlement.

The second technique is in my view the single most characteristic feature of Defoe's prose in his works of fiction. If a 'new' novel were to turn up, putatively ascribed to Defoe, this would be as reliable a test as any I know to check its authenticity. I refer to a pair of allied usages which might be termed respectively *approximating* and *alternative* counts. The former is the use of a figure with some expression of vagueness – as in 'about a mile', 'near two hours', 'almost six o'clock', 'in a week or less', 'towards midnight'. The last example does not strictly involve a figure, and there are allied usages which I have excluded ('about the middle of May', for instance). I also omit from calculation the formula 'no less than a mile', which generally seems to indicate one mile exactly rather than a mile plus. The *alternative* count takes the form 'two or three', 'once or twice', 'a week or two', 'that week or the next', '60 or 80 barrels', and so on. Sometimes the two techniques occur together, as in 'about four or five days later'. In that event I have entered the phrase in both calculations.[23]

The results are little short of astonishing (an appropriate construction). In *RC1* I have noted 110 approximating phrases, though there must be more; in *RC2* the tally is 197. The count for alternative expression is *RC1* 111, *RC2* 165. Again, these are sure to be underestimates. They occur consistently throughout the book; there are occasional thick clusters, as when Crusoe is stocking up or beating the bounds, but there is never a gap of more than (shall I say) two or three pages. We have already encountered both techniques in crucial episodes such as that of the money and the footprint.

The ubiquity of these formulas casts a strange light on Defoe's well-known love for quantifying and specifying. There is a kind of verisimilitude, perhaps, in vagueness concerning the details of an event which took place forty years prior to the supposed narration. But this cannot be the justification for many approximating phrases. When Crusoe says that the wreck had been driven aground 'about two Miles on my right Hand' (p. 48), he can never have known the *exact* distance; no one would have assumed if he had said merely 'two Miles' that he had verified the precise figure with an accurate measuring instrument. The vagueness is supererogratory; it goes beyond the real communicative needs of the passage. There is, however, a distinct advantage when Crusoe can afford a measure of sudden precision: the sixty pieces of eight paid for Xury (p. 33) or the 'eight and twenty Years, two Months, and 19 Days' of captivity (p. 278), whose exactitude happens to be a miscount. I should add that the technique is equally apparent in other novels; I have discussed its appearance in *Moll Flanders*,[24] and it stands out very clearly in *Roxana* and the *New Voyage*. This studied vagueness became a tic which Defoe could not control, and indeed he was probably quite aware of its prevalence in his books. (There is less evidence of the mannerism in his non-fiction, although by no means unknown: there are scores of examples in the *Tour*.) The effect is often to suggest compulsive mensuration even where accurate counting is not possible.

The main feature of the style is a kind of dogged fidelity, not just to fact but also to *impression*. Watt is certainly right to emphasise the direct registration of concrete particulars, and the relatively subdued role allotted to colour, texture or flavour. Starr is equally correct in pointing to a subjective element in the writing, which filters facts through the narrator's consciousness. The appeal of the book lies in its immediacy of observation allied to a reflective awareness – a strong present-tense quality infused with a sense of retrospection. At its best the writing has a muddled accuracy and an organised spontaneity. Take for example the first storm off Yarmouth roads:

By this Time it blew a terrible Storm indeed, and now I began to see Terror and Amazement in the Faces, even of the Seamen themselves. The Master, tho' vigilant to the Business of preserving the Ship, yet as he went in and out of his Cabbin by me, I could hear him softly to himself say several times, *Lord be merciful to us, we shall be all lost, we shall be undone*; and the like. During these first Hurries, I was stupid, lying still in my Cabbin, which was in the Steerage, and cannot describe my Temper: I could ill reassume the first Penitence, which I had so apparently trampled upon, and harden'd myself against: I thought the Bitterness of Death had been past, and that this would be nothing too like the first. But when the Master himself came by me, as I said just now, and said we should be all lost, I was dreadfully frightened; I got up out of my cabbin, and look'd out; but such a dismal Sight I never saw; The Sea went Mountains high, and broke upon us every three or four Minutes: When I could look about, I could see nothing but Distress round us: Two Ships that rid near us we found had cut their Masts by the Board, being deep loaden; and our Men cry'd out, that a ship which rid about a Mile a-head of us was foundered. Two more Ships being driven from their Anchors, were run out of the Roads to Sea at all Adventures, and that was not a Mast standing. The light Ships fared the best, as not so much labouring in the Sea; but two or three of them drove, and came close by us, running away with only their Sprit-sail out before the Wind. (pp. 10–11)

There are awkward repetitions here ('terrible'/'Terror'); the second sentence is a tangle of dislocated syntax; the third is limply constructed with insufficient connectives; and so on. But these defects are overcome by the directness of observation, by which the jumble of impressions (approximating and alternative counts to the fore) is conveyed to us. Defoe locates with remarkable skill, deploying simple prepositions like 'up', 'out' and 'by' with great effect. We have a clear picture of the frightened youth skulking in the cabin; but we are equally made aware of the adult narrator ('as I said just now'). The style is all elbows; yet it is superbly fitted for rendering the flux of experience. There were plenty of gifted prose writers about in 1719: Swift, Berkeley, Bolingbroke, Congreve, whilst Addison lay on his deathbed. None of them would have been capable of writing this passage, for their eloquence stifled incoherence at birth. One of the great things about *Robinson Crusoe* is the way the prose never quite gets a firm hold on its materials: the style has a struggle on its hands, just as the hero does.[25]

Consider finally a passage occurring at the centre of Crusoe's island solitude:

June 28. Having been somewhat refresh'd with the Sleep I had had, and the Fit being entirely off, I got up; and tho' the Fright and Terror of my Dream was very great, yet I consider'd, that the Fit of Ague wou'd return again the next Day, and now was my Time to get something to refresh and support my self when I should be ill; and the first Thing I did, I fill'd a large square Case Bottle with Water, and set it upon my Table, in Reach of my Bed; and to take off the chill or aguish Disposition of the Water, I put about a Quarter of a Pint of Rum into it, and mix'd them together; then I got me a Piece of the Goat's Flesh, and broil'd it on the Coals, but could eat very little; I walk'd about, but was very weak, and withal very sad and heavy-hearted in the Sense of my miserable Condition; dreading the Return of my Distemper the next day; at Night I made my Supper of three of the Turtle's Eggs, which I roasted in the Ashes, and eat, as we call it, in the Shell; and this was the first Bit of Meat I had ever ask'd God's Blessing to, even as I cou'd remember, in my whole Life.

The prose capitalises on standard 'diary' elements, such as the mention of time of day, or the staccato presentation of different events. We are reminded of the terrible dream which Crusoe had endured on the previous day, and then impelled to think of the fever's likely return on the following day. This has the effect of fixing 28 June in a particular sequence of happenings: the style draws a graph of physical and spiritual rhythms, just as Puritan self-examination would prompt. Words like 'Condition' are, of course, apt both to medical and religious concerns. Defoe's subtler skill lies in his use of the apparently rambling journal entry to enact Crusoe's listless and apprehensive state of mind.

At the start of the passage, Crusoe is positive enough, making plans and taking prudent courses of action – 'I considered', 'now was my Time', 'to take off the chill'. But this purposeful mood, established by 'then', 'now', 'yet', is dispelled when he tries to eat: suddenly we have 'I walk'd about', without the familiar introductory particle. The loose participial phrase which begins 'dreading the Return' has an absolute, untethered air to it. The slackness of Defoe's syntax is not always a virtue, but here it brilliantly evokes the mood of ominous waiting. On the other hand, the last part of the sentence is quite tautly constructed. Defoe has Crusoe insert his parenthetic thought, 'even as I cou'd remember', just where it will be most effective. The placing emphasises his concluding words, 'in my whole Life'; but it also reinforces his vague neglect of God in earlier years.

The style is indeed concrete and particular ('a large square Case Bottle'). The approximating phrase 'about a Quarter of a Pint of Rum' conveys the sense that Crusoe was concocting his own recipe, without any accurate measuring-vessels to hand. The three eggs suggest husbanded resources and, once more, a kind of medicinal regime. But the specifics are all governed by a general awareness of Crusoe's melancholy state. Throughout *RC1* Defoe shows an extraordinary power of verbal realisation: the hero's inner and outer health controls every nervous inflection of the prose. We perceive, with Crusoe, his partial recovery from the fever before we witness his decision to get up; the goat's meat is chosen and cooked, and then the sentence runs out of energy as Crusoe's appetite languishes. There is perhaps no book in the English language where the rhythm and ordering of words twine so closely around event and impression. Put alongside *Crusoe*, *Mrs Dalloway* seems to me an abstracted and distant rendition of feeling.

NOTES

1   Hunter, pp. ix–xn. For other views on the relationship between *RC1* and *RC2*, see Everett Zimmerman, *Defoe and the Novel* (Berkeley, Calif., 1975), pp. 35–9. For *RC3* as 'put together to cash in on the great success' of its predecessors, see Watt, pp. 92–3.

2 E. M. W. Tillyard, *Shakespeare's History Plays* (London, 1944; Harmondsworth, 1969), p. 269.

3 D. Brooks, *Number and Pattern in the Eighteenth-Century Novel* (London, 1973), pp. 18–20; Ellis, pp 12–13.

4 Brooks, *Number and Pattern*, pp. 22–6.

5 Starr, pp. 36–7.

6 D. Genzel, 'Chronology in *Robinson Crusoe*', *PQ*, Vol. XL (1961), pp. 495–512; Ellis, P. 14.

7 William H .Halewood believes that the structure is paratactic: 'There is no single point to which rising action rises and from which falling action falls' ('Religion and intention in *Robinson Crusoe*'. reprinted in Ellis, p. 84).

8 J. J. Richetti, *Defoe's Narratives* (Oxford, 1975), pp. 50–2.

9 For the contrast between earlier security and later anxiety, see Crusoe's reflections in *RC1*, p. 196.

10 Hunter, pp. 180–2.

11 Ellis, p. 14.

12 Brooks, *Number and Pattern*, pp. 20–2. It is interesting that Brooks does not attempt to make anything of the 364 pages in the first edition, a bait few numerologists could resist.

13 P. Rogers, *The Augustan Vision* (London, 1974), pp. 260–1, 265.

14 *Examiner*, No. 16 (23 November 1710), in *The Prose Works of Jonathan Swift*, ed. Herbert Davis (Oxford, 1939–68), Vol. III, p. 23; answered by a rival Whig balance-sheet drawn up in the *Medley* on 4 December 1710: see *The Medleys for the Year 1711*, octavo edn (London, 1712), pp. 112–13.

15 Dreams might be regarded as one such device, although I cannot regard these as quite so fundamental as do Brooks and some other critics.

16 G. L. Lannert, *The Language of Robinson Crusoe* (Uppsala and Cambridge, 1910), pp. xix–xx, 3, 6, 18; Franz Horten, *Studien über die Sprache Defoe's* (Bonn, 1914), pp. 3–104.

17 J. T. Boulton (ed.), *Daniel Defoe* (London, 1965; reprinted as *Selected Writings*, Cambridge, 1975), pp. 1–22.

18 Ian Watt, 'Defoe as novelist', *From Dryden to Johnson*, ed. B. Ford (Harmondsworth, 1957), p. 207; cf. Watt, pp. 105–6.

19 Arthur Sherbo, *Studies in the Eighteenth Century English Novel* (East Lansing, Mich., 1969), pp. 159–65. Sherbo provides an astringent alternative to the more uncritical readings of Defoe.

20 G. A. Starr, 'Defoe's prose style: 1. The language of interpretation', *MP*, Vol. LXXI (1974), pp. 277–94.

21 E. Anthony James, *Daniel Defoe's Many Voices* (Amsterdam, 1972), pp. 165–99.

22 Daniel Defoe, *Robinson Crusoe* (London, 1945), p. 366.

23 Vague expressions like 'some hours', where no figure is indicated, are not counted.

24 P. Rogers, 'Moll's memory', *English*, Vol. XXIV (1975), pp. 67–72. I have discussed the stress on quantity in the *Tour* in an article, 'Literary art in Defoe's *Tour*: the rhetoric of growth and decay', *ECS*, Vol. VI (1973), pp. 153–85.

25 Relevant here is Zimmerman's view that Defoe's writing 'is not always perfectly adapted to Crusoe': see his interesting argument in *Defoe and the Novel*, pp. 25–6.

CHAPTER 7

Critical History*

THE EIGHTEENTH CENTURY

If one were to judge simply by the mass of opprobious references, Defoe was already one of the least popular authors who ever lived when he came to write *Robinson Crusoe*. Evidence for this statement can be found in W. L. Payne's 'Bibliography of eighteenth-century pamphlets mentioning Daniel Defoe by name, initials, or the title of one of his works'. This runs to 165 items, and it in fact covers only the years 1700–31 – *ad hominem* criticism would dry up almost immediately with Defoe's death, but not, as we shall see, all references. Moreover, Payne's list excludes newspaper comments, which are numerous, and even within its limits the compiler admits that it is far from complete. (My own 'Selective List', published in *CH* a year earlier, included several items not in Payne, and since then other items have come to light.) Despite these considerations, Payne did assemble as many as 165 examples, the overwhelming majority of them hostile in tone. It is worth recalling that J. V. Guerinot, who may well have scored nearer to the maximum, could find only 158 pamphlet attacks on Alexander Pope – not the best-loved man of his time – in addition to a short appendix of more friendly items.[1]

Robinson Crusoe had very little to do with this tide of abuse. The heaviest concentration appears in the first fifteen years of the century and, though the phrasing is often pointed and personal, the real thrust of these attacks is political. Some of the animus died away as the topical issues faded; in 1719–20 the hack compiler of a biographical dictionary called *The Poetical Register* thought two poems worth mention as 'very much admir'd by some Persons' – they were *The True-Born Englishman* and *Jure Divino*, 'a Poem of considerable Bulk in Folio'.[2] Defoe thus joined such eminent contemporaries as Mr Henry Crisp, Sir William Dawes (Archbishop of Canterbury), the Reverend James Gardiner, the Honourable Simon Harcourt, Mr G. Jacob (the hack compiler in person), Doctor K. (a gentleman, author of a poem upon marriage), Mr John Oldmixon, Mr Ridout (a Chirurgeon), Mr Charles Tooke ('a Gentleman, I think, now living') and Mrs Wharton. Several of these get

---

* Fuller references to works discussed will be found in the Bibliography.

longer entries than Mr Daniel De Foe, whose name was also omitted
from the contents list – unlike those of Henry Crisp and the others.

At this stage it might appear natural for me to dilate upon the contemporary debate. In fact there was scarcely anything which could qualify
for such a description. Pope, who had put Defoe into *The Dunciad*
(1728) – for which he has still not been forgiven in some quarters – told
Joseph Spence that 'Defoe wrote many things, and none bad, though
none excellent'. He isolated *RC1* as 'good'.[3] For the rest, *Crusoe* is
treated mainly as a popular hack production; but so on the whole was
The Pilgrim's Progress. One contemporary, who had known Defoe for
over thirty years, wrote thus in 1728:

> The Itch of Answering is so great, that some Authors have taken it in
> Dudgeon, not to have been thought worthy of an Answer; and to
> prevent such Disgrace a second Time, have written on Purpose that
> they might answer themselves. I have heard, that the learned and
> ingenious *Robinson Crusoe* is in the Number of these.[4]

Here the critic perhaps has Defoe's earlier pamphleteering in mind, and
uses Robinson Crusoe simply as a variant for Defoe himself – unless he
can have supposed that Gildon's attack came from Defoe's pen, which
seems extraordinary. For the most part people were inclined to think
that works of fiction belonged in the servants' quarters:

> Down in the kitchen, honest Dick and Doll
> Are studying Colonel Jack and Flanders Moll.[5]

Nobody at that time could have predicted that the novel would come to
occupy a prime suite in the house of literature, or that Crusoe and Moll
would rise so far in the world.

Contemporary readers were rebuked because they would 'waste their
Time about such Stuff as *Robinson Cruso's*, *Gullivers*, *&c.*'[6] The book
was seen as part of a process of entropy; *Richard Falconer* (see p. 12)
carried a preface deploring the sight of Shakespeare and Ben Johnson
giving way to *Robinson Crusoe* and *Colonel Jack*, 'as well as *Dryden*
and *Otway* to *Moll Flanders* and *Sally Salisbury*'.* Oddly, to our way of
thinking, *Crusoe* was often aligned with criminal lives:

> Such are the fabulous Adventures and Memoirs of *Pirates*, *Whores*,
> and *Pickpockets*, wherewith for some time past the Press has so
> prodigiously swarmed. Your *Robinson Crusoe's*, *Moll Flanders's*, *Sally
> Salisbury's*, and *John Shephard's*, have afforded notable Instances how

---

* Sally Salisbury, *née* Pridden (*c.*1690–1724), a courtesan, was accused of
stabbing a lover; she died in Newgate. There are many biographies more or less
tied to reality; it is not inconceivable that Defoe may have contributed to this
flood.

easy it is to gratify our Curiosity, and how indulgent we are to the *Biographers* of *Newgate*, who have been as greedily read by People of the better sort, as the Compilers of *Last Speeches* and *Dying Words* by the Rabble.[7]

Defoe was a contributor to both branches of writing; apparently *Crusoe* belonged to the up-market end of popular reading, but nobody thought of the novel as any sort of high literature.

There is one shining exception to this paucity of comment. Soon after *Crusoe* appeared, it provoked on 28 September 1719 something between a critique and a parody, entitled *The Life and Strange Surprizing Adventures of Mr D—— De F—, of London*. This deservedly famous riposte was anonymous, but it has always been identified as the work of Charles Gildon (1665–1724), a professional writer of many years' standing on topics ranging from deism to drama.[8] The first part of the *Life* comprises a dialogue between Crusoe, Man Friday and Defoe himself; then comes an epistle 'to D—— D' F—e, the Reputed Author of Robinson Crusoe', dealing in turn with *RC1* and *RC2* (this last now some five weeks old). The publisher was James Roberts, whose name appears in the imprint of forty-odd Defoe items.[9] Elsewhere Gildon and Defoe were liable to find themselves yoked together in satiric portrayals of Grub Street, as happened indeed in *The Dunciad*. It is a piquant thought that the sharpest retort to *Crusoe* came from a fellow-scribbler, not from one of the lordly Augustans.

The opening dialogue is set near Newington Green (the novelist's home) in the early hours of the morning. Defoe enters, brandishing a pair of pistols, and finds himself approached by two strangely garbed men with muskets. These are, needless to say Crusoe and Friday. Defoe makes to run off, but his progeny reveal themselves and pour out a series of complaints. Crusoe laments the fact that he was created a 'strange whimsical, inconsistent Being . . . to ramble over three Parts of the World after I was sixty-five' – a dig principally at *RC2*. Defoe defends himself in a splendid burst of rhetoric, imitating perhaps the speech given to Edmund Curll in a prose satire by Pope three years earlier. A much-quoted snatch of dialogue ensues:

> *D——l.* You are my Hero, I have made you, out of nothing, fam'd from *Tuttle-Street* to *Limehouse-hole*; there is not an old Woman that can go to the Price of it, but buys thy Life and Adventures, and leaves it as a Legacy, with the *Pilgrim's Progress*, the *Practice of Piety*, and *God's Revenge against Murther*, to her Posterity.
> *Cru.* Your Hero! your Mob Hero! your *Pyecorner* Hero! On a Foot with *Guy* of *Warwick*, *Bevis* of *Southampton*, and the *London Prentice*! for *M-w-r* has put me in that Rank, and drawn me much better. . . .

D——l. Then know, my dear Child, that you are a greater Favorite
to me than you imagine; you are the true Allegorick Image of thy
tender Father D——1; I drew thee from the Consideration of my own
Mind; I have been all my Life that Rambling, Inconsistent Creature,
which I have made thee.*

Defoe then describes his own career in terms well established by
pamphleteers and critics in the previous twenty years; he is made to
present himself as a projector, a dabbler, a hackney author, a turncoat,
and so on. His style also comes in for sharp satire. Ultimately Crusoe
and Friday decide to make their creator swallow his own volumes, and
then toss him in a blanket – incidents which once more recall the Pope–
Curll skirmishes of 1716. Soon after Defoe emerges from a swoon and
finds he has been dreaming; but the fright he has experienced has caused
him to befoul himself – yet another parallel with the Curll story.[10]
Amusing as the dialogue is, only one important critical point emerges:
the suggestion of a personal allegory which remains a live issue even
today (see Chapter 4). The epistle proper which follows (including a
stop-press addition, covering *RC2*) is a more substantial attempt to come
to terms with the novel itself. Many of Gildon's points are literal and
some are trivial – small inconsistencies or failures of continuity. He is on
firmer ground when criticising Defoe's handling of the 'original sin';
though his insistence on the 'open' and 'disinterested' nature of seamen
has something of Thomas Rymer about it, yet he casts reasonable doubts
on the preferability of Crusoe's alternative profession, that of attorney.
Equally, he discerns real difficulties in the portrayal of Crusoe's repentance, and in the way Providence is employed to mark out Crusoe's path
for him. Gildon claims to be no enemy to 'Fables' as such, but he
condemns Defoe for telling improbable stories, with poorly motivated
characters, without any worthwhile moral to control the direction of his
narrative. Some of Gildon's objections still crop up, couched in different
language, and seldom so entertainingly argued. He probably stung Defoe,
and he undoubtedly stung the novel's official admirers for generations to
come. Sneering at the religious reflections (put in 'to swell the Bulk of

---

* Tuttle Street and Limehouse Hole were insalubrious quarters of London,
the former in Westminster, a little to the west of the Abbey, and the latter down-
river where the West India docks came subsequently to be built. *The Practice of
Piety* (1613) by Lewis Bayly and *God's Revenge against Murder* (1621–4) were
exceedingly popular Puritan manuals of conduct: see Hunter, p. 21. The works
mentioned by Crusoe were all famous folk-tales, well known as broadside ballads
and in chapbook versions. The first two were vulgarised romances, while the last
is presumably the seventeenth-century ballad used as the basis of George Lillo's
successful play *The London Merchant* (1731). M-w-r should be an engraver or
printseller, but I cannot identify him. *Pyecorner* has connotations of refuse and
street-trafficking; a real Pye Corner lay at the south end of Smithfield market.

your Treatise up to a five Shilling Book'), and identifying 'the Canaille' as the work's natural audience, Gildon inaugurated a hostile line of comment which will never quite die out.[11]

Defoe died in April 1731 – an event that drew from the Pope party's *Grub-street Journal* a sharp reference to 'that ancient ornament' of the scribbling fraternity.[12] In the following years Defoe's name was kept alive by successive versions of *The Dunciad* and occasional barbed comment. *Crusoe*, as we have seen (above, pp. 7–10), still appeared at regular intervals, although anonymously; Defoe's name is not regularly attached to the book until the nineteenth century. Other works frequently reprinted were *The Family Instructor* (Volume 1 reached what was called the 'sixteenth' edition in 1766: these are sometimes underestimates), *Religious Courtship* (at least twenty-two editions by 1800), and *The Complete English Tradesman*. The *Tour* was revised and augmented by Samuel Richardson; Defoe's name first appears on the title-page of the seventh edition (1769). The *History of the Pyrates* was much translated and abridged; often it was tacked on to lives of highwaymen and other criminals. Not until 1972 did this work appear with Defoe named as the compiler. Nor were the so-called secondary novels entirely lost to the world, although they commonly made their entrance as chapbooks or otherwise mangled. *Moll Flanders* was transmogrified into *Fortune's Fickle Distribution* and *The History of Laetitia Atkins*. Crusoe, at all events, was famous enough not to have to sail under borrowed colours. The book survived while the author was drifting into obscurity.

Defoe was, it is true, granted a place in *The Lives of the Poets* (1753), attributed to Theophilus Cibber but now ascribed to Robert Shiels. The first attempt to catalogue Defoe's works resulted in a meagre haul of thirteen items (one spurious); *Crusoe* and *Colonel Jack* are the only novels mentioned. Most of the entry, naturally, is devoted to Defoe as satiric poet; a good deal of weight is placed on his 'resolute temper' in facing adversity, a prefiguring of the Victorian hero. The general verdict is more complimentary than might have been expected at this date:

The natural abilities of the author (for he was no scholar) seem to have been very high. He had a great knowledge of men and things, particularly what related to the government, and trade of these kingdoms. He wrote many pamphlets on both, which were generally well received, though his name was never prefixed. His imagination was fertile, strong, and lively, as may be collected from his many works of fancy, particularly his Robinson Crusoe, which was written in so natural a manner, and with so many probable incidents, that, for some time after its publication, it was judged by most people to be a true story. It was indeed written upon a model entirely new, and the success and esteem it met with, may be ascertained by the many editions it has sold, and the sums of money which have been gained by it. Nor was he less remarkable in his writings of a serious and religious turn, witness his Religious Courtship, and his Family Instructor; both of which strongly inculcate the worship of God, the relative duties of husbands, wives, parents, and children, not in a dry dogmatic manner, but in a kind of dramatic way, which excites curiosity, keeps the attention awake, and is extremely interesting, and pathetic.[13]

By the standards of a popular handbook, at any date, this is excellent criticism; and one might be tempted to speculate that Samuel Johnson (who is believed to have given Shiels a fair amount of help) contributed some of these ideas. The only certain evidence of Johnson's opinions is to be found in *obiter dicta* reported by Boswell or Mrs Thrale. Once he compiled a list of Defoe's works of imagination, 'allowing a considerable share of merit to a man, who, bred a tradesman, had written so variously and so well. Indeed his *Robinson Crusoe* is enough of itself to establish his reputation.' On another occasion he delivered a more famous verdict: 'Was there anything yet written by mere man that was wished longer by its readers, excepting *Don Quixote, Robinson Crusoe,* and the *Pilgrim's Progress*?'[14]

Most mid-century comment is more patronising; Smollett refers contemptuously to 'a scurrilous party-writer in very little estimation'. It is chastening to think that this is very likely the reputation Defoe would still bear, had he died at the age of 58 – a slightly more successful Old-mixon or a more pious Toland. Goldsmith introduces Crusoe's longboat into *The Vicar of Wakefield* but omits all mention of Defoe in his estimate of Augustan literature. In the 1780s James Beattie attempted to find a home for *Crusoe* in the new literary province of prose fiction; 'serious romance' was as near as he could get, while he concurred with Rousseau in believing that 'this is one of the best books that can be put in the hands of children'.[15] Rousseau's tribute had come in the third book of *Emile* (1762), where he chooses *Crusoe* as the first (and for some time only) book to be studied by the growing boy: a course of practical living in a natural environment, away from society and 'all artificial aids', a symbolic experiment in natural education. Even Rousseau's critics found eloquence in such passages.[16]

THE BIOGRAPHERS

In the history of Defoe studies, biographers have taken an unusually large part. Rather as with Shakespeare, it was only when certain questions of fact – chronology, attribution, physical locations, etc. – had been sorted out that serious aesthetic consideration could begin. Many famous writers gave their view of *Crusoe,* as the next section will show.

Still, the most influential readings were those enshrined in large, earnest and pious works of biography. Between 1785 and 1925 there were eight full-length studies of Defoe, that is, general assessments rather than specialised monographs. Almost all of these were predominantly biographical, not critical. Each devoted considerable space to *Crusoe*, and indeed *RC1* furnished a hidden key to its author for some of these biographers. When Crusoe is not required in any other mythical role, he can be made without much trouble to play the part of an abstracted and idealised Defoe.

The first major contribution was that of George Chalmers (1742–1825), a Scottish antiquarian, who practised law at Baltimore for a time before returning to Britain. He wrote a good deal on colonial and commercial matters, besides a life of Tom Paine. In 1785 he published *The Life of Daniel De Foe*, which was subsequently reprinted with editions of the *History of the Union* (1786) and *Robinson Crusoe* (1790). The progress of Defoe studies can be gauged partly from the number of books confidently ascribed to him: Chalmers lists eighty, of which only two or three are now regarded as spurious, plus twenty-one dubious items, with more right than wrong attributions. Chalmers inquired what the particular charm of *Crusoe* was, to account for its astonishing popularity, and answered that 'few books have ever so naturally mingled amusement with instruction. The attention is fixed either by the simplicity of narration, or by the variety of the incidents; the heart is amended by *a vindication of the ways of God to man*: and the understanding is informed, by various examples, how much utility ought to be preferred to ornament: the young are instructed, while the old are amused.' A Ciceronian touch, not altogether appropriate to Defoe. Chalmers takes issue with Gildon and assesses the debt to Selkirk's story:

> Thus he may fairly have acquired the fundamental incident of Crusoe's life; but, he did not borrow the various events, the useful moralities, or the engaging style. . . . It was the happiness of De Foe, that . . . he excelled in narrating adventures by sea, with such felicities of language, such attractive varieties, such insinuative instruction, as have seldom been equalled, but never surpassed.

Chalmers saw Defoe a little in his own image – a 'learned and intelligent' historian, a writer on trade possessing 'originality and depth', a witty controversialist. The 'professed' poems are quickly dispatched, but 'if we regard the adventures of Crusoe, like the adventures of Telemachus, as a poem, his moral, his incidents, and his language, must lift him high on the poet's scale'. This was perhaps the first time that *Crusoe* was elevated to the epic kind. In his final summary Chalmers pronounces Defoe 'one of the ablest and most useful writers of our island'. The second epithet is noteworthy: nobody called Swift or Fielding 'useful' authors. Chalmers means not just didactic, but positive and morally healthy, too.[17]

If some self-identification may have got in the way of Chalmers, this was nothing beside the distractions imposed on the next biographer, Walter Wilson, by his religious preoccupations. Wilson (1781–1847) had been a bookseller as well as an India Office clerk; he had come to know Charles Lamb, whom he consulted during the making of his three-volume *Memoirs of the Life and Times of Daniel De Foe* (1830). Speaking generally, we must admire the treatment of the times rather more than that of the life. Twenty years earlier Wilson had written a history of dissent in London, and there are moments in the *Memoirs* when he seems to have reverted to the former subject. It is a ponderous, slow-wheeling galleon of a book, moralistic and wordy. All the same, it marked a real advance in understanding Defoe's career, particularly on the religious background. The checklist of works now runs to 210 items.

As for *Crusoe*, Wilson is notable for his high praise of the structure (he has *RC1* only in mind): 'As a narrative replete with incidents, it stands unrivalled for its natural and easy transitions from one part of the story to another, unincumbered by irrelative matter, or display of useless ornament. The whole machinery is strictly subservient to the main object of the story, and its various parts are so nicely adjusted, that nothing is wanting, to complete the chain, nor to heighten the interest.' Similarly he argues that the moral lessons of *Crusoe* 'are closely interwoven with the story, and are so just and pertinent in themselves, that they cannot be passed over, but the attention is irresistibly rivetted to them as an essential part of the narrative'. Wilson concludes:

> As De Foe wrote for the common people, who form the most numerous class of readers, he selected his subjects in accommodation to their habits and ideas; and his language is the fittest in the world to recommend them to their attention. Let the same stories be told in the classical style of our purest writers, and they would at once lose their impressive attraction; the charm would be broken, and they would bear about the same comparison with the great original, as [Simon] Patrick's *Parable of the Pilgrim* [1664], by the side of the *Pilgrim's Progress*.[18]

In a way this could be termed the start of the sociological approach to the novels: Wilson seems predictably hazy about the nature of Defoe's audience, but he is happy to assess the literary merits of *Crusoe* by reference to this group. Many reviewers took Wilson to task for his nonconformist bias, and one even produced a High Church version of events to counter him. A *Westminster Review* notice wondered whether

'the courageous exercise of their reasonable powers by men of the perse-
vering and untameable spirit of De Foe has not done more to distinguish
and exalt Great Britain than all the Horatian felicity or Cervantic
humour [Pope and Swift] . . . have ever displayed'.[19] The patriotic hero
Defoe is creeping up on us.

A better-known figure historically is John Forster (1812–76), the
friend and biographer of Dickens. Forster was well versed in the
eighteenth century; he composed lives of Goldsmith and Swift (incomplete) along with much miscellaneous journalism. His essay on Defoe
first appeared in the *Edinburgh Review* in 1845, as a review of two
editions of the works. It subsequently came out as the first half of a
production entitled *Daniel De Foe and Charles Churchill* (1855). The
essay is gracefully written, sharp and clear in its judgements. Its attitudes
are, to say the least, very much those of its time; for example, this
passage:

> De Foe is our only famous politician and man of letters, who
> represented, in its inflexible constancy, sturdy dogged resolution,
> unwearied perseverance, and obstinate contempt of danger and of
> tyranny, the great Middle-class English Character. We believe it to be
> no mere national pride to say, that, whether in its defects or its
> surpassing merits, the world has had none other to compare with it.

Wilson's true blue Protestant writer is never far away, and Forster
combines this with an unctuous allegorisation:

> And when he now retreated from the world Without to the world
> Within, in the solitariness of his unrewarded service and integrity, he
> had assuredly earned the right to challenge the higher recognition of
> Posterity. He was walking towards History with steady feet; and might
> look up into her awful face with a brow unabashed and undismayed.

It is a critical prose worthy of Florence Dombey. The heroic martyrdom
of Daniel De Foe was by now a received fact.

Naturally *Robinson Crusoe* elicits stirring sentiments from Forster:

> It is the romance of solitude and self-sustainment, and could only so
> perfectly have been written by a man whose life had for the most part
> been passed in the independence of unaided thought, accustomed to
> great reverses, of inexhaustible resource in confronting calamities,
> leaning ever on his Bible in sober and satisfied belief, and not afraid
> at any time to find himself Alone, in communion with nature and with
> God. Nor need we here repeat, what has been said so well by many
> critics, that the secret of its fascination is its Reality.

Forster was an intelligent man, whose life of Dickens allows many of the dark touches to show through when the pressures for hagiography must have been intense. But when he wrote of Defoe he could see little but persecuted virtue and injured merit: he mentioned with pointed relevance 'the fact that there is now living in Kennington, in deep though uncomplaining poverty, James De Foe, aged 77, the great grandson of the author of Robinson Crusoe'. *Crusoe* is seen as morally more beneficial than the ancient classics: 'Neither the *Iliad* nor the *Odyssey*, in the much longer course of ages, has incited so many to enterprise, or to reliance on their own powers and capacities.'[20]

One of the more engaging biographies was published in 1859. *The Life and Times of Daniel De Foe, with Remarks Digressive and Discursive* is the work of William Chadwick, of Arksey near Doncaster, a man about whom little seems to be known. Within a page or two Chadwick has given us a sample of his lively style, together with some interesting causes and effects:

> The pillory and the gaol shut up the hosier's shop, and gave us *Robinson Crusoe*. Yes! the grinder's wheel was stopped in Bedford streets and lanes; and years of imprisonment in the borough gaol gave us the *Pilgrim's Progress* instead. Blindness, neglect, and persecution, gave us the *Paradise Lost*. . . . Yes, and I verily believe that a good ducking in the Thames or Serpentine would force John Bright, the patriot of Rochdale, upon my Reform Bill, in the place of his own.

The author informs us that the book, composed by an 'untried' hand, took its origin from an excursion to the Yorkshire dales; in a sale-room he came across 'a book of travels through England, by some party unknown'. This proved to be Defoe's *Tour*, and it stimulated Chadwick's interest, resulting in 'deeper investigation into the erratic waywardness of this ingenious [author] . . . the writer of *Robinson Crusoe*, and (may I add also?) of the *Complete Tradesman* – a work which I consider second to none in the English language, and the work which formed the groundwork of the character of the great Benjamin Franklin, for that work is Franklin all over'. Such was Chadwick's introduction to 'the hero of these pages . . . one of Britain's greatest of geniuses'.

Just 440 pages later the biographer has traced the splendours and miseries of Defoe's first fifty-nine years, with – as promised – many remarks digressive and discursive. Defoe has been shown as an apostle of Free Trade, a doughty Whig (opposed by many a 'Tory-madman'), a patriot contending against papists and others in the French pay, a staunch dissenter surrounded by sycophantic tufthunters among the Anglican clergy. Defoe has been compared, not to his discredit, with Ebenezer Elliott; celebrated, above all, as a champion of liberty, a nineteenth-century liberal born before his time. We have learnt that Chadwick himself has been a tile-maker 'and about as successful as Defoe'. What we have not had is any discussion of Defoe's best-known books, that is, the series of novels and socio-economic works he wrote in his last twelve years. Chadwick must be the only critic ever to have devoted more space to *RC3* than to the first two parts: he actually gives a single page to *RC1*, the same amount to *RC2*, and then a further ten to *RC3*, mostly direct quotation of the text. This is assuredly one of the strangest items in the entire critical history, and yet it illuminates the context in which many Victorians must have read *Crusoe*. It was the very peak of Defoe's reputation as noble victim and visionary projector of the British Empire, a 'poor neglected genius' and a 'great and good' man born before his time.[21]

An inconvenient thing happened a few years later. Defoe managed to survive the use made of him in the first volume of *Das Kapital* (1867), but then William Lee, an official at the Board of Health, published his findings in the State Papers and elsewhere. The result was *Daniel Defoe: His Life and Recently Discovered Writings* (1869). Lee had found something nasty in Defoe's woodshed, that is, his work for the ministry after the accession of George I. He was led to these discoveries by the correspondence between Defoe and Charles Delafaye,[22] and went on to attribute many new items, including a whole series of periodical contributions which were reprinted in the second and third volumes of his work. This was certainly the most satisfactory biography to date, based on a far more comprehensive understanding of Defoe's complex nature than any predecessor had commanded. Lee was able to raise the total of Defoe books to 254 items, most of them attributed on safe grounds.

The biographer himself was not inclined to judge Defoe with immoderate harshness on the basis of this new evidence. But when word got through to his contemporaries the Victorian faith in Defoe began to experience its own mood of doubt. Lee's own concern was to set the record straight; he thought that Wilson had failed to bring out 'the large-hearted Catholicity of [Defoe's] religious character and principles', which is a considerable understatement.[23] On all factual points, including the circumstances which surrounded the appearance of *Crusoe*, Lee attains a far greater dependability than earlier biographers. He scotches the theory of Harley's composition, and goes some way to unravel the publishing history. He has nothing much to say about the novel from the critical angle, but he had done enough by dispelling legends and confusions. In fact Lee had performed a great service, merely by setting in motion a reappraisal of the old idealised image of a Daniel Defoe who could do no wrong. He was, incidentally, the first biographer to write 'Defoe' as one word, a change which somehow reflects the loss of critical innocence.

Ten years later came a volume in the English Men of Letters series, edited by John Morley. Its author was William Minto (1845–93), a Scottish journalist who later became a professor at Aberdeen University. The renown of this series guaranteed a wide readership; when the book was issued in a uniform edition (1885) copies had already reached their tenth thousand. As a popular guide Minto has much to commend him; he is less idolatrous than the early Victorians, but he writes with sympathy and a certain dry precision. From our present vantage-point the most important section is clearly the penultimate chapter, which is called 'The place of Defoe's fictions in his life'. It emphasises Defoe's background as a journalist, later something of a cliché but then a reasonable point to make. Minto's belief is that 'Defoe's novel-writing . . . grew naturally out of his general literary trade'; he argues the case with some care. His discussion of *Crusoe* is the most acute of any biographer so far considered. The central paragraph runs thus:

> But whatever it was that made the germ idea of *Robinson Crusoe* take root in Defoe's mind, he worked it out as an artist. Artists of a more emotional type might have drawn much more elaborate and affecting word-pictures of the mariner's feelings in various trying situations, gone much deeper into his changing moods, and shaken our souls with pity and terror over the solitary castaway's alarms and fits of despair. Defoe's aims lay another way. His Crusoe is not a man given to the luxury of grieving. If he had begun to pity himself, he would have been undone. Perhaps Defoe's imaginative force was not of a kind that could have done justice to the agonies of a shipwrecked sentimentalist; he has left no proof that it was; but if he had represented Crusoe bemoaning his misfortunes, brooding over his fears, or sighing with Ossianic sorrow over his lost companions and friends, he would have spoiled the consistency of the character. The lonely man had his moments of panic and his days of dejection, but they did not dwell in his memory. Defoe no doubt followed his own natural bent, but he also showed true art in confining Crusoe's recollections as closely as he does to his efforts to extricate himself from difficulties that would have overwhelmed a man of softer temperament. The subject had fascinated him, and he found enough in it to engross his powers without travelling beyond its limits for diverting episodes, as he does more or less in all the rest of his tales. The diverting episodes in *Robinson Crusoe* all help the verisimilitude of the story.

If this seems a rationalistic and stoical kind of Crusoe, who might well have spent his formative years at Aberdeen University, it is a fact that the Victorians chose to emphasise the strength and not the vulnerability of the hero. His fears on the island – a motif which so much preoccupies recent critics – hardly seem to exist for the nineteenth-century reader. It is of a piece with this emphasis that Minto should describe *all* Defoe's heroes and heroines as 'animated by [the] practical spirit' of the *Complete English Tradesman*: they are, he asserts, 'all tradesmen who have strayed into unlawful courses'. Finally he is puzzled by the power such heroic creatures hold over our mind. In some ways Minto is the first critic to ask the awkward questions about Defoe; his answers are, to modern taste, unduly comfortable, but that was to be expected.[24]

The next decade saw valuable biographical work by G. A. Aitken and Henry Morley (whose *Earlier Life and Chief Early Works* (1889), remains useful). It was not until 1894 that a major life appeared, however: its author was Thomas Wright (1859–1936), principal of the Cowper School, Olney, and a well-known authority on the poet Cowper. Wright's book was curiously organised in 100 short sections, each headed by the works Defoe produced in that phase. An appendix presented Lee's list of books, with a few small revisions. Almost forty years later, in 1931, Wright brought out a bicentenary edition or, rather, an extensive revision of the *Life* with fuller detail and the checklist now augmented to 258 items. There are good things in Wright's biography, and he had important new evidence (for example, information on Defoe's last years from his correspondence with Henry Baker, derived from descendants of the family). Unfortunately, he was apt on occasion to put more credence in theories than the evidence warranted.

This was the case with the story of Defoe's dealings with Selkirk. In his preface Wright asserted boldly, 'Thanks to the kindness of Mr Richard Champion Rawlins, I am able to settle once and for ever the vexed question as to whence Defoe obtained the bulk of the material upon which "Robinson Crusoe" is founded, and I give a photograph of the house of Mrs Damaris Daniel in Bristol, where Defoe met Selkirk'. Such contentious issues are commonly reluctant to lie down when the critic so bids them, and few authorities today would accept Wright's narrative as reliable. He placed the interview as taking place late in 1711 or early in 1712, at the home of Mrs Daniel in St James's Square, Bristol. Wright was clearly unaware, incidentally, that Damaris Wade did not become Mrs Daniel until 1752, forty years after the supposed meeting; in 1711 she had not yet married John Coysgarne, the Bristol merchant who himself did not move to St James's Square until 1715. Wright was positive that Selkirk did hand over his papers to Defoe, that there was nothing surreptitious about the transaction, and that Defoe did not pay out a large sum in return. Since there is no proof that any papers ever existed, let alone that Defoe met Selkirk in Bristol or anywhere else, it would be redundant to explore the terms of such a negotiation.

Wright was one of the few biographers to accept *Crusoe* as an allegorical reworking of Defoe's own life. He did not scruple, either, to

admit the 'probable accuracy' of the tale that Defoe hawked his manuscript round most of the London book trade before Taylor agreed to
publish it. He spins a pretty fable concerning Taylor's 'buxom widow',
which supplements the meagre facts with charming invention. There is
not much serious attempt at criticism; merely a collection of unsolicited
testimonials from Dr Johnson, Scott and others. Wright is inclined to
place *RC2* more nearly on a par with the original than most readers have
done; he remarks that 'the fascination of style is the same [in *RC2*], and
passages quite as fine as those in the first [part], if not finer, are
scattered up and down its pages'. Equally, 'the verisimilitude that is so
prominent in the first volume of "Crusoe" is as much in evidence in the
second'. Nor, in the final sections, 'does the interest anywhere flag'. Few
would be so positive on *that* point. Wright's uncritical approach is
encapsulated in a vehement exclamation, 'Is not every reader of [*Crusoe*]
its panegyrist!'[25] There is something deadening about such unrelieved
idolatry.

A more balanced picture emerges from W. P. Trent's *Daniel Defoe:
How to Know Him* (1916), the first major American contribution. Trent
had written a useful chapter on 'Defoe: the newspaper and the novel' in
the *Cambridge History of English Literature*, Volume 9 (1913), and had
supplied a checklist of 370 items. His book marks the advent of the
professional scholar in Defoe studies, with a sceptical and precise treatment of the accredited legends. Following the plan of the series in which
it appeared, Trent's biography is interlarded with quotations from books
and pamphlets by Defoe. There are four excerpts from *Crusoe*, including
one from *RC2* and one from *RC3*. Elsewhere Trent's rather prudish
notions tended to get in the way of critical vision, as on *Moll Flanders*:
'It is not a book to be recommended to young readers – perhaps it is not
a book to be recommended to any one, which is one of the reasons why
no selections are given in the present volume from it or from *Roxana*.'
But he has apt things to say about *Crusoe*, and made one memorable
comment regarding 'this wonderful story': namely, 'When a new
language is invented, *Robinson Crusoe* is one of the first books published
in it'.[26]

Another important figure in the history of Defoe scholarship produced
a biography in 1924. This was Paul Dottin, whose *De Foe et ses romans*
appeared in three volumes in Paris; a one-volume abridged translation
was published four years later as *The Life and Strange Surprising
Adventures of Daniel Defoe*. The first volume is the biography proper;
the second concerns *Crusoe* alone; whilst the third deals with the
'secondary' novels, and also contains a checklist of 380 items. Dottin
usefully scotched the legend of Defoe's hawking the manuscript around
unwilling booksellers. More doubtful is his view that Taylor offered him
'une forte somme' for a third volume he did not care to write as 'le sujet

l'ennuyait'. All the signs are that in writing *RC3* Defoe was engaged on a congenial task, not a wearisome labour imposed on him by the success of its predecessors. However, Dottin remains an instructive guide to *Crusoe* and, indeed, to Defoe throughout his literary career.[27]

More recent work can be dealt with in summary fashion. James Sutherland's *Defoe* (1937; revised edition 1950) is amongst other things the best-written of all the biographies; as a whole writers on Defoe have not been conspicuous for elegance of style. But it is also the shrewdest and critically most sensitive in the line; this book remains by far the soundest introduction to Defoe's career, unsupplanted even by Sutherland's own later contributions. A very different work is John Robert Moore's *Daniel Defoe: Citizen of the Modern World* (1958); it contains not a sustained biographical narrative but a series of essays on Defoe under one guise or another (merchant, reporter, projector, and so on). As such it is undoubtedly the fullest compendium of information on Defoe. Some readers are disturbed by Moore's strongly partisan feeling for Defoe, but in my view it needs only a little allowance to be made for the balance to adjust itself. It is impossible to read Moore's book without a greatly enriched sense of the complex ideas and inner experiences which went to the making of *Crusoe*.[28] Finally, there are more popular lives by William Freeman (1950), Francis Watson (1952) and Brian Fitzgerald (1954), the last of which is one of a number of Marxist readings of Defoe. Among this group Watson is the most reliable and Fitzgerald the most provocative. *Crusoe* naturally looms large for all three writers, but nowadays there is more competition from the other novels – *Moll Flanders* and increasingly *Roxana*. The fortunes and misfortunes of the famous Daniel Defoe continue to attract fresh generations of students of the novel.

ROMANTIC AND VICTORIAN

Strangely – as some might think – it was the Romantic movement which lifted prosaic old Daniel Defoe, controversialist and compiler, to the status of a major artist.[29] Chalmers's *Life* had prepared the way; between 1800 and 1840 the writer's reputation climbed dramatically. Even with the loss of faith in Defoe as a man which succeeded Lee's biography, the books themselves were never again to fall back into the obscurity that shrouded them in the eighteenth century. It was the 'secondary' novels (a term invented by Charles Lamb) which benefited most spectacularly, but *Crusoe*, too, began to receive more serious attention as a literary work, and not just as a moral document.

At the beginning of this shift, as in other phases of taste, a prominent place belongs to Walter Scott. His involvement in the eighteenth century was to become manifest in the editions of Dryden and Swift which he supervised; and, more inwardly, through the great novels dealing with Scottish history during Jacobite times. The twelve-volume Ballantyne edition of Defoe (Edinburgh, 1810) enlisted Scott's aid to an indeterminate extent, but the introductory study, is certainly his. Very acute it is, moreover, observant on Defoe's language, and sharply evocative with regard to the extraordinary *plausibility* of Defoe's imaginative flights. 'All the usual scaffolding and machinery employed in composing fictitious history are carefully discarded', according to Scott. This is not the currently fashionable view, but Scott's notion of an artless art was to influence successive generations of readers. His discussion of *Crusoe* contains some robust good sense, as in a passage such as this:

> The assistance which De Foe derived from Selkirk's history, seems of a very meagre kind. It is not certain that he was obliged to the real hermit of Juan Fernandez even for the original hint; for the putting mutineers or turbulent characters on shore upon solitary places, was a practice so general among the bucaniers, that there was a particular name for the punishment; it was called *marooning* a man. De Foe borrowed, perhaps, from the account in Woodes Rogers, the circumstance of the two huts, the abundance of goats, the clothing made out of their skins; and the turnips of Alexander Selkirk may have perhaps suggested the corn of Robinson Crusoe. Even these incidents, however, are so wrought up and heightened, and so much is added to make them interesting, that the bare circumstances occurring elsewhere, cannot be said to infringe upon the author's claim to originality. On the whole, indeed, Robinson Crusoe is put to so many more trials of ingenuity, his comforts are so much increased, his solitude is so much diversified, and his account of his thoughts and preoccupations so distinctly traced, that the course of the work embraces a far wider circle of investigation into human nature, than could be derived from that of Selkirk, who, for want of the tools and conveniences supplied to Crusoe by the wreck, relapses into a sort of savage state, which could have afforded little scope for delineation.

Commonplace later, this emphasis was itself a new one in 1810. Scott was enough a man of his time to wish to portray Defoe as an 'original' writer, and this the Romantic critics found a possible task in several directions.[30]

Coleridge – like his great predecessor Samuel Johnson – gave only brief indications of his verdict on Defoe. Most of his comments are indeed marginalia, rescued by his son in the 1830s from a copy of the 1812 edition (a Ballantyne set which also included *Gulliver's Travels* and *Peter Wilkins*). As Scott had done, Coleridge proposed a comparison between Swift and Defoe, finding the latter distinctly superior; in a famous sentence he wrote that Defoe's skill was to make the reader 'forget [his] *specific* class, character, and circumstances' and to raise him 'into the universal man'. 'You became a man while you read,' Coleridge roundly declares. Defoe is praised as a natural theologian, as 'a true philanthropist' and even as a geological observer. His description of Crusoe's moment of hesitation over whether to take the money from his wreck (*RC1*, p. 57) earns the comment, 'Worthy of Shakespeare' – a eulogy not dimmed by our knowledge that Taylor's text had a comma instead of the celebrated semi-colon. (See p. 80.) More than anything else, Coleridge's remarks are notable for the stress laid on the 'exquisite judgment' displayed by Defoe and 'the fine tact of genius' in his writing:

> The *Robinson Crusoe* is like the vision of a happy nightmare such as a denizen of Elysium might be supposed to have from a little excess of his nectar and ambrosia supper. Our imagination is kept in full play, excited to the highest, yet all the while we are touching or touched by a common flesh and blood.

After this, conventional talk of 'realism' and the like comes to seem very thin praise indeed.[31]

In 1830 William Hazlitt wrote a notice of Wilson's biography in the *Edinburgh Review*. It is not among Hazlitt's most impressive critical essays, for there is a sense that he cannot quite find the key to Defoe's special power. *Crusoe* is allowed pre-eminence, but Hazlitt is content to see this as caused by the fact that 'the subject mastered his prevailing bias to religious controversy, and the depravity of social life, by confining him to the unsophisticated views of nature and the human heart'. In the other novels Hazlitt could find 'no sentiment, no atmosphere of imagination' surrounding the depiction of squalor or evil. Only *A Journal of the Plague Year* was exempted, as possessing 'an epic grandeur, as well as heart-breaking familiarity, in its style and matter'.[32]

By contrast Charles Lamb found in Defoe a congenial subject. As already indicated, he was consulted by Walter Wilson during the preparation of the latter's biography; and his impressionistic accounts of the novels immediately foreshadow Victorian taste. He sees all Defoe's fiction as 'romantic', by which he appears to mean exotic and replete in incident. For Lamb there is a special quality of sympathy for the outcast which recalls 'the tenderness of Bunyan'. His picture of Defoe as a profound chronicler of guilt and isolation is, naturally, couched in different language from that of twentieth-century psychological criticism; but it emphasises the same features of Defoe's technique. In fact Lamb's Defoe is an educator of the heart, a Wordsworthian teacher who imparts morality through the exploration of feeling.[33] These are still in the 1970s thoroughly familiar attitudes among critics of the novel.

Wordsworth himself made a few references to Defoe, notably a comment around 1840 to the effect that Crusoe was – contrary to general belief – a truly uncommon man in his 'extraordinary energy and resource'. For De Quincey, at about the same time, there is a lingering unease over the assumed historicity of Defoe's stories. The insertion of small details which work 'by their apparent inertness of effect' produced for De Quincey an unsettling 'double character' in the books: 'He makes them so amusing that girls read them for novels; and he gives them such an air of verisimilitude that men read them for histories.' Meanwhile W. S. Landor composed two short poems more or less identifying Defoe with Crusoe: again, the stress is on the work as character-builder or repository of national virtue ('A Rodney and a Nelson may/Without him not have won the day.')The antecedent of 'him' is probably Crusoe, but 'persecuted, brave Defoe' with his 'mutilated frame' would fit the sense just as well.[34]

Just as vehement but more convincing testimony to the book's appeal came from George Borrow in *Lavengro* (1851), where the reader was invited to identify the work in question:

> . . . a book which has exerted over the minds of Englishmen an influence certainly greater than any other of modern times, which has been in most people's hands, and with the contents of which even those who cannot read are to a certain extent acquainted; a book from which the most luxuriant and fertile of our modern prose writers have drunk inspiration; a book, moreover, to which, from the hardy deeds which it narrates, and the spirit of strange and romantic enterprise which it tends to awaken, England owes many of her astonishing discoveries both by sea and land, and no inconsiderable part of her naval glory.
>
> Hail to thee, spirit of De Foe! What does not my own poor self owe to thee!

This kind of tribute might seem to us more appropriately bestowed on, say, *Westward Ho!*, with its conscious patriotism and high pitch of feeling. But Borrow spoke for a generation when he asserted that his intellectual curiosity was first stirred by *Crusoe*: 'In this manner . . . I first took to the paths of knowledge.'[35] Another partial autodidact, Charles Dickens, was less flattering about the novel, which he found deficient in emotional range and expressive warmth.[36] Incidentally, W. M. Thackeray, a close student of the eighteenth century who was on the most familiar terms with Dick Steele and Harry Fielding, showed no interest in Defoe whatsoever. The campaigns in which Henry Esmond took part were the subject of many pamphlets and papers, but of Dan De Foe we hear nothing. The omission is pointed; we are almost back with 'the Fellow that was *pilloryed*, I have forgot his Name'.

An important advance occurred in 1856, when a long article on Defoe appeared in the *National Review*. In my judgement it is very likely, though not incontrovertibly, the work of Walter Bagehot. At all events it is one of the most impressive discussions we have, full of penetrating comment and sharp in its discriminations. The critic detects a kinship in all Defoe's leading characters, and asserts that there is a 'remarkably full and explicit' degree of 'unconscious self-revelation'. He distinguishes between the isolation bred of some great purpose, 'too great for the sympathy of a man's compeers', and the loneliness which comes 'from a want of warmth in the emotions'. For the *National Review* critic, Defoe endured both kinds of solitude; the first was a vein of self-sufficiency which enabled him to conceive his masterpiece, the second a failure in temperament which limited his range as a novelist. It is an account with which every student of Defoe's art must come to terms.[37]

A better-known essay was contributed by Leslie Stephen to the *Cornhill Magazine* in 1868. Reprinted in the first series of Stephen's *Hours in a Library* (1874), it became almost the standard critical version of Defoe as a novelist. Stephen displayed strong reservations as to Defoe's standing as an imaginative artist: phrases like 'little or no dramatic power', 'little enough of a poet', 'extremely straightforward and prosaic view of life' are sprinkled through the discussion. There is an Arnoldian capacity for dismissal:

De Foe, even in *Robinson Crusoe*, gives a very inadequate picture of the mental torments to which his hero is exposed. He is frightened by a parrot calling him by name, and by the strangely picturesque incident of the footmark on the sand; but, on the whole, he takes his imprisonment with preternatural stolidity. His stay on the island produces the same state of mind as might be due to a dull Sunday in Scotland. For this reason, the want of power in describing emotion as compared with the amazing power of describing facts, *Robinson Crusoe* is a book for boys rather than men, and, as Lamb says, for the kitchen rather than for higher circles. It falls short of any high intellectual interest. . . . But for people who are not too proud to take a rather low order of amusement *Robinson Crusoe* will always be one of the most charming of books.

Stephen's view of the book as exhibiting 'the most unflinching realism' is today regarded as narrow, if not misleading; and his emphasis on mere reportage ('a plain statement of the facts') needs to be qualified. However, his lucid and forceful essay forms a distinct landmark in the history of Defoe's reputation.[38]

Two other nineteenth-century critiques deserve attention. One is found in Taine's highly influential *Histoire de la littérature anglaise* (1863), where five thoughtful pages are devoted to the 'Presbyterian and plebeian' themes of the novels. Like Stephen, Taine sees Defoe's mind as 'entirely destitute of refinement'. Indeed, 'his imagination was that of a man of business, not of an artist'. However, Taine is more ready to accept the spiritual implications than Stephen: he concludes that in Crusoe's world 'religion consecrates labour, piety feeds patience; and man, supported on one side by his instincts, on the other by his beliefs, finds himself able to clear the land, to people, to organise and civilise continents'. Four years later, in the first volume of *Das Kapital*, Karl Marx used Crusoe as a particularly clear demonstration of value as related to the 'labour time' involved. There is nothing striking or controversial about the passage, but it helped to confirm *Crusoe* as a document, supposedly, of economic theory in action.[39]

THE MODERN AGE

Early in the present century Defoe had relatively few ardent admirers; but they included distinguished names. Two seemingly unlikely allies were Virginia Woolf and James Joyce. In fact Joyce's comments on the novelist, composed in 1911, were not published until 1964, by which time Defoe had already achieved a more exalted station. Joyce was most impressed by *Moll Flanders*, still a work to be commended with caution in Edwardian times, but he paid tribute also to *Crusoe* as a prophetic and mythical insight into the course of empire.[40] Virginia Woolf perhaps inherited her interest in Defoe from her father, Leslie Stephen. Her two best-known essays in this area were published in the first and second *Common Reader* (they derive originally from journalism).

'Defoe', written to commemorate the bicentenary of *Robinson Crusoe*, 'the perennial and immortal', in 1919, is the more relaxed and entertaining piece. In celebrating *Crusoe's* anniversary, the critic observed, 'we are making a slightly unnecessary allusion to the fact that, like Stonehenge, it is still in existence'. On the other hand, the essay makes high claims for *Moll Flanders* – indeed, this is perhaps the beginning of Moll's apotheosis. Concerned to argue that Defoe 'was not, as he has been accused of being, a mere journalist and literal recorder of facts with no conception of the nature of psychology', Virginia Woolf yet conceded that he was 'often dull' and ended by placing him in 'the school of Crabbe and of Gissing'.[41]

The second essay, entitled simply '*Robinson Crusoe*', adopts a more searching approach. Mrs Woolf sees *Crusoe* as a masterpiece 'largely because Defoe has throughout kept to his own sense of perspective'. As a central symbol – comparable in some respects with Wallace Stevens's jar in Tennessee – she takes one of Crusoe's domestic utensils: 'There are no sunsets and no sunrises; there is no solitude and no soul. There is, on the contrary, staring us full in the face nothing but a large earthen-ware pot.' God has shrivelled into a remote magistrate 'only a little way above the horizon'; 'Nature does not exist'. Indeed, 'nothing exists except an earthenware pot'. At the heart of this achievement lies a 'genius for fact', which allows Defoe to attain effects beyond 'any but the great masters of descriptive prose'. In conclusion:

> Thus Defoe, by reiterating that nothing but a plain earthenware pot stands in the foreground, persuades us to see remote islands and the solitudes of the human soul. By believing fixedly in the solidity of the pot and its earthiness, he has subdued every other element in his design; he has roped the whole universe into harmony.

Later critics have restored God to the heavens and have discerned both solitude and soul in Crusoe. But Virginia Woolf's essay remains a brilliant evocation of one aspect that still fascinates readers: it is the most eloquent statement of the 'magnificent downright simplicity' that somehow pervades a book with deep roots and complex literary relations.[42]

Admiration for Defoe has not been confined to British novelists: André Gide, François Mauriac, and Cesare Pavese are among writers to have recorded their appreciation.[43] But, with them as with E. M. Forster (in *Aspects of the Novel*) and William Faulkner, it is Moll who occupies the most prominent place. Poets who have written about Defoe include W. H. Davies, Edmund Blunden and Walter de la Mare, whose *Desert Islands and Robinson Crusoe* (1930) spins an elaborate tracework of allusion around the castaway theme. Otherwise the interwar years were notable for helpful and rather unadventurous scholarship: biography was still a major focus of attention, whilst Defoe's relation to his political and intellectual milieu received fuller treatment than it had previously been given. A trickle of work on the religious background began to emerge with an article by James Moffatt (1919), followed by R. G. Stamm's workmanlike study *Der aufgeklärte Puritanismus Defoes* (1936), with its careful analysis of politics, religion, ethics, aesthetics and socio-economic themes.

Several writers attempted exploration of the supposed personal allegory in *Crusoe*, most directly G. Parker (1925). 'Realism' continued to be the most overworked concept, and a number of critics approach *Crusoe* along this well-beaten track. Language was another popular aspect, generally treated in a philological rather than stylistic fashion. Herman Ullrich* made a special study of the history and influence of the novel, especially

---

* His name is commonly spelt 'Ulrich', but the title page has *Ullrich*.

the vogue of Robinsonades. Source studies were perhaps the most numerous of all – two separate theses appeared in Germany during a single year (1909) devoted to the models on which *Crusoe* might have been based. Here the pioneering phase was brought to a decisive end by the appearance of A. W. Secord's *Studies in the Narrative Method of Defoe* (1924). Debate now rages, as we have seen, over the weight to be placed on the sources in any literary assessment of *Robinson Crusoe*; but no one doubts that Secord remains the best all-round guide.

The thirties represented a period of consolidation. There was no critical book to rank with Sutherland's biography, and even J. R. Moore's important bibliographical work lay for the most part on the margins of Defoe as novelist. A useful article on the intellectual background by H. W. Häusermann came out in 1936, spread across two issues of the *Review of English Studies*. Another valuable essay by H. H. Andersen, on 'The paradox of trade and morality in Defoe', appeared in 1941, a year which also saw the publication of J. F. Ross's well-conceived exercise in comparing and contrasting, *Swift and Defoe: A Study in Relationship*. During the late forties other facets of Defoe were effectively treated at book length, for example, in W. L. Payne's *Mr Review* (1947). Bonamy Dobrée helped to give a more literary turn to discussions of Defoe's language; whilst scholarship and bibliography seemed for a time to have run out of energy, except in the prolific research of Secord and Moore.

Modern Defoe criticism may be said to date from the 1950s. Harbingers of this development were articles by Mark Schorer (1950) and Benjamin Boyce (1953), and the decisive moment arrived soon afterwards. A. D. McKillop's *The Early Masters of English Fiction* (1956) contained a well-written and sensitive appraisal. Its opening sentence read: 'Defoe's contribution to fiction has never been fully analyzed, interpreted, or even identified.' McKillop did much to remedy this situation: after a general overview of Defoe's career, seeking to discern the elements which contributed to the formation of the novelist specifically, he discussed the major works of fiction in turn – beginning with *A Journal of the Plague Year* and moving through to *Roxana* (*A New Voyage* was omitted). A final section considered Defoe's place in the history of fiction, and the taste to which his novels appealed. *Crusoe* was given thorough and intelligent coverage, although *Moll Flanders* perhaps suited McKillop's method better. In the critic's view 'The way of life on the island establishes a dominant pattern seldom to be found in Defoe. The situation makes Defoe substitute a tighter analysis of a situation for the loose travel and adventure formula, enables him to attain the range and variety of adventure within the compass of the strictly relevant.' More predictable at this date was the assertion, 'Even though Defoe does not use elaborate psychological notation, Crusoe's anxiety and anguish are vividly presented, and interest us more than his heavy piety'.[44]

McKillop hinted that the novel lay closer to epic than to romance (borrowing terms from W. P. Ker), and thus came close to forestalling an emphasis shortly to be laid by E. M. W. Tillyard. In his book *The Epic Strain in the English Novel* (1958) Tillyard made a strong case for *Crusoe*, which he regarded as 'read too little and prized too low', as the best-constructed and deepest of the novels. A brisk argument found 'an intensity in the way [Defoe] apprehended his story, a steady seriousness', which led Tillyard to align the novel with epic rather than any other literary kind. For Defoe, he asserted, 'voices the "accepted unconscious metaphysic" of a large group of men'; the book is the 'choric expression' of the middle-class ethos.[45]

If McKillop had proved influential, his impact now appears limited in comparison with that of Ian Watt, whose *The Rise of the Novel* came out in 1957. Quite apart from its provocative treatment of general issues concerning early fiction (see Chapter 5 above), this study contained two chapters devoted specifically to Defoe. Each has continued to stimulate debate, and there are no signs of a let-up after twenty years. Watt's estimate of *Moll Flanders* was lower than that of many contemporaries, with the result that this chapter prompted more dissent than assent. On the other hand, his section on '*Robinson Crusoe*, individualism, and the novel' elicited a more complicated response. Here Watt sought to demonstrate: (1) that Crusoe's character 'depends very largely on the psychological and social orientations of economic individualism' – by which Watt means the new freedom of action for people to determine their own worldly and spiritual ends, as against the traditional modes of life based on corporate authority; (2) that the island story illustrates Crusoe finding satisfaction in undertaking a variety of tasks which increasing 'economic specialisation' (roughly, the division of labour) denied to most men and women; (3) that a secularised Puritan version of individualism, placing special emphasis on consciousness of the self, lies behind Crusoe's spiritual experience. It is possible to pick holes in the details of this argument, and Diana Spearman is one critic to have done so with some success, but the chapter remains an outstandingly intelligent discussion of *Crusoe* in its historical bearings.[46]

Ian Watt had already published one important essay, '*Robinson Crusoe* as a myth' (1951), which overlaps to some degree with the chapter just discussed. The essay places great stress on the novel's universal – one might again say epic – meaning: Crusoe is seen as the 'culture-hero' of a self-sufficient, isolated and joyless capitalism. Not long afterwards, in 1957, Watt returned to the theme in an excellent chapter he contributed to the *Pelican Guide to English Literature*; again, Crusoe's material conquests are set against 'spiritual loneliness and social alienation'. The judgement does, of course, raise larger political and social questions – it is possible to believe that Watt characterises a real element in Crusoe's make up without accepting his strong distaste for this self-sufficiency. Nevertheless, it is Watt's version of Crusoe which stands at the centre of recent criticism; he has provided the most coherent and credible hero for *our* times.[47]

After Watt came a flood of rejoinders, revaluations and reconsiderations. In the early 1960s it was Moll Flanders who held the centre of the stage, and the main bustle of critical activity went on around her person.[48] In the last decade, however, Crusoe has regained some of his former pre-eminence, and any general estimate of Defoe will again bestow particular importance on the meaning of this novel. In earlier chapters of this book I have rehearsed many of the arguments which came to the surface during this period, and it would be redundant to go fully into these matters at such a late stage. Briefly, then, the most recent phase has been dominated by four monographs with special relevance to *Crusoe*. Two are the work of Maximillian E. Novak, the outstanding Defoe scholar now professionally active. *Economics and the Fiction of Daniel Defoe* (1962) has been the more widely challenged, perhaps because its findings are based on less abstruse sources. By comparison *Defoe and the Nature of Man* (1963), which explores Defoe's relation to natural law, drew its store of background ideas from writers such as Samuel Pufendorf, Hugo Grotius and Hobbes. The former book, in addition, had a clear relation to Watt, in so far as it was designed to combat certain versions of Defoe's economic thinking expressed or mentioned in *The Rise of the Novel*. In the long term it may be that *Defoe and the Nature of Man* will prove the more fertile stimulus to students of Defoe, not least in its final discussion of Defoe's search for a fully individuated and convincing hero (or heroine).

The two other seminal works have both figured prominently in this book (see Chapter 3). George A. Starr's *Defoe and Spiritual Autobiography* (1965) was quickly followed by J. Paul Hunter's *The Reluctant Pilgrim* (1966), an intriguing and significant coincidence. Starr spreads himself more widely over the novels, but confines himself to a single form; whereas Hunter concentrates exclusively on *Crusoe*, but brings several different models as evidence. In my judgement Starr is the more moderate and cogent, but both books are essential bases for any serious contemporary reading. Subsequently Starr brought out *Defoe and Casuistry* (1971), in which *Crusoe* receives only glancing attention. Other monographs on Defoe, by Rodney M. Baine and Michael Shinagel, likewise leave their principal emphasis elsewhere.

Three recent books which do contain frontal treatment of *Robinson Crusoe* are those of John J. Richetti, E. Anthony James and Everett Zimmerman; the last of these may prove to be the most durable. James's special concern is language and rhetoric, treated in a somewhat piecemeal fashion. Richetti adopts a Hegelian scheme, with results closer to Watt than to Starr or Hunter: he concludes drily that Crusoe's worldly gains (at the end of *RC1*) combine 'freedom and innocence in a manner rather difficult to achieve in the real economic world'. The hero is seen as 'a converter, turning an ideology to the uses of survival and autonomy'.[49] A more original view is that of Zimmerman, who describes Crusoe as 'the kind of figure who is the butt of much of the satire of Swift and Pope', a morally confused being of 'chaotic energy'.[50] In addition Zimmerman writes more convincingly of *RC2* than do most of the critics. A shorter study by Pierre Nordon, *Robinson Crusoe: unité et contradictions* (1967), contains a brisk review of familiar themes (myth, realism, modernity), noting that despite his fortuitous isolation Crusoe emerges with his sociability unimpaired. It may be added that the Critical Heritage volume (1972) prints excerpts of criticism up to 1880 – with *RC1* the main focus of attention – and offers a brief appraisal of twentieth-century developments. A similar appraisal is found in three casebooks on Defoe which appeared between 1969 and 1976.

During this period the scholarly and critical journals have equally carried a large body of relevant comment. Probably the most important general study here is Homer O. Brown's article, 'The displaced self in the novels of Daniel Defoe', speculative and provocative. On *Crusoe* itself there have been some attempts, only partly successful in my view, to construct a four-square religious allegory: notable here are the essays listed in the bibliography by Martin J. Greif (1966) and Robert W. Ayers (1967). Perhaps the best article in this area is William H. Halewood's 'Religion and invention in *Robinson Crusoe*' (1964). Symbolism rather than allegory is the concern of E. B. Benjamin (1951); a more recent Marxist approach is that of Stephen Hymer (1971). As well as James, several critics have discussed Defoe's prose style, with valuable contributions made by James T. Boulton (1965) and George A. Starr (1974). Maximillian E. Novak's article on 'Defoe's theory of fiction' (1964) broaches a surprisingly neglected topic.

Scholarship in the past twenty years is headed by the final works of two major figures in the history of this subject, A. W. Secord and J. R. Moore. Moore's *Checklist* first appeared in 1960, bringing something like order to a previously chaotic field. His final tally of more than 550 items will not go unchallenged; indeed certain additions and subtractions have already been essayed. But it is certainly the most comprehensive and reliable list yet assembled. Secord's collection, *Robert Drury's Journal and Other Studies*, appeared posthumously in 1961; it contains the fruits of many hours of skilled research, though little that bears directly on *RC1*. This period also saw the appearance of seven books by Defoe in the Oxford English Novels series; the standard of editing is variable, but the best is very good indeed. Other works such as the *History of Pyrates* and the *Tour* have appeared in annotated editions.

Most important of all, the long-awaited collected edition is now in preparation; the general editors are two distinguished scholars, Maximillian E. Novak and Manuel Schonhorn, and the publishers the University of Southern Illinois Press. This will be a major advance which should, when completed, give Defoe studies a new direction and momentum. *Robinson Crusoe* has now been in the world for well over 250 years, and continues to show rude health. The density of scholarship is one indication, but so are the abridgements, the films and the dramatised versions. A book with such staying power must command our respect, but luckily it is fresh enough on each reading to inspire our affection as well.

NOTES

References are supplied only in the case of direct quotations. Fur fuller details concerning critical studies mentioned in the text, see the Bibliography below.

1 See W. L. Payne, 'Defoe in the pamphlets', *PQ*, Vol. LII (1973), pp. 85–96; *CH*, pp. 209–19; J. V. Guerinot, *Pamphlet Attacks on Alexander Pope 1711–1744* (London, 1969).

2 *The Poetical Register*, 2nd edn (London, 1723), Vol. II, p. 293; *CH*, p. 48.

3 For the treatment of Defoe by Pope, Swift and their friends, consult *CH*, pp. 38–40.

4 John Oldmixon, *An Essay on Criticism* (London, 1728; reprinted Los Angeles, Calif., 1964), p. 88.

5 Quoted by Sutherland, p. 236, from the *Flying Post*, 1 March 1729.

6 John Oldmixon, *The Arts of Logick and Rhetorick* (London, 1728; reprinted Hildesheim, 1976), p. 27.

7 Quoted by A. D. McKillop, *The Early Masters of English Fiction* (Lawrence, Kans., 1956), pp. 43–4: the second quotation is drawn from the *Dublin Journal* (an essay written in 1725).

8 See Paul Dottin's introduction to *Robinson Crusoe Examin'd and Criticis'd* (London and Paris, 1973).

9 Roberts (1668/9–1754) was mainly a distributor and did not generally own the copyright of books 'published' by his firm. He is associated with pro-Defoe and anti-Defoe items, and the same applies to him in respect of Pope and Swift.

10 Gildon, pp. viii–x. For the Pope–Curll parallels, see *The Prose Works of Alexander Pope*, ed. N. Ault (Oxford, 1936), Vol. I, pp. 259–66, 275–85; and Ralph Straus, *The Unspeakable Curll* (London, 1927), pp. 49–76.

11 Gildon, pp. 2, 31–2. See the fuller extracts in *CH*, pp. 41–7.

12 *CH*, p. 40, quoting *Grub-street Journal* of 29 April 1731.

13 Theophilus Cibber (?), *The Lives of the Poets of Great Britain and Ireland* (London, 1753; reprinted Hildesheim, 1968), Vol. IV, pp. 322–3; *CH*, pp. 49–51, reproduces other extracts.

14 *CH*, pp. 58–9, quoting Boswell's *Life* under 10 April 1778 and *Johnsonian Miscellanies*, ed. G. B. Hill (Oxford, 1897), Vol. I, p. 332.

15 For this phase, consult *CH*, pp. 13–14, 59–61.

16   *CH*, pp. 52–3, reproduces the main passage in translation; it can be found
  in *Emile*, ed. Michel Launay (Paris, 1966), pp. 238–40. Paul Nourrisson,
  Jean-Jacques Rousseau et Robinson Crusoé (Paris, 1931), discusses the
  theme of solitude in Rousseau with incidental reference to Defoe.
17   George Chalmers, 'The life of Daniel De Foe', in *Robinson Crusoe*
  (London, 1790), Vol. II, pp. 422–3, 426, 433–40. See also *CH*, pp. 61–5.
18   Walter Wilson, *Memoirs of the Life and Times of Daniel De Foe*
  (London, 1830), Vol. III, pp. 441–3, 636. For extensive quotation from
  Wilson, consult *CH*, pp. 90–106.
19   ibid., p. 112.
20   John Forster, *Daniel De Foe and Charles Churchill* (London, 1855), pp.
  132–3, 139–40, 145n; see also *CH*, pp. 119–22.
21   William Chadwick, *The Life and Times of Daniel De Foe* (London, 1859),
  pp. vi, 1–2, 56, 463–4; cf. *CH*, p. 20. For Benjamin Franklin, see ibid.,
  p. 12; for other criticism of the mid-century, ibid., pp. 150–60.
22   See *Letters*, pp. 450–61.
23   Lee, Vol. I, pp. xxii–xxiii. For fuller extracts from Lee, consult *CH*, pp.
  177–90.
24   William Minto, *Daniel Defoe* (London, 1885), pp. 137, 145–6, 156; fuller
  quotations are given in *CH*, pp. 203–8.
25   Thomas Wright, *The Life of Daniel Defoe* (London, 1894), pp. xvi, 230–
  40, 245–7. Wright quotes a passage from Alphonse Daudet (pp. 239–40),
  expressing particular admiration for Defoe's capacity to render the effects
  of *terror* – a new emphasis.
26   William P. Trent, *Daniel Defoe: How to Know Him* (Indianapolis, Ind.,
  1916), pp. 186, 215. Trent's insistence that *Crusoe* was almost certainly
  written at Stoke Newington (p. 183) supplied another healthy corrective.
27   P. Dottin, *De Foe et ses romans* (Paris, 1924), Vol. II, pp. 309, 353; Vol.
  III, pp. 802–49. The three 'volumes' are continuously paginated.
28   Sutherland, pp. 227–50, sets the novel in the context of Defoe's career up
  to 1719; see also the same author's *Daniel Defoe: A Critical Study*
  (Cambridge, Mass., 1971), pp. 123–43. Moore's chief treatment of the
  novel occurs in *Citizen*, pp. 222–8.
29   General assessment of this phase will be found in *CH*, pp. 14–18.
30   Lengthy extracts from Scott's essay, taken from his *Miscellaneous Works*
  (Edinburgh, 1834), Vol. IV, pp. 248–81, are reproduced in *CH*, pp. 66–
  79; see also *Swift: The Critical Heritage*, ed. Kathleen Williams (London,
  1970), pp. 307–8, for a comparison by Scott of Swift and Defoe.
31   Quotations from *CH*, pp. 80–5, where the text is taken from *Coleridge's
  Miscellaneous Criticism*, ed. T. M. Raysor (London, 1930).
32   *CH*, pp. 107–11; also available in Hazlitt's *Works*, ed. A. R. Waller and
  A. Glover (London, 1904), Vol. X, pp. 355–85.
33   *CH*, pp. 87–8, drawing on *The Works of Charles and Mary Lamb*, ed.
  E. V. Lucas (London, 1903–5), Vol. I, pp. 325–7.
34   *CH*, pp. 115–18; see also p. 89 for Carlyle's comments.
35   ibid., pp. 123–4, quoting chapter 3 of *Lavengro*. For the Victorian climate,
  see the discussion in *CH*, pp. 19–22.
36   ibid., p. 21; see also Forster's *Life of Charles Dickens*, ed. J. W. T. Ley
  (London, 1928), p. 611n.
37   *CH*, pp. 125–50, reproduces the bulk of this essay from the *National
  Review*, Vol. III (1856), pp. 380–410. It is not included in the recent
  Collected Works of Bagehot, where the canon is established on impressionistic grounds.

38 *CH*, pp. 169–77, where the text is based on *Hours in a Library* (London, 1892), Vol. I, pp. 17–46.

39 *CH*, pp. 160–6, quotes the translation of Taine's *Histoire* by H. Van Laun (Edinburgh, 1873), Vol. II, pp. 153–7; and the translation of *Das Kapital* by Samuel Moore and Edward Aveling (London, 1915), Vol. I, pp. 88–91.

40 James Joyce, 'Daniel Defoe', trans. and ed. Joseph Prescott, in *Buffalo Studies*, Vol. I (1964), pp. 3–25. The text is based on a lecture in Italian, delivered at Trieste in 1912.

41 Virginia Woolf, *The Common Reader* (London, 1925), pp. 89–97; reprinted in Byrd, pp. 15–22. (First published in *TLS*, 24 April 1719, pp. 217–18.) For family readings in the Stephen household, see Quentin Bell, *Virginia Woolf: A Biography*, Vol. I (London, 1972), pp. 26–7.

42 Virginia Woolf, *The Second Common Reader* (London, 1932), pp. 51–8; reprinted in Ellis, pp. 19–24.

43 *CH*, pp. 25–8, gives a general assessment of twentieth-century trends in Defoe criticism.

44 McKillop, *The Early Masters of English Fiction*, pp. 20–5.

45 E. M. W. Tillyard, *The Epic Strain in the English Novel* (London, 1958), pp. 31–50; reprinted in Ellis, pp. 62–78.

46 Watt, pp. 62–96; see also his witty and thought-provoking 'Serious reflections on *The Rise of the Novel*', *Novel: A Forum on Fiction*, Vol. I (1968), pp. 205–18. Extracts from the book appear in Byrd, pp. 51–9, and Ellis, pp. 39–54.

47 Ian Watt, '*Robinson Crusoe* as a myth', *EIC*, Vol. I (1951), pp. 95–119; 'Defoe as novelist', *From Dryden to Johnson*, ed. B. Ford (Harmondsworth, 1957), pp. 203–16.

48 See Ian Watt, 'The recent critical fortunes of *Moll Flanders*', *ECS*, Vol. I (1967), pp. 109–26.

49 J. J. Richetti, *Defoe's Narratives* (Oxford, 1975), pp. 23, 61–2.

50 Everett Zimmerman, *Defoe and the Novel* (Berkeley and Los Angeles, Calif., 1975), p. 47.

Woodes Rogers's Narrative of Selkirk

This account first appeared in Rogers's *Cruising Voyage Round the World* (1712), which reached a second edition in 1718. See pages 17–19 above. A good modern edition is by G. E. Manwaring (1928). The extract reprinted here deals with events following the arrival of *Duke* and *Dutchess* on 1 February 1709. For Thomas Stradling, Robert Fry (first lieutenant in *Duke*) and Thomas Dover, see Little, *passim*. The reference on page 158 is to Basil Ringrose's continuation of Exquemelin's *Bucaniers of America* (1685), which contains the story of 'the dangerous voyage and bold attempts of Captain Bartholomew Sharp' over the isthmus of Darien (Panama). For the Dampier reference, see page 31.

In the afternoon we hoisted our pinnace out; Captain Dover, with the boat's crew, went in her to go ashore, though we could not be less than four leagues off. As soon as the pinnace was gone, I went on board the *Dutchess*, who admired our boat attempting going ashore at that distance from land. 'T was against my inclination, but to oblige Captain Dover I consented to let her go. As soon as it was dark we saw a light ashore. Our boat was then about a league from the island, and bore away for the ships as soon as she saw the lights. We put our lights abroad for the boat, though some were of opinion the lights we saw were our boat's lights; but as night came on, it appeared too large for that. We fired our quarter-deck gun and several muskets, showing lights in our mizen and fore shrouds, that our boat might find us whilst we plied in the lee of the island. About two in the morning our boat came on board, having been two hours on board the *Dutchess*, that took them up astern of us; we were glad they got well off, because it began to blow. We are all convinced the light is on the shore, and design to make our ships ready to engage, believing them to be French ships at anchor, and we must either fight them or want water. We stood on the back side along the south end of the island, in order to lay in with the first southerly wind, which Captain Dampier told us generally blows there all day long. In the morning, being past the island, we tacked to lay it in close aboard the land, and about ten o'clock opened the south end of the island, and ran close aboard the land that begins to make the north-east side. . . . We sent our yawl ashore about noon, with Captain Dover, Mr Fry, and six men, all armed. Meanwhile we and the *Dutchess* kept turning to get in, and such heavy flaws came off the land, that we were forced to let go our topsail sheet, keeping all hands to stand by our sails, for fear of the wind's carrying them away; but when the flaws were gone we had little or no wind. These flaws proceeded from the land, which is very high in the middle of the island. Our boat did not return; so we sent our pinnace, with the men armed, to see what was the occasion of the yawl's stay, for we were afraid that the Spaniards had a garrison there, and might have seized them. We put out a signal for our boat, and the *Dutchess* showed a French ensign. Immediately our pinnace returned from the shore, and brought abundance of cray-fish, with a man clothed in goat's skins, who looked wilder than the first owners of them. He had been on the island four years and four months, being left there by Captain Stradling in the *Cinque Ports*; his name was Alexander Selkirk, a Scotchman, who had been master of the *Cinque Ports*, a ship that came here last with Captain Dampier, who told me that this was the best man in her; so I immediately agreed with him to be a mate on board our ship. 'T was he that made the fire last night when he saw our ships, which he judged to be English. During his stay here he saw several ships pass by, but only two came to anchor. As he went to view them, he found them to be Spaniards, and retired from them, upon which they shot at him. Had they been French, he would have submitted, but chose to risk his dying alone on the island rather than fall into the hands of the Spaniards in these parts; because he apprehended they would murder him, or make a slave of him in the mines, for he feared they would spare no stranger that might be capable of discovering the South Seas.

The Spaniards had landed before he knew what they were, and they came so near him that he had much ado to escape; for they not only shot at him, but pursued him to the woods, where he climbed to the top of a tree, at the foot of which they made water, and killed several goats just by, but went off without discovering him. He told us that he was born at Largo, in the county of Fife, in Scotland, and was bred a sailor from his youth. The reason of his being left here was a difference betwixt him and his captain; which, together with the ship's being leaky, made him willing rather to stay here than go along with him at first; and when he was at last willing, the captain would not receive him. He had been in the island before to wood and water, when two of the ship's company were left upon it for six months till the ship returned, being chased thence by two French South Sea ships.

He had with him his clothes and bedding, with a firelock, some powder, bullets, and tobacco, a hatchet, a knife, a kettle, a Bible, some practical pieces, and his mathematical instruments and books. He diverted and provided for himself as well as he could, but for the first eight months had much ado to bear up against melancholy, and the terror of being left alone in such a desolate place. He built two huts with pimento trees, covered them with long grass, and lined them with the skins of goats, which he killed with his gun as he wanted, so long as his powder lasted, which was but a pound; and that being almost spent, he got fire by rubbing two ticks of pimento wood together upon his knee. In the lesser hut, at some distance from the other, he dressed his victuals; and in the larger he slept and employed himself in reading, singing psalms, and praying; so that he said he was a better Christian while in this solitude than ever he was before, or than, he was afraid, he should ever be again.

At first he never ate anything till hunger constrained him, partly for grief, and partly for want of bread and salt. Nor did he go to bed till he could watch no longer; the pimento wood, which burnt very clear served him both for firing and candle, and refreshed him with its fragrant smell. He might have had fish enough, but could not eat them for want of salt, because they occasioned a looseness; except crayfish, which are there as large as lobsters, and very good. These he sometimes boiled, and at other times broiled, as he did his goats' flesh, of which he made very good broth, for they are not so rank as ours. He kept an account of 500 that he killed while there, and caught as many more, which he marked on the ear, and let go. When his powder failed, he took them by speed of feet; for his way of living and continual exercise of walking and running cleared him of all gross humours; so that he ran with wonderful swiftness through the woods, and up the rocks and hills, as we perceived when we employed him to catch goats for us. We had a bulldog, which we sent, with several of our nimblest runners, to help him in catching goats; but he distanced and tired both the dog and the men, catched the goats, and brought them to us on his back.

He told us that his agility in pursuing a goat had once like to have cost him his life: he pursued it with so much eagerness that he catched hold of it on the brink of a precipice, of which he was not aware, the bushes hiding it from him; so that he fell with the goat down the said precipice, a great height, and was so stunned and bruised with the fall that he narrowly escaped with his life; and when he came to his senses, found the goat dead under him. He lay there about twenty-four hours, and was scarce able to crawl to his hut, which was about a mile distant, or to stir abroad again for ten days.

He came at last to relish his meat well enough without salt or bread; and in the season had plenty of good turnips which had been sowed there by Captain Dampier's men, and have now overspread some acres of ground. He had enough of good cabbage from the cabbage trees, and seasoned his meat with the fruit of the pimento trees, which is the same as Jamaica pepper and smells deliciously. He found also a black pepper called malageta, which was very good to expel wind, and against griping of the guts.

He soon wore out all his shoes and clothes by running through the woods; and at last, being forced to shift without them, his feet became so hard that he ran everywhere without difficulty, and it was some time before he could wear shoes after we found him; for, not being used to any so long, his feet swelled when he came first to wear them again.

After he had conquered his melancholy, he diverted himself sometimes by cutting his name on the trees, and the time of his being left, and continuance there. He was at first much pestered with cats and rats, that bred in great numbers from some of each species which had got ashore from ships that put in there to wood and water. The rats gnawed his feet and clothes whilst asleep, which obliged him to cherish the cats with his goats' flesh, by which many of them became so tame, that they would lie about him in hundreds, and soon delivered him from the rats. He likewise tamed some kids, and to divert himself would, now and then, sing and dance with them and his cats; so that, by the care of Providence, and vigour of his youth, being now about thirty years old, he came at last to conquer all the inconveniences of his solitude, and to be very easy.

When his clothes wore out, he made himself a coat and a cap of goat's skins, which he stitched together with little thongs of the same, that he cut with his knife. He had no other needle but a nail; and when his knife was wore to the back, he made others, as well as he could of some iron hoops that were left ashore, which he beat thin and ground upon stones. Having some linen cloth by him, he sewed himself shirts with a nail, and stitched them with the worsted of his old stockings, which he pulled out on purpose. He had his last shirt on when we found him on the island.

At his first coming on board us, he had so much forgot his language, for want of use, that we could scarce understand him, for he seemed to speak his words by halves. We offered him a dram, but he would not touch it, having drank nothing but water since his being there; and 't was some time before he could relish our victuals.

He could give us an account of no other product of the island than what we have mentioned, except small black plums, which are very good, but hard to come at, the trees which bear them growing on high mountains and rocks. Pimento trees are plenty here, and we saw some of sixty feet high, and about two yards thick and cotton trees higher, and more than four fathom round in the stock.

The climate is so good that the trees and grass are verdant all the year. The winter lasts no longer than June and July, and is not then severe, there being only a small frost and a little hail, but sometimes great rains. The heat of the summer is equally moderate, and there's not much thunder or tempestuous weather of any sort. We saw no venomous or savage creature on the island, nor any other sort of beast, but goats, &c., as above mentioned, the first of which had been put ashore here on purpose for a breed by Juan Fernandez, a Spaniard, who settled there with some families for a time, till the continent of Chili began to submit to the Spaniards; which, being more profitable, tempted them to quit this island, which is capable of maintaining a good number of people, and of being made so strong that they could not be easily dislodged.

Ringrose, in his account of Captain Sharpe's voyage, and other buccaneers, mentions one who had escaped ashore here, out of a ship which was cast away with all the rest of the company, and says he lived five years alone, before he had the opportunity of another ship to carry him off. Captain Dampier talks of a Mosquito Indian that belonged to Captain Watlin, who, being a-hunting in the woods when the captain left the island, lived there three years alone, and shifted much in the same manner as Mr Selkirk did, till Captain Dampier came hither in 1684 and carried him off. The first that went ashore was one of his countrymen, and they saluted one another, first by prostrating themselves by turns on the ground, and then embracing. But whatever there is in these stories, this of Mr Selkirk I know to be true; and his behaviour afterwards gives me reason to believe the account he gave me how he spent his time, and bore up under such an affliction, in which nothing but the Divine Providence could have supported any man.

Richard Steele's Narrative of Selkirk

The account which follows appeared in Richard Steele's paper *The Englishman* which was published three times a week over two series between 1713 and 1715. This occupies number 26 of the first series, for Thursday, 3 December 1713. The text is taken from *The Englishman*, ed. Rae Blanchard (Oxford, 1955), pp. 106–9, which is based on the original issue.

The motto is from the *Aeneid*, Bk III, l. 690: 'such were the things he [Achaemenides] pointed out in retracing his earlier wanderings'.

Talia monstrabat relegens errata retrorsum. *Virg.*

Under the Title of this Paper, I do not think it foreign to my Design, to speak of a Man born in Her Majesty's Dominions, and relate an Adventure in his Life so uncommon, that it's doubtful whether the like has happen'd to any other of human Race. The Person I speak of is *Alexander Selkirk*, whose Name is familiar to Men of Curiosity, from the Fame of his having lived four Years and four Months alone in the island of *Juan Fernandez*. I had the pleasure frequently to converse with the Man soon after his Arrival in *England*, in the Year 1711. It was a matter of great Curiosity to hear him, as he is a Man of good Sense, give an Account of the different Revolutions in his own Mind in that long Solitude. When we consider how painful Absence from Company for the space of but one Evening, is to the generality of Mankind, we may have a sense how painful this necessary and constant Solitude was to a Man bred a Sailor, and ever accustomed to enjoy and suffer, eat, drink, and sleep, and perform all Offices of Life, in Fellowship and Company. He was put ashore from a leaky Vessel, with the Captain of which he had had an irreconcileable difference; and he chose rather to take his Fate in this place, than in a crazy Vessel, under a disagreeable Commander. His Portion were a Sea Chest, his wearing Cloaths and Bedding, a Fire-lock, a Pound of Gun-powder, a large quantity of Bullets, Flint and Steel, a few Pounds of Tobacco, an Hatchet, a Knife, a Kettle, a Bible, and other Books of Devotion, together with Pieces that concerned Navigation, and his Mathematical Instruments. Resentment against his Officer, who had ill used him, made him look forward on this Change of Life, as the more eligible one, till the Instant in which he saw the Vessel put off; at which moment his Heart yearned within him, and melted at the parting with his Comrades and all Human Society at once. He had in Provisions for the Sustenance of Life but the quantity of two Meals, the Island abounding only with wild Goats, Cats and Rats. He judged it most probable that he should find more immediate and easy Relief, by finding Shell-fish on the Shore, than seeking Game with his Gun. He accordingly found great quantities of Turtles, whose Flesh is extremely delicious, and of which he frequently eat very plentifully on his first Arrival, till it grew disagreeable to his Stomach, except in Jellies. The Necessities of Hunger and Thirst, were his greatest Diversions from the Reflection on his lonely Condition. When those Appetites were satisfied, the Desire of Society was as strong a Call upon him, and he appeared to himself least necessitous when he wanted every thing; for the Supports of his Body were easily attained, but the eager Longings for seeing again the Face of Man during the Interval of craving bodily Appetites, were hardly supportable. He grew dejected, languid, and melancholy, scarce able to refrain from doing himself Violence, till by Degrees, by the Force of Reason, and frequent reading of the Scriptures, and turning his Thoughts upon the Study of Navigation, after the Space of eighteen Months, he grew thoroughly reconciled to his Condition. When he had made this Conquest, the Vigour of his Health, Disengagement from the World, a constant, chearful, serene Sky, and a temperate Air, made his Life one continual Feast, and his Being much more joyful than it had before been irksome. He now taking Delight in every thing, made the Hutt in which he lay, by Ornaments which he cut down from a spacious Wood, on the side of which it was situated, the most delicious Bower, fann'd with continual Breezes, and gentle Aspirations of Wind, that made his Repose after the Chase equal to the most sensual Pleasures.

I forgot to observe, that during the Time of his Dissatisfaction, Monsters of the Deep, which frequently lay on the Shore, added to the Terrors of his Solitude; the dreadful Howlings and Voices seemed too terrible to be made for human Ears; but upon the Recovery of his Temper, he could with Pleasure not only hear their Voices, but approach the Monsters themselves with great Intrepidity. He speaks of Sea-Lions, whose Jaws and Tails were capable of seizing or breaking the Limbs of a Man, if he approached them: But at that Time his Spirits and Life were so high, and he could act so regularly and unconcerned, that meerly from being unruffled in himself, he killed them with the greatest Ease imaginable: For observing, that though their Jaws and Tails were so terrible, yet the Animals being mighty slow in working themselves round, he had nothing to do but place himself exactly opposite to their Middle, and as close to them as possible, and he dispatched them with his Hatchet at Will.

The Precaution which he took against Want, in case of Sickness, was to lame Kids when very young, so as that they might recover their Health, but never be capable of Speed. These he had in great Numbers about his Hutt; and when he was himself in full Vigour, he could take at full Speed the swiftest Goat running up a Promontory, and never failed of catching them but on a Descent.

His Habitation was extreamly pester'd with Rats, which gnaw'd his Cloaths and Feet when sleeping. To defend him against them, he fed and tamed Numbers of young Kitlings, who lay about his Bed, and preserved him from the Enemy. When his Cloaths were quite worn out, he dried and tacked together the Skins of Goats, with which he cloathed himself, and was enured to pass through Woods, Bushes, and Brambles with as much Carelessness and Precipitance as any other Animal. It happened once to him, that running on the Summit of a Hill, he made a Stretch to seize a Goat, with which under him, he fell down a Precipice, and lay senseless for the Space of three Days, the Length of Time he Measured by the Moon's Growth since his last Observation. This manner of Life grew so exquisitely pleasant, that he never had a Moment heavy upon his Hands; his Nights were untroubled, and his Days joyous, from the Practice of Temperance and Exercise. It was his Manner to use stated Hours and Places for Exercises of Devotion, which he performed aloud, in order to keep up the Faculties of Speech, and to utter himself with greater Energy.

When I first saw him, I thought, if I had not been let into his Character and Story, I could have discerned that he had been much separated from Company, from his Aspect and Gesture; there was a strong but chearful Seriousness in his Look, and a certain Disregard to the ordinary things about him, as if he had been sunk in Thought. When the Ship which brought him off the Island came in, he received them with the greatest Indifference, with relation to the Prospect of going off with them, but with great Satisfaction in an Opportunity to refresh and help them. The Man frequently bewailed his Return to the World, which could not, he said, with all its Enjoyments, restore him to the Tranquility of his Solitude. Though I had frequently conversed with him, after a few Months Absence he met me in the Street, and though he spoke to me, I could not recollect that I had seen him; familiar Converse in this Town had taken off the Loneliness of his Aspect, and quite altered the Air of his Face.

This plain Man's Story is a memorable Example, that he is happiest who confines his Wants to natural Necessities; and he that goes further in his Desires, increases his Wants in Proportion to his Acquisitions; or to use his own Expression, *I am now worth 800 Pounds, but shall never be so happy, as when I was not worth a Farthing.*

APPENDIX C
The Illustrators of
Robinson Crusoe

No full investigation has yet been made of the history of illustrations to *Crusoe*. A beginning was made by George S. Layard, 'Robinson Crusoe and his illustrators', *Bibliographica*, vol. II (1896). I am engaged in a fuller study of the topic; the present checklist simply records some of the principal illustrators up to 1900, in chronological order. The date is that of the earliest edition using given illustrations that I have located; 'Ullrich' numbers refer to the items as listed in Hermann Ullrich, *Robinson und Robinsonaden* (Weimar, 1898).

Stothard, Thomas (1755–1834), RA, chiefly known as an illustrator; designed plates for Stockdale edition (1790). Ullrich 27.

Medland, Thomas (d.1833), engraver and draughtsman, engraved Stothard's illustrations (1790). Ullrich 27.

Heath, Charles (1785–1848), engraver, son of James Heath; engraved the Stothard plates (1820). Ullrich 44.

Cruikshank, George (1792–1878), the celebrated artist and caricaturist (1831). Ullrich 51.

Harvey, William (1796–1866), engraver and designer, pupil of Bewick (1831). Ullrich 52.

'Grandville', i.e. Jean Ignace Isidore Gérard (1803–47), French caricaturist and illustrator; designed plates for *Gulliver's Travels* and other works (1840). Ullrich 58.

Doyle, C. A., son and pupil of the Irish painter John Doyle, executed many illustrations in mid-Victorian era (1859). Ullrich 76.

Wehnert, Edward H. (1813–68), watercolourist and illustrator (1861). Ullrich 87.

'Phiz', i.e. Hablôt K. Browne (1815–82), the famous illustrator of Dickens (1861). Ullrich 85.

Zwecker, Johann Baptist (1814–76), Frankfurt-born painter, etcher and illustrator who settled in London (1861). Ullrich 88.

Nicholson, Thomas Henry (d.1870), wood-carver and sculptor (1862). Ullrich 93.

Watson, John Dawson (1832–92), painter and watercolourist (1864). Ullrich 101.

Griset, Ernest Henry (1844–1901), French-born illustrator active in England (1869). Ullrich 114.

Halswelle, Keeley (1832–91), painter and illustrator (1871). Ullrich 122.

Mouilleron, Adolphe (1820–81), French illustrator (1882). Ullrich 146.

Brown, Gordon (b.1859), painter and illustrator (1884). Ullrich 168.
Paget, Walter, illustrator of Scott and other authors (1891). Ullrich 180.
Yeats, J. B. (1839–1922), father of the poet W. B. Yeats, painter (1895). Ullrich 192.

Among the most important of the illustrations were those of Stothard, Cruikshank, Watson, Ernest Griset and Grandville. Twentieth-century artists to have illustrated the book include Eleanore Plaisted Abbott, C. E. Brock, Savile Lumley, George Soper, Milo Winter and N. C. Wyeth.

APPENDIX D

Table of Dates

Major Events	Age	Defoe's Career
1660 Charles II restored to throne		Born (? autumn) in London, son of James Foe
1662 Act of Uniformity forces non-subscribers out of Church of England		
1665 Great Plague in London	5	Possibly evacuated to the country
1666 Great Fire of London		
1674	14	Attends Newington Academy (c.1674–9).
1678 Popish Plot alleged by Titus Oates		
1683 Rye House plot	23	Enters business in London (c.1682–3).
1684	24	Marries Mary Tuffley (1 January)
1685 Death of Charles II; accession of James II; Monmouth Rebellion; Battle of Sedgmoor (6 July); Bloody Assizes	25	Joins Monmouth rising and is captured (subsequently given royal pardon)
1688 William of Orange encouraged to 'invade' England; James II in effect abdicates	28	Admitted to Butchers' Company; rides to meet William's invading army
1692	32	Bankrupt for £17,000 through losses in marine insurance during war with France; committed to Fleet prison (October)
1694 Death of Queen Mary		
1695	35	Obtains official posts and adopts name 'Defoe'
1697 Treaty of Ryswick (respite in war); William Dampier, A New Voyage Round the World	37	Travels as agent of William III; An Essay upon Projects, first important literary work
1701	41	The True-Born Englishman attains great popularity; presents Legion's Memorial to Parliament

1702	Death of William III; accession of Queen Anne; War of the Spanish Succession begins	42	*The Shortest Way with the Dissenters*, often miscon-strued; in Fleet prison again (May)
1703		43	Arrested, tried, condemned to pillory and Newgate prison; released through Harley's influence; brick works bankrupt
1704	Battle of Blenheim; Swift's *Tale of a Tub* published; Alexander Selkirk marooned	44	Begins his journal *The Review* (running until 1713)
1705		45	*Apparition of Mrs Veal*; tours England on behalf of Harley
1706	Battle of Ramillies	46	Begins to spend long periods in Scotland to promote Union and government interest; *Jure Divino*
1707	Act of Union between English and Scottish Parliaments		
1708	Fall of Harley	48	Serves Godolphin, the Lord Treasurer
1709	Battle of Malplaquet; Sacheverell's sermon; Woodes Rogers' expedition rescues Selkirk from Juan Fernandez		
1710	Fall of Godolphin; Harley administration takes power; Sacheverell trial		
1711	South Sea company formed; Swift's *Conduct of the Allies; The Spectator* (1711–12)	51	Political pamphlets for Harley
1712	Pope's *Rape of the Lock* first published in two cantos; accounts by Rogers and Cooke of the Selkirk story		
1713	Steele's narrative of Selkirk; Treaty of Utrecht	53	Arrested for libels, released after further prison-term
1714	Death of Queen Anne, accession of George I; Whig ministry begins; Pope, *Rape of the Lock* in five cantos	54	Arrested again

1715	Jacobite Rising; Dampier dies	55	*Family Instructor*; illness at start of the year
1716		56	Pamphlets on Jacobites
1717	New edition of Dampier's *Voyages*; Harley released after two years in the Tower		
1718	New edition of Rogers's *Cruising Voyage*; war with Spain		
1719	Jacobite attempt; Handel, *Acis and Galatea*	59	*ROBINSON CRUSOE*, Parts 1 and 2
1720	South Sea Bubble; plague in Marseilles	60	*ROBINSON CRUSOE*, Part 3; *Captain Singleton*; *Memoirs of a Cavalier*; Life of Ralegh
1721	Walpole gains ascendancy; death of Selkirk	61	Active in journalism
1722	Atterbury plot; Wood's patent for Irish coin	62	*Moll Flanders*; *A Journal of the Plague Year*; *Colonel Jack*
1724	Swift, *Drapier's Letters*	64	*Tour*, Vol 1; *Roxana*; *History of Pyrates*, Vol 1; *A New Voyage Round the World*
1725		65	*Tour*, Vol 2; criminal biographies (1724–5); *Complete English Tradesman*
1726	Swift, *Gulliver's Travels*	66	*Tour*, Vol 3; *History of the Devil*
1727	Death of George I accession of George II	67	*The History of Apparitions*
1728	Gay, *The Beggar's Opera*; Pope, *The Dunciad*	68	*A Plan of the English Commerce*; *History of Pyrates*, Vol 2; *Atlas Maritimus & Commercialis*
1729	Swift, *A Modest Proposal*	69	*Robert Drury's Journal*
1730	Fielding, *Tom Thumb*	70	Edits *The Political State*
1731		71	Dies in London (24 April); buried in Bunhill Fields; library sold (15 November)
1732	Woodes Rogers dies; Hogarth, *The Harlot's Progress*		

APPENDIX E

Gazetteer

Entries are confined to places directly involved in the narratives of *RC1*.
Page references apply to the first mention in the text, where there is
more than one.

All Saints Bay, see *Todos los Santos, Bay of*.

Bahia, see *St Salvador*.

Bremen (p. 5), 53°N 8°E, port on the River Weser, a leading town in
the Hanseatic league, held by Sweden and Denmark until acquired
by Hanover in 1731. The home-town of Crusoe's father.

Fernando de Noronha (p. 41), 4°S 32°W, island off the coast of Brazil.

Guinea (p. 16), loosely applied to a wide area stretching from Gambia
to Cameroun; sometimes more specifically the central region of the
Gold Coast (modern Ghana). The main location of the slave trade,
with Portuguese, Dutch, French and English settlements. See *History
of Pyrates*, pp. 180*ff*., and map on pp. 184–5. The Royal African
Company headquarters were at Cape Coast Castle (see *Captain
Singleton*, OEN, p. 137), where Dalby Thomas was Agent-General.

Hull (p. 3), 53°N 0°W, large port in Yorkshire, described in the *Tour*
(Vol. II, pp. 651–4) as notable for the volume of its business, for its
coastal shipping, its 'Trade to all parts of the known World' and
its 'Market stored with an infinite plenty of all Sorts of Provision'.
The exchange was filled with 'a Confluence of real Merchants, and
many Foreigners, and several from the Country'. Crusoe's father was
in trade here, and the son sailed from the port on first leaving home.

Lisbon (p. 35), 38°N 9°W, capital city of Portugal, and base of the
Portuguese overseas empire; an important British factory before and
after the Methuen Treaty of 1703.

Orinoco (p. 41), the 'Great River', flowing mainly northwards through
modern Venezuela to its delta, 9°N 61°W. Discovered by Columbus in
1498; remained an area of Spanish influence until the time of Bolivar,
when a Venezuelan republic was founded (1818). Crusoe's island has
been wrongly identified with Tobago; it is meant to lie 100 miles
farther south, in the mouth of the Orinoco itself (see *RC1*, p. 215),
about 50 miles south-east of Trinidad. It is in fact an imaginary
location.

Pampeluna (p. 290), 42°N 1°W, town in northern Spain, ancient capital
of Navarre, later scene of battle during the Peninsular War. A staging-
post for Crusoe on his journey across the Pyrenees to Toulouse.

St Augustino, Cape (p. 41), on the coast of Brazil, evidently in the
vicinity of Pernambuco (7°S 35°W).

St Salvadore (p. 38), 13°S 38°W, or Bahia, colonial capital of Brazil
until 1762, centre of sugar-producing area, a slave-port, visited by
Dampier in 1699; from here Crusoe sailed on his fateful voyage that
was to end in shipwreck.

Sallee (p. 18), 34°N 7°W, port in Morocco, in theory the northern limit
of possessions governed by the Royal African Company; long a nest
of corsairs, attacked by the British in 1632 and many captives
released.

Todos los Santos, Bay of (p. 34), the inlet on which Bahia is situated;
see also *Captain Singleton*, OEN, p. 5.

Yarmouth (p. 10), 52°N 1°E, fishing and coasting port; the shallow
'road' off Winterton Ness, ten miles north, figures in *The Storm*
(1704), pp. 266–70, and the Tour, Vol. I, pp. 69–72.

York (p. 3), 54°N 1°W, cathedral city whose 'Antiquity' is stressed
by Defoe in the *Tour*, Vol. II, pp. 635–43. Crusoe's father retired
there, possibly seeking gentility: 'York is full of Gentry and Persons
of Distinction. . . . Here is no Trade indeed, except such as depends
upon the Confluence of the Gentry'.

APPENDIX F

Biographical Index

Aitken, G. A. (1860–1917). Home Office civil servant and a notable eighteenth-century scholar; made several contributions to the study of Defoe, including the first examination of *Library*.

Chalmers, George (1742–1825). Scottish lawyer and miscellaneous writer; lived for a time in Baltimore. Author of the first serious biography of Defoe: see p. 133.

Cruso, Timothy (?1656–97). Supposed original of Crusoe's name; Presbyterian minister and Defoe's schoolfellow: see p. 60.

Dampier, William (1652–1715). Mariner, privateer and travel-writer, whose *Voyages* supplied material for *RC2* especially: see p. 30.

Farewell, Phillips or Philips (1687/8–1730). Educated at Westminster; Fellow of Trinity College, Cambridge, 1712–30. Divine whose books were auctioned along with Defoe's and catalogued in *Library*.

Forster, John (1812–76). Biographer and friend of Dickens: see p. 135.

Gildon, Charles (1665–1724). Miscellaneous writer satirised in *The Dunciad*, and probable author of first critique of *Crusoe*: see p. 129.

Harley, Robert, first Earl of Oxford (1661–1724). Statesman and important patron for Defoe: see p. 3.

Lee, William. Superintending Inspector in the Board of Health. Author of one of the major biographies: see p. 137.

Minto, William (1845–93). Scottish man of letters and professor at Aberdeen University; wrote life of Defoe in English Men of Letters series: see p. 138.

Moore, John Robert (1890–1973). A leading Defoe scholar, professor at Indiana University, and author of the standard *Checklist*: see p. 14.

Morley, Henry (1822–94). Author and teacher of literature; wrote account of Defoe's early years: see p. 139.

Morton, Charles (1627–98). Puritan minister, subsequently master of Stoke Newington dissenting academy in Defoe's time there, and later still vice-president of Harvard College: see p. 59.

Rogers, Woodes (1678/9–1732). Seaman and colonial governor, who led expedition which rescued Alexander Selkirk: see p. 17.

Secord, Arthur Wellesley (1891–1957). A major figure in Defoe scholarship, who pioneered source-study of *Crusoe* and prepared the modern edition of *The Review*: see p. 151.

Selkirk, Alexander (1676–1721). Seaman, marooned on Juan Fernandez between 1704 and 1709; supposed prototype for Robinson Crusoe: see p. 17.

Steele, Richard (1672–1729). Essayist and dramatist, who wrote an early account of Selkirk's life on Juan Fernandez: see p. 159.

Stephen, Leslie (1832–1904). Critic and editor of the *Dictionary of National Biography.* Author of one of the most influential studies of Defoe: see p. 145.

Taylor, William (d.1724). Bookseller in Paternoster Row, and publisher of original editions of *Crusoe*: see p. 4.

Thomas, Dalby. Projector, African Company official, and early patron of Defoe: see p. 45.

Trent, William P. (1862–1939). Professor at Columbia University and a well-known Defoe scholar: see p. 140.

Wilson, Walter (1781–1847). Writer on London dissent and author of a three-volume life of Defoe: see p. 134.

Woolf, Virginia (1882–1941). Novelist and critic; wrote two widely read appreciations of Defoe: see p. 146.

Wright, Thomas (1859–1936). Resident of Olney and an active student of the poet Cowper; author of a biography of Defoe, later revised: see p. 139.

BIBLIOGRAPHY

A TEXTS

Collected editions containing *Crusoe*:
Romances and Narratives by Daniel Defoe, ed. G. A. Aitken, 16 vols (London, 1895).
The Works of Daniel Defoe, ed. G. H. Maynadier, 16 vols (Boston, Mass., 1903–4).
Novels and Selected Writings of Daniel Defoe, 14 vols (Oxford, 1927–8); omits *RC3*.

RC1 has been edited for the Oxford English Novels by J. Donald Crowley (London, 1972). Other novels by Defoe in this series are *Roxana*, ed. Jane H. Jack (1964); *Colonel Jack*, ed. S. H. Monk (1965); *Captain Singleton*, ed. S. K. Kumar (1969); *A Journal of the Plague Year*, ed. L. A. Landa (1969); *Moll Flanders*, ed. G. A. Starr (1971); and *Memoirs of a Cavalier*, ed. J. T. Boulton (1973). The last three are the most helpful of these editions.

There is a facsimile edition of *The Review*, ed. A. W. Secord, 22 vols (New York, 1938); see also the *Index* by W. L. Payne (New York, 1948).

Other works by Defoe which exist in modern annotated editions are: *A General History of the Pyrates*, ed. M. Schonhorn (London, 1972). *A Tour through the Whole Island of Great Britain*, abridged edn by P. Rogers (Harmondsworth, 1971). The full text of the *Tour*, unannotated, is provided with an introduction by G. D. H. Cole (London, 1927; reprinted 1968).

Useful selections are found in the following:
Daniel Defoe, ed. J. T. Boulton (London, 1965, reprinted Cambridge, 1975).
Selected Poetry and Prose of Daniel Defoe, ed M. F. Shugrue (New York, 1968).

B BIBLIOGRAPHY AND REFERENCE

The standard source is J. R. Moore, *A Checklist of the Writings of Daniel Defoe* (Bloomington, Ind., 1960; rev. edn 1971). There are probable omissions and some certainly mistaken inclusions, whilst the bibliographical description is sometimes unorthodox; but it remains an indispensable guide.

A concise listing, with critical studies published up to 1969, will be found in M. E. Novak, 'Daniel Defoe', in *The New Cambridge Bibliography of English Literature*, ed. G. Watson (Cambridge, 1971), Vol. II, cols 880–917.

For Defoe's poetry, see D. F. Foxon, *English Verse 1701–1750* (Cambridge, 1975), Vol. I, pp. 167–75.

The sale catalogue of Defoe's library has been edited by H. Heidenreich as *The Libraries of Daniel Defoe and Phillips Farewell* (Berlin, 1970). See also G. A. Aitken, 'Defoe's library', *The Athenaeum*, 1 June 1895, pp. 706–7.

The publishing history of *Crusoe* is treated in the following:

L. L. Hubbard, 'Text changes in the Taylor editions of *Robinson Crusoe* with remarks on the Cox edition', *PBSA*, vol. XX (1926), pp 1–76.

H. C. Hutchins, *Robinson Crusoe and Its Printing 1719–1731* (New York, 1925).

H. C. Hutchins, 'Two hitherto unrecorded editions of *Robinson Crusoe*', *The Library*, vol. VIII (1928), pp. 58–72.

K. I. D. Maslen, 'The printers of *Robinson Crusoe*', *The Library*, vol. VII (1952), pp. 124–31.

K. I. D. Maslen, 'Edition quantities for *Robinson Crusoe*, 1719', *The Library*, vol. XXIV (1969), pp. 145–50.

For the history of Defoe's reputation, see the following:

C. E. Burch, 'British criticism of Defoe as a novelist', *Englische Studien*, vol. LXVII (1932), pp. 178–98.

C. E. Burch, 'Defoe's British reputation 1869–94', *Englische Studien*, vol. LXVIII (1934), pp. 410–23.

W. L. Payne, 'Defoe in the pamphlets', *PQ*, vol. LII (1973), pp. 85–96.

P. Rogers (ed.), *Defoe: The Critical Heritage* (London and Boston, Mass., 1972).

P. Rogers, 'John Oldmixon on Swift and Defoe', *Texas Studies in Literature and Language*, vol. XXV (1972), pp. 33–43.

On the reception abroad, the major studies are these:

O. Deneke, *Robinson Crusoe in Deutschland 1720–80* (Göttingen, 1934).

W. E. Mann, *Robinson Crusoé en France* (Paris, 1916).

W. H. Staverman, *Robinson Crusoe in Nederland* (Groningen, 1907).

W. H. Staverman, 'Robinson Crusoe in Holland', *English Studies*, vol. XIII (1931).

H. Ullrich, *Robinson und Robinsonaden* (Weimar, 1898).

H. Ullrich, *Defoes Robinson Crusoe: die Geschichte eines Weltbuches* (Leipzig, 1924).

A recent article is U. Broich, 'Robinsonade und science fiction', *Anglia*, vol. XCIV (1976), pp. 140–62.

See also C. S. Brigham, *A Bibliography of American Editions of Robinson Crusoe to 1830* (1958).

C LETTERS

See the excellent edition by G. H. Healey, *The Letters of Daniel Defoe* (Oxford, 1955). For a small addendum, see P. Rogers, 'Two unrecorded letters by Daniel Defoe', *Papers on Language and Literature*, vol. VII (1971), pp. 298–9.

D BIOGRAPHY

The first biographical sketches are contained in Theophilus Cibber [or Robert Shiels?], *The Lives of the Poets* (1753), Vol. IV, pp. 313–25; and the article by Joseph Towers in *Biographia Britannica*, Vol. V, 2nd edn (1778–93), pp. 45–75.

Historically the most important works are these:
G. Chalmers, *The Life of De Foe* (1786), with *The History of the Union*; first separate edn 1790.
W. Wilson, *Memoirs of the Life and Times of Daniel Defoe*, 3 Vols (1830).
J. Forster, *Daniel De Foe and Charles Churchill* (1855); two separate studies from the *Edinburgh Review*. Also in Forster's *Historical and Biographical Essays,* Vol 2 (1858).
W. Chadwick, *The Life and Times of Daniel De Foe* (1859).
W. Lee, *Daniel Defoe: His Life, and Recently Discovered Writings*, 3 Vols (1869); reprinted Hildesheim, 1968.
W. Minto, *Daniel Defoe* (1879).
H. Morley, *The Earlier Life and the Chief Earlier Works of Daniel Defoe* (1889).
T. Wright, *The Life of Daniel Defoe* (1894; rev. edn 1931).
W. P. Trent, *Daniel Defoe: How to Know Him* (Indianapolis, Ind., 1916).
P. Dottin, *De Foe et ses romans*, 3 Vols in one (Paris, 1924); trans. into English as *The Life and Strange Surprising Adventures of Daniel Defoe*, 1 Vol (1928).
J. Sutherland, *Defoe* (1937; 2nd edn 1950). (Extract in Ellis.)
J. R. Moore, *Daniel Defoe: Citizen of the Modern World* (Chicago, Ill., 1958). (Extract in Ellis.)

E GENERAL STUDIES

For pre-1900 criticism see *CH*.

On Defoe's language, see:
J. T. Boulton, 'Daniel Defoe: his language and rhetoric', in *Daniel Defoe* (London, 1965; reprinted as *Selected Writings*, Cambridge, 1975), pp. 1–22.
B. Dobrée, 'Some aspects of Defoe's prose', in *Pope and His Contemporaries*, ed J. L. Clifford and L. A. Landa (Oxford, 1949), pp. 171–84.

Franz Horten, *Studien über die Sprache Defoe's* (Bonn, 1914).

E. A. James, *Daniel Defoe's Many Voices: A Rhetorical Study of Prose Style and Literary Method* (Amsterdam, 1972).

G. L. Lannert, *The Language of Robinson Crusoe Compared with that of Other 18th Century Writers* (Uppsala and Cambridge, 1910).

G. A. Starr, 'Defoe's prose style: 1. The language of interpretation', *MP*, Vol. LXXI (1974), pp. 277–94.

General assessments include:

H. H. Anderson, 'The paradox of trade and morality in Defoe', *MP*, Vol. XXXIX (1941), pp. 23–46.

R. M. Baine, *Defoe and the Supernatural* (Athens, Ga, 1968).

B. Boyce, 'The question of emotion in Defoe', *SP*, Vol. I (1953), pp. 45–53. (In Byrd.)

Homer O. Brown, 'The displaced self in the novels of Daniel Defoe', *ELH*, Vol. XXXVIII (1971), pp. 562–90.

Max Byrd (ed.), *Daniel Defoe: A Collection of Critical Essays* (Englewood Cliffs, NJ, 1976).

W. de la Mare, *Desert Islands and Robinson Crusoe* (London, 1930).

B. Dobrée, *English Literature in the Early Eighteenth Century 1700–1740* (Oxford, 1959), pp. 408–31.

P. Earle, *The World of Defoe* (London, 1976).

D. Genzel, 'Chronology in *Robinson Crusoe*', *PQ*, Vol. XL (1961), pp. 495–512.

W. T. Hastings, 'Errors and inconsistencies in Defoe's *Robinson Crusoe*', *MLN*, Vol. XXVII (1912), pp. 161–6.

James Joyce, 'Daniel Defoe', trans. and ed. Joseph Prescott, *Buffalo Studies*, Vol. I (1964), pp. 3–25.

A. D. McKillop, *The Early Masters of English Fiction* (Lawrence, Kans., 1956; reprinted 1968): pp. 1–46 on Defoe.

J. R. Moore, *Defoe in the Pillory and Other Studies* (Bloomington, Ind., 1939).

J. R. Moore, *Defoe's Sources for Robert Drury's Journal* (Bloomington, Ind., 1943). Parallels between *Crusoe* and the *Journal* are noted, pp. 55–60.

M. E. Novak, *Economics and the Fiction of Daniel Defoe* (Berkeley and Los Angeles, Calif., 1962; reprinted New York, 1976): pp. 32–67 have special reference to *Crusoe* and incorporate articles published elsewhere. (Extracts in Byrd and Ellis.)

M. E. Novak, *Defoe and the Nature of Man* (Oxford, 1963). The most direct treatment of *Crusoe* occurs on pp. 22–64.

M. E. Novak, 'Defoe's theory of fiction', *SP*, Vol. LXI (1964), pp. 650–68.

W. L. Payne, *Mr Review* (New York, 1961).

J. J. Richetti, *Defoe's Narratives: Situations and Structures* (Oxford, 1975): pp. 21–62 on *Crusoe*.

G. Roorda, *Realism in Defoe's Novels of Adventure* (Wageningen, 1929): pp. 25–93 concern *Crusoe*.

J. F. Ross, *Swift and Defoe: A Study in Relationship* (Berkeley, Calif., 1941).

A. W. Secord, *Studies in the Narrative Method of Defoe* (Urbana, Ill., 1924; reprinted New York, 1963).

A. W. Secord, *Robert Drury's Journal and Other Studies* (Urbana, Ill., 1961).

M. Shinagel, *Daniel Defoe and Middle-Class Gentility* (Cambridge, Mass., 1968). See especially pp. 126–41 on *Crusoe*.

R. G. Stamm, *Der Aufgeklärte Puritanismus Daniel Defoes* (Zürich and Leipzig, 1936).

R. G. Stamm, 'Daniel Defoe: an artist in the Puritan tradition', *PQ*, Vol. XV (1936), pp. 225–46.

G. A. Starr, *Defoe and Spiritual Autobiography* (Princeton, NJ, 1965): pp. 74–125 concern *Crusoe*. (Extracts in Byrd and Ellis.)

G. A. Starr, *Defoe and Casuistry* (Princeton, NJ, 1971).

J. Sutherland, *Daniel Defoe: A Critical Study* (Cambridge, Mass., 1971): pp. 123–43 on *Crusoe*.

I. Watt, *The Rise of the Novel* (London, 1957); paperback, Harmondsworth, 1963). (Extract on *Crusoe* in Byrd and Ellis.)

I. Watt, 'Serious reflections on *The Rise of the Novel*', *Novel: A Forum on Fiction*, Vol. I (1967), pp. 205–18.

I. Watt, 'Defoe as novelist', in *The Pelican Guide to English Literature, Vol 4, From Dryden to Johnson*, ed B. Ford (Harmondsworth, 1957), pp. 203–16.

V. Woolf, 'Defoe', *The Common Reader* (London, 1925), pp. 89–97. (In Byrd.) Also in her *Collected Essays* (London, 1966), pp. 62–8.

E. Zimmerman, *Defoe and the Novel* (Berkeley and Los Angeles, Calif., 1975): pp. 20–47 on *Crusoe*.

F   SPECIAL STUDIES OF ROBINSON CRUSOE

R. W. Ayers, '*Robinson Crusoe*: "allusive allegorick history"', *PMLA*, Vol. LXXXII (1967), pp. 399–407.

E. B. Benjamin, 'Symbolic elements in *Robinson Crusoe*', *PQ*, Vol XXX (1951), pp. 206–11. (In Ellis.)

E. Berne, 'The psychological structure of space with some remarks on *Robinson Crusoe*', *Psychoanalytic Quarterly*, Vol XXV (1956), pp. 549–57. (Extract in Ellis.)

D. Brooks, *Number and Pattern in the Eighteenth-Century Novel* (London, 1973): pp. 18–26 on *Crusoe*.

W. B. Carnochan, *Confinement and Flight* (Berkeley, Calif., 1977): pp. 29–45 on *Crusoe*.

F. H. Ellis (ed.), *Twentieth Century Interpretations of Robinson Crusoe* (Englewood Cliffs, NJ, 1969).

P. H. Geissler, *Is Robinson Crusoe an Allegory?* (Pirna, 1893).

M. J. Greif, 'The conversion of Robinson Crusoe', *SEL*, Vol VI (1966), pp. 551–74.

W. H. Halewood, 'Religion and invention in *Robinson Crusoe*', *EIC*, Vol. XIV (1964), pp. 339–51. (In Ellis.)

Bibliography 177

H. W. Häusermann, 'Aspects of life and thought in *Robinson Crusoe*', *RES*, Vol XI (1935), pp. 229–312, 439–56.

J. P. Hunter, *The Reluctant Pilgrim: Defoe's Emblematic Method and Quest for Form in Robinson Crusoe* (Baltimore, Md, 1966). (Extracts in Byrd and Ellis.)

J. P. Hunter, 'Friday as convert: Defoe and the accounts of Indian missionaries', *RES*, Vol XIV (1963), pp. 243–8.

S. Hymer, 'Robinson Crusoe and primitive accumulation', *Monthly Review*, Vol XXIII (1971), pp. 11–36.

J. Laird, *Philosophical Incursions into English Literature* (Cambridge, 1946): pp. 21–33 on *Crusoe* as *tractatus theologicus-politicus*.

J. Moffatt, 'The religion of Robinson Crusoe', *Contemporary Review*, Vol. CXV (1919), pp. 664–9.

J. R. Moore, '*The Tempest* and *Robinson Crusoe*', *RES*, Vol XXI (1945), pp. 52–6.

P. Norden, '*Robinson Crusoe: unité et contradicitions*', *Archives des lettres modernes*, Vol III (1967), pp. 1–40.

G. Parker, 'The allegory of Robinson Crusoe', *History*, Vol X (1925), pp. 11–25.

G. Pire, 'Jean-Jacques Rousseau et Robinson Crusoe', *Revue de littérature comparée*, Vol XXX (1956), pp. 479–96.

P. Rogers, 'Crusoe's home', *EIC*, Vol XXIV (1974), pp. 375–90.

E. D. Seeber, 'Oroonoko and Crusoe's Man Friday', *MLQ*, Vol XII (1951), pp. 286–91.

E. M. W. Tillyard, *The Epic Strain in the English Novel* (London, 1958): pp. 31–50 on *Crusoe* (In Ellis.)

I. Watt, 'Robinson Crusoe as a myth', *EIC*, Vol I (1951), pp. 95–119. Reprinted in *Eighteenth-Century English Literature: Modern Essays in Criticism*, ed. J. L. Clifford (New York, 1959), pp. 158–79.

V. Woolf, '*Robinson Crusoe*', *The Second Common Reader* (London, 1932), pp. 51–8. (In Ellis.) Also in her *Collected Essays* (London, 1966), pp. 69–75.

G BACKGROUND

On travel and discovery, see the following:

W. H. Bonner, *Captain William Dampier* (Stanford, Calif., 1934).

P. Earle, *Corsairs of Malta and Barbary* (London, 1970).

B. Little, *Crusoe's Captain* (London, 1960). The life of Woodes Rogers.

R. L. Mégroz, *The Real Robinson Crusoe* (London, 1939). The life of Alexander Selkirk.

J. C. Shipman, *William Dampier: Seaman-Scientist* (Lawrence, Kans., 1962).

Consult further *The New Cambridge Bibliography of English Literature*, Vol II, 1389–1486.

Modern editions include the following:

W. Dampier, *Voyages*, ed. J. Masefield (London, 1906); ed. Sir A. Gray *et al.* (London, 1927–31).

R. Knox, *An Historical Relation of the Island Ceylon*, ed. J. Ryan (Glasgow, 1911).

W. Rogers, *A Cruising Voyage Round the World*, ed. G. E. Manwaring (London, 1928).

L. Wafer, *A New Voyage*, ed. L. E. Elliott Joyce (Oxford, 1933).

Literary influences:

P. G. Adams, *Travelers and Travel Liars 1660–1800* (Berkeley, Calif., 1962).

W. A. Eddy, *Gulliver's Travels: A Critical Study* (Princeton, NJ, 1923; reprinted New York, 1963).

R. W. Frantz, *The English Traveller and the Movement of Ideas 1660–1732* (Lincoln, Nebr., 1934).

P. B. Gove, *The Imaginary Voyage in Prose Fiction* (New York, 1941; rev. edn. 1961).

For religious background, see especially:

W. Haller, *The Rise of Puritanism* (New York, 1938).

The standard work on dissenting academies is still:

H. McLachlan, *English Education under the Test Acts* (Manchester, 1931).

For social and political cross-currents, see:

I. Kramnick, *Bolingbroke and His Circle: The Politics of Nostalgia in the Age of Walpole* (Cambridge, Mass., 1968): pp. 188–200 are devoted specifically to Defoe.

Literary background is provided by these works:

E. A. Baker, *The History of the English Novel*, Vol 3 (London, 1929; reprinted New York, 1950).

F. W. Chandler, *The Literature of Roguery* (Boston, Mass., 1907; reprinted New York, 1958). On rogue biography, etc.

A. Kettle, *An Introduction to the English Novel*, Vol 1 (London, 1951). A Marxist account.

R. Paulson, *Satire and the Novel in Eighteenth-Century England* (New Haven, Conn., 1967). Sidelights on realism and the picaresque.

J. J. Richetti, *Popular Fiction before Richardson* (Oxford, 1969): especially pp. 60–118.

P. Rogers, *Grub Street: Studies in a Subculture* (London, 1972): pp. 311–27 on Defoe's relation to Grub Street.

P. Rogers, *The Augustan Vision* (London, 1974): pp. 245–66 on the rise of the novel and Defoe's part in this.

M. S. Røstvig, *The Happy Man* (Oslo, 1954–8; 2nd edn. 1971). On retirement and the *beatus ille* theme.

D. Spearman, *The Novel and Society* (London, 1966): pp. 154–78 on Defoe.

L. Stephen, *English Literature and Society in the Eighteenth Century* (London, 1903). A classic analysis.

I. Watt (ed.), *The Augustan Age* (Hamden, Conn., 1968). Valuable perspectives on the era in which Defoe lived.

GENERAL INDEX

Single references, unless of special interest, are omitted from the index, as are all references in the notes at the end of each chapter.

Addison, Joseph (1672–1719) 106–8, 123

Aitken, G. A. (1860–1917) 139, 170

Annesley, Samuel (c.1620–96) 54, 59–60

Applebee, John 93, 95

Austen, Jane (1775–1817) vii, 97

Ayers, R. W. 64, 151

Baker, E. A. vii, 31

Bayley, Lewis (d.1631) 54, 130n

Behn, Aphra (1640–89) vii, 92–3

Bolinbroke, Henry St John, Viscount (1678–1751) 74, 105–6, 123

Boswell, James (1740–95) 11, 132

Boulton, J. T. 120, 151

Boxer, C. R. x, 39

Brooks, Douglas 111–13, 115–16

Brown, Homer O. 89–90, 151

Bunyan, John (1628–88) viii, 52–3, 57, 104, 120, 143
   Grace Abounding 53
   The Pilgrim's Progress viii, 89, 103, 128, 132, 134, 136

Caslon, Thomas (d.1783) 11, 104

Chadwick, William 136–7

Chalmers, George (1742–1825) 133–4, 141, 170

Cibber, Theophilus: *for* Lives of the Poets (*1753*), *falsely ascribed to Cibber, see under* Shiels

Coleridge, Samuel Taylor (1772–1834) 13, 78, 80, 88, 142–3

Congreve, William (1670–1729) 99–101, 123

Cooke, Edward 17, 19–20, 33

Cowper, William (1731–1800) 19–20, 139

Cox, Thomas (d.1754) 7–8, 104

Cruso, Timothy (c.1656–97) 54, 60, 170

Curll, Edmund (1683–1747) 10, 129–30

Dampier, William (1652–1715) 8, 25, 30–2, 34, 38–9, 107, 155–7, 159, 170

Defoe, Daniel (1660–1731)
   biography 1–4, 58–60, 67–8
   pseudonyms 5–6, 93
   interest in travel 25–7
   colonial schemes 26–7
   reading 26, 30–1
   attitude to trade 41, 46
   attitude to slavery 42–4
   on American colonies 44
   interest in disasters 56–7
   dissenting background 58–60
   political views 74–5, 106–7
   economic views 77–8, 80
   social views 82–4
   criminal writing 93
   domestic manuals 94–5
   journalism 95–6
   social contacts 102–3
   stylistic characteristics 116–17, 119–23
   contemporary reputation 127–31
   posthumous reputation 131–48
   recent and current estimates 148–52
   career in outline 165–7
   Robinson Crusoe compared with *Pilgrim's Progress* viii
   early editions of *RC1* 4–10
   early editions of *RC2* 8–9
   early editions of *RC3* 9
   piracies, serialisations and abridgements 7–10, 15
   rights sold 10
   imitations, *Robinsonades* 10–16
   translations 12–14
   children's versions 15
   composition 16–22
   the Selkirk story 17–20
   theories of authorship by another 21–2
   travel and colonial background 25–50
   sources and models 27–34
   doubtful relevance of *The English Rogue* 28, 93
   theme of piracy 34–8
   imperial powers 39–41

Crusoe as governor 44–6
Puritan inheritance 51–7
spiritual autobiography 53–4
guide tradition 54–5
providential narratives 55–8
missionary stories 58
Friday's role 58, 68, 93, 115
source of Crusoe's name 60
Crusoe's 'original sin' 61–6
allegorical readings 66–70
social and philosophic themes 73–91
the middle station 73–7
economic readings 77–82
'money' episode 77, 80–2
solitude and retirement 85–90
self-preservation and self-help 82–5
absence of sex 89
literary background 91–109
contemporary narrative forms 91–6
romance 91–2
picaresque 93
adventure stories 93–4
biographies 96
rise of the novel 96–101
comparison with *Incognita* 99–101
reading public 101–5
commercial success 104–5
comparison with Scriblerian group 105–8
comparison with *Gulliver's Travels* 107
comparison with Addison 107–8
structure 110–13
relation of *RC1* and *RC2* 110–11
footprint episode 113–16
expressive devices 116–19
style 119–25
false adversatives 121–2
approximating phrases 122–3
critical history 127–52
eighteenth-century views 127–32
early biographers 132–41
Romantic and Victorian criticism 141–6
twentieth-century views 146–52
illustrators 163–4
works other than *Robinson Crusoe*
Appeal to Honour and Justice 5, 59, 67
Augusta Triumphans 106

Caledonia 5, 102
Captain Singleton 4, 26, 29, 34, 36–7, 41, 68
Colonel Jack 1, 4, 41, 43–4, 83, 96, 99, 128, 131
Complete Art of Painting 5
Complete English Gentleman 4, 25, 55, 119
Complete English Tradesman 4, 75–6, 78, 131, 136, 139
Conjugal Lewdness 69
Consolidator, The 47
Daniel Defoe's Hymn 5
De Foe's Answer to Dyer's Scandalous News Letter 5
Essay upon Projects 3, 74–5, 78
Family Instructor 53, 55, 94, 131–2
General History of Trade 78
Historical Account of the Voyages and Adventures of Sir Walter Raleigh 4, 27
History of the Pyrates 4, 30, 34, 37, 131, 152
History of the Union 5
Journal of the Plague Year 2, 4, 57, 74, 148
Jure Divino 74, 82, 102
Life of Jonathan Wild 1, 128
Madagascar: or Robert Drury's Journal 21, 34, 37
Meditacions 16, 60
Memoirs of a Cavalier 4, 116
Memoirs of Captain George Carleton 96
Memoirs of John, Duke of Melfort 96
Memoirs of Major Alexander Ramkins 96
Memoirs of the Duke of Shrewsbury 96
Memoirs of Daniel Williams 54, 96
Mere Nature Delineated 42
Moll Flanders 1, 4, 41, 44, 52, 68, 83, 96, 101, 104, 116–17, 123, 128, 131, 140–1, 146–8
Narrative of the Robberies of Jack Sheppard 1, 128
New Voyage Round the World 25–6, 37, 116, 123, 148
Plan of the English Commerce 36, 46, 106
Reformation of Manners 43–4

Religious Courtship 131–2
Review, The 3, 79, 95, 106, 117
Robert Drury's Journal see *Madagascar*
Roxana 4, 52, 83, 104, 116, 123, 140–1, 148
Shortest Way with the Dissenters 3
Storm, The 56–7
Tour through the whole Island of Great Britain 4, 75–6, 131, 136, 152
True-Born Englishman 1, 3
Wars of Charles XII 96
de la Mare, Walter (1873–1956) 33, 147
Dickens, Charles (1812–70) 97, 119, 135–6, 144
Dottin, Paul 140–1
Dover, Thomas (1660–1742) 18, 155
Drury, Robert 21
Dryden, John (1631–1700) 33, 103, 105, 141
Dunton, John (1659–1733) 96, 117

Earle, Peter ix, 16, 42, 44, 80
Ellis, F. H. 27, 112, 115
Exquemelin (*or* Esquemeling), Alexandre Olivier 28, 34, 36, 155

Farewell, Phillips (1687/8–1730) 169
Fielding, Henry (1707–54) 6, 97–8, 104, 111, 119, 134, 144
Fisher, James 59–60
Forster, John (1812–76) 135–6, 169
Franklin, Benjamin (1706–90) 75, 136

Gay, John (1685–1732) 6, 103–4, 106–7
Gildon, Charles (1665–1724) 8, 42, 44, 51, 66–7, 69, 95, 103, 128–31, 169
Godolphin, Sidney, Earl (1645–1712) 3, 22, 103

Halewood, William H. 79, 81, 151
Harley, Robert, Earl of Oxford (1661–1724) 3, 5, 19, 21–2, 27, 103, 106, 137, 169
Haywood, Eliza (c.1693–1756) 91, 97, 102
Hobbes, Thomas (1588–1679) 74, 150
Hunter, J. Paul ix, 33, 47, 52–5, 57, 60, 63, 69, 90, 111, 113, 115, 150–1

Hutchins, H. C. 6, 8–10

James, E. Anthony 120–1, 150–1
Johnson, Samuel (1709–84) 96, 132, 140, 142
Joyce, James (1882–1941) vii, 119, 146

Knox, Robert (1641–1720) 28–30
Kramnick, Isaac 74–7, 105–6

Lamb, Charles (1775–1834) 13, 134, 141, 143, 145
Law, William (1686–1761) 54–5
Lee, William 137, 141, 170
Lintot, Bernard (1675–1736) 4, 19
Locke, John (1632–1704) 74, 78, 120
Longman, Thomas (1699–1755) and family 7, 10–11, 104

Marx, Karl (1818–83) 51, 78, 84, 146
McKillop, A. D. 148–9
Mears, William 7, 9
Milton, John (1608–74) 52
Minto, William (1845–93) 137–8, 170
Mist's *Weekly Journal* 16, 95
Moll, Herman (d.1732) 26
Moore, John Robert (1890–1973) ix, 1, 20, 33, 59, 87, 107, 141, 148, 151, 170
Morley, Henry (1822–94) 139, 170
Morton, Charles (1627–98), 57, 59–60, 170

Nashe, Thomas (1567–1601) vii, 93
Novak, Maximillian E. ix, 35, 45–6, 62, 78–9, 81, 83–5, 150, 152

Oldmixon, John (c.1673–1742) 79, 96, 127–8, 132
Osborn, John (d.1739) and family 7, 9–10

Parker, Henry 6–7
Payne, W. L. 127, 148
Pope, Alexander (1688–1744) 6, 78, 103, 105–7, 127–8, 131, 135, 151

Ralegh, Walter (c.1552–1618) 4, 27
Richardson, Samuel (1689–1761) 6, 97–8, 102, 131
Richetti, John J. 62, 64, 88–9, 94, 113, 150–1
Rogers, Woodes (1678/9–1732) 8, 12, 17–18, 18n, 19–20, 25, 31, 33–4, 37, 45, 142, 155–9, 170
Rousseau, Jean-Jacques (1712–78) 84, 104, 132

Salisbury, Sally (c.1690–1724) 93, 128
Scott, Walter (1771–1832) 140–2
Secord, Arthur W. (1891–1957) ix, 1, 27–33, 57, 148, 151, 170
Selkirk, Alexander (1671–1721) 17–20, 30–1, 55, 139, 142, 155–62, 170
Shakespeare, William (1564–1616) 33, 132
Sheppard, Jack (1702–24) 1, 93, 96, 128
Shiels, Robert (d.1753) 104, 131
Shinagel, Michael 75–6, 89, 150
Spark, Muriel 15–16
Spearman, Diana 77–8, 80, 98–9, 149
Starr, George A. ix, 4–5, 62–3, 111–12, 120, 123, 150–1
Steele, Richard (1672–1729) 12, 17, 19, 33, 106, 144, 159–62, 170
Stephen, Leslie (1832–1904) 145–6, 171
Sterne, Laurence (1713–68) viii, 97, 111
Swift, Jonathan (1667–1745) 6, 78, 103, 105–7, 117, 123, 134–5, 141–2, 151
  Gulliver's Travels 6, 47, 104, 107, 128
Sunderland, Charles Spencer, Earl of (1674–1722) 21–2

Sutherland, James ix, 68, 87, 141, 148

Tawney, R. H. (1880–1962) 51–2, 62
Taylor, William (d.1724) 4, 6–10, 140, 143, 171
Thomas, Dalby 45, 76, 171
Tillyard, E. M. W. (1889–1962) 110–11, 149
Trent, W. P. (1862–1939) 140, 171

Ulrich (*or* Ullrich), H. 12–13, 147

Walpole, Robert (1676–1745) 75–6, 105–6, 108
Watt, Ian ix, 51, 61–2, 64, 77, 80–1, 84, 87–9, 97–8, 101–2, 120, 123, 149–51
Weber, Max (1864–1920) 51, 62
Wild, Jonathan (c.1683–1725) 1, 93–4
William III, King of England (1650–1702) 2–3, 26, 59, 75
Wilson, Walter (1781–1847) 134–5, 137, 143, 171
Woodward, Thomas 7, 9
Woolf, Virginia (1882–1941), 146–7, 171
Wordsworth, William (1770–1850) 144
Wright, Thomas (1859–1936) 67, 139–40, 171